DUSTIN

DUSTIN

A BIOGRAPHY OF DUSTIN HOFFMAN

Michael Freedland

VIRGIN

Phototypeset by Input Typesetting Ltd, London
Printed and bound in Great Britain by
Mackays of Chatham Plc, Corkswood, Chatham, Kent
for the Publishers, W. H. Allen & Co. Plc
Sekforde House, 175/9 St John Street, London EC1V 4LL

ISBN 0 491 03784 8

FOR MY MOTHER
With love, devotion, admiration and gratitude

ACKNOWLEDGEMENTS

For once, a biographer is stumped. It is absolutely impossible to list all the people who helped in the production of this book – mainly because a number of them did not want to be officially identified. But this Dustin Hoffman biography is the result of a detailed research in both the United States and Great Britain and is possible only because so many people, named and unnamed, offered their help. Among them, I am pleased to be able to list: Larry Adler, Jarvis Astaire, the late George Coulouris, the late Bob Fosse, Susan George, Sir Peter Hall, Anne Byrne Hoffman Kronenfeld, Peter Noble, Harry Dean Stanton, and Timothy West.

There are thanks due, to Merle Kessler and the librarians of the National Library, London, the British Film Institute and of the Academy of Motion Picture Arts and Sciences, Los Angeles.

Michael Freedland
London, 1989

PICTURE CREDITS

Unless otherwise marked all illustrations are courtesy of the National Film Archive, London.

DUSTIN

1

The Shrine Auditorium on Jefferson Boulevard, Los Angeles, is one of those dinosaur places that America loves so much. It is huge – so big that those people sitting in the balcony for a movie feel as if they are taking part in a ritual that most of the history books say died out a couple of generations earlier.

It was there that the epic *Napoleon* had its West Coast première following its rediscovery sixty years after being lost.

The annual ritual known as the Oscar ceremonies sometimes looks just as ancient – as indeed it is. But it is ancient in the way that a religious service is. It is an event on which television screens all over the world focus to the obvious delight of the viewers. The cameras ignore the lesser folk in the balcony and concentrate on the first few rows, where stars and directors and others who have been nominated for what are still officially known as the Academy Awards sit, chewing their nails and clapping the competitors who walk off with statuettes they know should have been theirs. They smile as they stifle tears and rage, while patting backs they would dearly have loved to have stabbed.

In March 1989, a name was called from the podium that brought perhaps more applause than was usual – and if there was venom in the eyes of his competitors it was shielded from view.

Dustin Hoffman's was one of seven Oscars for his new film *Rain Man*, and somehow a strange thing had happened: the industry declared that it approved. It was indeed strange, for Dustin Hoffman had rarely been everybody's favourite person. People admired his acting ability and his attitude to his work could easily have been included in some manual on the technique of movie and stage performing. If dedication was regarded as a distinct requirement for an actor, then it was generally accepted that Hoffman had it.

But he was a perfectionist – a word that practically everybody uses about him. They used to use the same word about Fred Astaire. But then it was the done thing to love Fred Astaire, or at least to say so. Dustin Hoffman was almost 51 – old enough to have achieved a fair volume of work, but still young enough to have enemies who resented the way that that perfectionism had been practised. The dubbing of Dustin Hoffman at work as a microsurgeon was not intended as a compliment.

Now, though, Hollywood was ready to applaud and more than ready to be seen doing so. The three and a half million dollars Hoffman had received for his part as the middle-aged autistic 'idiot *savant*' was perhaps nothing to what he could charge for his next product, without anyone claiming that his talent was also subject to inflation.

A 'savant' is defined as a learned man. The character Dustin played in *Rain Man* was astonishingly 'learned' in one respect only: he had a mathematical brain so acute that he could beat the system at Las Vegas and declare in a split second the square root of some huge number posed by a psychiatrist; but he didn't know how much change he would get from a dollar when he bought a hamburger for 50 cents. In a way, Hoffman's career has been like that, too. He has achieved success beyond most actors' dreams using a talent that is given to very, very few. Yet he is said by some to have no knowledge of the way human relations work.

Perhaps the psychiatrists he has patronised over the years with the frequency other men used to visit their tailors would have the answer to that. Maybe they see his early childhood and the received wisdom of a family which had suffered the torment of escaping pogroms before even his parents were born as having something to do with it. If there were such reasons, then those events were responsible for creating perhaps the most outstanding actor of the age, a man who could shine on stage as well as screen and who could look forward to achieving the status of the biggest star and most impressive performer of the 1990s.

2

The Depression of 1929 had an effect on America that virtually nothing else has ever had. It destroyed the cosiness of a life that some people had begun to take for granted and wrecked their very attitudes to living.

For Harry Hoffman it also provided an excuse to get out of Chicago, which to him and the surviving members of his family had never been anything more than a temporary way-station.

Harry was a first-generation American. His parents had come over from Romania, a country where his father had considered life to revolve around his holy books – and which his mother knew was no environment in which to bring up a family. Chicago for them was just another stop on the wanderings which had become so familiar to Jews.

Harry was nine years old when his father died in Chicago – a barber who had never made a decent living and who died in a mental hospital, still dreaming of a place where streets were paved with gold, or of another place in another world where he could hide away with his books.

The young Hoffman wanted no part of that life. For that reason, he wanted virtually no part of his father's Judaism. What he did want was to get away to the one place where the Depression had seemed not to hit – to California, the centre of the industry that positively thrived while all was desolation around it. People who could afford nothing else could usually find the price of a movie ticket. Unemployed men who were ashamed not to have anywhere to go in the mornings would spend their days in the cinema, hoping no one would notice. Harry Hoffman was going to be one of the people who made those films.

He also had a girl who was going to be with him. Her name was Lillian.

They married. Soon after their wedding, Lillian was pregnant. But it was not until their first child, a son they named Ronald, was five that they actually made the trip west. Harry and Lillian piled all their worldly goods into an old Model T Ford, with Ron sitting in the back seat, trying to be amused by the sights outside the window. It was an amusement that was perilously short-lived. By the time, several days later, that the car steamed into Los Angeles – it was very hot work for the engine – tempers were as frayed as the cloth covering their belongings. But come to California they had. Harry was ready to improve the film industry.

When people cheered Franklin D. Roosevelt as he prepared for his second inauguration, Harry and Lillian were shouting with the best of them. Happy days were going to be really here again.

Harry was determined to show that he was going to be master in his own house – something his father had never been. And Lillian made it known that she was happy to allow him to take on that role, while she concentrated on dressing and making-up to please him.

He was, after all, going to step into the shoes of the Warner Bros. or Adolph Zukor and such an important man had to be suitably pampered. He couldn't go wrong. He had the ambition and, she knew, the brains as well. How could such things be thwarted, especially now that he had got himself a job?

Harry took to the studio life with all the enthusiasm of a cat thrown into a pool of water. For although his job was attached to Harry Cohn's Columbia studios, it was that word 'attached' that presented the problems. Harry was attached to Columbia by the sewerage pipes on which he was working as a labourer. Eventually, he got off the sewer gang – which was perhaps inevitable, since Columbia hoped it would be in the business of making films, not drains.

In fact, Harry got a new job inside the studios, working as a props man. When he came home to his bride it was to talk movie talk, to talk about the movie people, all of which Lillian lapped up as she piled his plate with the cheapest meat or fish she could buy in the locality.

Lillian was the sort of woman about whom books were written and films made. She was intoxicated with Hollywood and all that she thought it represented, which was why their son had been named Ronald. It was a tribute to a life that allowed her regular escapes from reality, sitting in a darkened theatre, watching the most beautiful women in the world making love to that most handsome man with the enchanting English accent, Ronald Colman.

Ronald was the light of their eyes; a good-looking boy who proved in his first days of elementary school that he had a good brain and, just as he enjoyed sports, excelled in them.

Six and a half years after Ronald's birth, Lillian and Harry had another son. This one they called Dustin, which would be another demonstration of throwing off the old ways. Who ever heard of a Rabbi Dustin? In fact, very few people at all had ever heard the name. The only Dustin on record seemed to be Dustin Farnum, who had been the star of the first picture made in Hollywood, *The Squaw Man*, which had put an ill-assorted trio named Jesse Lasky, Jnr., Samuel Goldfish (later to be renamed Goldwyn) and Cecil B. De Mille in business.

The legend was that Mrs Hoffman named her Dustin after Mr Farnum, which would fit nicely into her star-struck image. But towards the end of her life she began denying it. How could she even have known about a star working a quarter of a century before her child was born? Were those the protests of a now ageing woman who did not enjoy being reminded of her advancing years? Probably.

Both of his parents used to say that their Dusty was a slow developer. He didn't talk until he was three years old. 'But he rode a scooter at one-and-half,' Lillian would recall proudly. 'And a two-wheeler at two-and-a-half.'

She said that she was not going to allow her children to be as affected by Hollywood as she was. Not true. At the age of eight, Ronald was working on a film set. He was an extra in the 1939 James Stewart blockbuster about political corruption, *Mr Smith Goes To Washington*.

Even so, Ronald showed no aptitude for or further interest in becoming a child actor and he never faced a professional movie camera again. Dustin, however, was much more keen on acting. In the seventh grade, he played Tiny Tim in the school's seasonal play, *A Christmas Carol*. To Tim's immortal speech, 'God bless us every one', Dustin added the word, 'Goddammit'. He did it as a bet – and was suspended from school for the privilege.

But there was not a lot that would upset Lillian where Dustin was concerned. He was her little 'Dustalah', an affectionate Yiddishism, which harked back to her own roots. Adding 'alah' to a name is to say, 'I love you – you may be naughty, but you're mine.' 'Dustalah' was her pride and joy. He was also his grandmother's, whom he called either Nanny or 'Red', a nickname which has never been adequately explained.

'Red' was an unusual Jewish grandmother, who worked in her husband's barber shop. She was cleverer than her husband had ever been. She realized that men who went to have their hair cut liked to talk or be talked to – and usually on one of two subjects, sex or ball-games. No self-respecting Jewish woman was going to talk sex to a man, but was it written anywhere that she shouldn't know anything about baseball? So she learned the rudiments of the game, found out how the scoring was done, and then studied the results. Her customers loved to talk games with her and, as a result, what had been a collapsing business in her husband's day became a huge success under 'Red's' supervision.

Dustin was happy at home. At least, happier than when he first found out he had to go to school. School wasn't easy for him, mainly because he knew that he didn't fit in. It might have been easier if he had been called Tom, Dick or even Ronald like his brother, but Dustin? As he told *Time* magazine in 1969, 'I always used to wish there was another Dustin in my class. When you're poked fun at, you either go inside yourself or become a clown.'

He was opting to become a clown, which was precisely why he improved on Charles Dickens and extended the Tiny Tim role beyond merely stomping about with his crutch and making people feel sorry for him.

No, Dustin was not a name to enjoy, especially since in a world where nicknames take hold like leeches, his was 'Dustbin'. He would forever wish that the more American term 'garbage can' had totally eclipsed the English word in America of the mid and late 1940s. Fortunately, he called *himself* 'Dusty' and his closest friends followed suit.

His behaviour as a clown at school made him the bane of his teachers. He would whisper to friends: 'At two-o-three, everybody cough.' Such was the power of this clown that at two-o-three precisely everybody at school did cough. The teacher knew who was responsible. Without having to think twice – it was like a scene from a Woody Allen movie, and probably one that he himself would have made had he been born Woody Allen – she would order: 'Hoffman to the office.' He went, but it was a triumph of sorts, nevertheless.

The problem was that he was never in a school long enough to have a lot of friends. The Hoffmans were constantly moving, and every time they moved, he had to change schools. Sometimes, they lived in Beverly Hills. That was when Harry had a good job. When he was financially tight, they had to find a home in a less fashionable area of Los Angeles. Dustin always recalled that those were the happier times for him. He had Mexican and black friends who were a lot nicer to him than his white, Anglo-Saxon classmates.

Life wasn't easier in other respects either. He had an adolescent fascination with girls and their anatomy, but didn't dare do anything about it. The nearest he got to having a romance while at school was sitting alone in assembly next to a girl. Intending it to seem casual and the most natural thing in the world, he placed his hand on the girl's budding right breast. She was so shocked she ran away. Dustin didn't know what to do. He just continued to sit – and to bang his head on the wall behind him.

He had only one aptitude, for sport, which at the time was not thought to be particularly masculine (or macho as it would be termed later). 'In high school, the other guys had hair on their chests and played football. I played tennis, had a big nose and acne so bad my face looked like a rifle range.'

He was not part of the school life any more than he really felt he fitted into his native city; the Hoffman wanderlust plainly struck him early. When he went to see films, it was to revel in the antics of the Bowery Boys led by Leo Gorcey, or his previous mob the Dead End Kids, a pack of dirty-faced youngsters (they were the Angels With Dirty Faces immortalized in the James Cagney film) who never saw sunlight, let alone palm trees.

Saturday afternoons with the Dead End Kids offered a much more potent form of paradise. As he said in that *Time* interview, he used to watch them and think, 'Wouldn't it be fun to swim in the East River and play in dirty streets.'

Social workers were meanwhile dreaming of ways of getting New York kids to keep away from the germ-ridden river and the filthy streets so that they could play in nice areas not unlike the middle-class sections of Los Angeles.

Dusty was not, as he said, an attractive child, although, teasing apart, he does not appear to have had very many problems that could turn a youngster into a psychiatric case. Perhaps choosing to be a clown rather than an introvert was a sensible move.

He was a firm believer in the point of view that it is far better to hear people say nasty things about him than to say nothing. If he could have articulated it that way, he would no doubt have added that if they were going to write about him, they only had to be sure that they spelled his name correctly. That was why at school dances he chose the fattest and ugliest girls to dance with. That way, he sure would be noticed. When his father complained about his not doing his homework, he could either shout or cry. He did neither of those things; he simply imitated him. That little bit of mimicry worked miracles, especially at moments when Harry's frustrations at not getting the work to which he believed he was entitled turned into depression.

Home life was not easy. The Hoffmans seemed to love each other, but they did not hide their feelings. When there were disagreements, there were verbal pyrotechnics. There was never any suggestion that fights had to be kept quiet and out of the way of the children. Dustin's impersonations had the effect of a one-child United Nations peace-keeping force.

That also said a lot about the kind of child that he was. There was enough insecurity in his appearance without the additional problems of marital discord. If he could make his parents laugh, they wouldn't want to fight, would they? The Hoffmans, if they had been brighter or more prescient than they were, could have seen the sensitivity of an unusually impressive actor in all this. It is fair to assume that they did not.

Playgirl magazine, assessing Dustin's childhood, came to the conclusion that had he been born in New York and not Los Angeles, he would have become Woody Allen instead of Woody Allen. That assumes that Jewish children have more problems at home than their WASP neighbours. There is no real justification for that suggestion. He never saw his father punch his mother or come home drunk, or her ever deprive him of a meal so that they could go out gambling. True, Lillian did not particularly enjoy cooking and as soon as she could scrape up the money for it, she persuaded Harry to get domestic help.

Dustin doesn't remember his childhood totally affectionately, nor does he completely think that way about his relationship with his father. 'We had some bad times,' he would recall, 'guys coming to the door when he was at work, pulling the furniture out, and then he'd get into fights at the finance department, saying, "Don't scare my wife and kids!" '

Dustin had sessions of introspection. He says he remembers spending hours peering at his reflection in the chromium-plated toaster, saying over and over again, 'Dusty, Dusty, Dusty'. The face he saw did not represent the perfectly formed, handsome features he envisaged for himself. But even when he contemplated the big nose that seemed to dominate his face, he could see the funny side of it. He had decided absolutely to enjoy life no matter what – even when school 'friends' called him a rat because of the way he looked.

Dustin certainly didn't have the difficulties that other Jewish youngsters faced. His parents did not allow religion to interfere with everyday life. In fact, it hardly existed for him at all. Neither Ronald nor his younger brother were bar mitzvah, for instance, although in middle age friends say Dustin has grown to regret his lack of Jewish attachment and has tried to rectify it.

About the only ceremonies which they did not take part in were the annual Passover Seder – one night, not two as is the Orthodox practice – and then mainly because it was the thing to do. It was an essential ritual in a Jewish environment not unlike Christmas dinner for Christians, and non-religious as well as religious people indulge in it more as an excuse for a good family meal than as an opportunity to recite the Haggadah that tells the story of the exodus of the Children of Israel from Egypt.

It was at one Seder that his Aunt Pearl achieved her place in theatrical history by becoming the first person to 'discover' Dustin Hoffman. 'What do you want to be when you grow up?' she asked him. 'An actor,' he replied. Everyone laughed. Dustin had not seriously thought of it himself until then.

But Pearl was ready to dissuade him from any such nonsense. 'You're not good-looking enough,' she added in a remark that was as unpalatable as the bitter herbs which form part of the Passover ritual.

What she did not know, or what Harry and Lillian couldn't accept, was that everything Dustin did at this time was a kind of acting, although then it might have just seemed like another game. He would pretend he was a boxer, constantly knocked to the floor, and then imagine he was good enough to come back to win.

While neither of his parents gave any indication of approving his career plans, there was too much in Lillian's background and her dream of one day dancing on a stage to dismiss his notions as childish idiocy. Dustin was to say that his mother was a 'closet flapper'. Through her children, she felt able to come out of that closet, as though vicariously starting her life all over again.

If she were happy with things that way, it is more than can be said for Dustin. He was to remember those years as anything but good ones. He once put it like this: 'I was skinny, sickly and short. I wanted to be tall, which I suspected I would probably never be.' Even so, that was not the be-all and end-all of the prime masculinity to which he aspired. The person he admired most in the world was Ron, who was on his way to becoming an economist. Ron's only drawback in his brother's eyes was that he was even shorter than Dustin.

But school was harder than simply being at home. Again and again, he has said it: 'I envy people who remember school fondly.'

He was certainly conscious of all his limitations. He hated the idea of being Jewish, even the kind of Jews that the Hoffmans were. As he put it: 'Most of my friends were Roman Catholics and I figured that's what I should be.' The nearest he got to it was trimming the Christmas tree – which shone throughout the second part of December whereas a Chanukah menorah never did. The impish Dustin Hoffman thought of a way of providing a compromise, as far as that was concerned – he hung a string of bagels from the tree. 'The tree wasn't very pretty, but from my guilt at wanting to be Gentile, I guess I figured we ought to do something ethnic.' The very fact that the only 'ethnic' thing he could think of was a bagel, a flat roll with a hole in the middle that is part of the staple diet of New York's Lower East side and in the Jewish areas of other cities in the world, gives some idea of the Judaism practised in his home.

It might be that an actor was simply an escape in Dustin's eyes. Except that it was several years before he thought of it seriously. In fact, apart from his expedition into dramatics with his *Christmas Carol* performance, he had barely given the theatre passing consideration, even though he had seen his first play at the age of six.

Fanny Brice, immortalized by Barbra Streisand in *Funny Girl*, was the star and Dustin enjoyed it immensely. As he later told *Pageant* magazine: 'I was impressed. We had good seats.'

One can never be sure whether that was the experience that fired the young Hoffman's dramatic ambitions, which despite Harry's hopes of being a director and Lillian's dreams of dancing on stage or on the screen, were not exactly encouraged at home.

They certainly would not have fitted in with the one way in which both parents were little different from other Jewish families living in their neighbourhood, or whom they had left behind in Chicago or whom their families had left behind in the old country: they were determined to get on – and Harry's seemingly glaring failure to do just that was to make an older Dustin Hoffman see in him the Willy Loman figure he himself later played in Arthur Miller's *Death of a Salesman*.

The movie prop man was going to experience better things, but couldn't quite get the hang of how to do it. He had one ambition in those days, stronger even than that of being a producer: he wanted to direct pictures; a role which in his heart he never really abandoned. Directors of his son's pictures could testify to that.

Harry tried hard, very hard indeed, to get jobs at the studio, but always met with a blank. How, he then compromised, about being an assistant director? It was obvious that he was a realist; much better to have a job from which he could surely advance – once the producers began to appreciate his talents – than staying in the prop department. Finally, a studio executive was blunt: 'Harry,' he told him, 'you'll never make a director and you'll never make an assistant director'.

It was cruelty beyond all imagination – except that the executive had a list in front of him that when shown to Hoffman made a lot of sense: it was of all the brothers, sisters, cousins and close friends of senior people at the studio, all of whom would have the assistant directors' jobs before he could get near them.

That was the decision that turned him away from films as a profession and directed him towards furniture. He found a job selling it. Before long, he was designing his own Danish-style tables and chairs and earning a fair living doing it. But if he could not be rich and successful, his sons could. Dustin for one would by My son, the doctor.

And that is how the youngest of the Hoffman family was brought up to see his own future. His parents had decreed that he would be a doctor and he could not imagine being anything else. The only trouble was that he didn't really want to be a doctor. Did he have to be one? Harry and Lillian declared that yes, he did. But they did not allow this decision to overpower everything Dustin did, although they cared about his appearance and possibly worried secretly about some of his seemingly less attractive features. They kept his teeth in braces for the best part of his childhood, a fact that might have commended itself to him in later years when he contemplated the effect uneven teeth could have on the face of a film star, even one named Dustin Hoffman.

In the meantime, he traded on his looks as they were. In the ninth grade at school, he stood for class president – using as a poster a picture of Mickey Mouse with his face superimposed on that of the cartoon rodent. It didn't help him to win the election, but it enabled him to make a point, if only to himself.

He tried to get into the high school social club, the Dragons. If you weren't a Dragon, you could never have been considered to have made it properly. He did not make it properly, or any other way. They rejected his application with all the cruelty that children can summon up.

'I guess I didn't fit their image,' he reflected as an adult, still slightly sore from the experience. 'That really jaded me. I became an outsider, an observer.'

The bright light on his horizon was a young girl called Fran, who offered him the comfort of being the only female who deigned to speak to him. But that was of short duration. Fran might have taken to him, but she did not take equally to a blond hulk of a brute who considered that his appearance should have made him the target of every girl's dreams. When he realized that Fran had no such feelings towards him, he acted – against Dustin.

Spotting Dustin in the street, wearing a pair of low-slung blue jeans (that was how they were worn in those days, he maintains), he went in to the attack. He pulled the Levi's to the ground, while a crowd of other boys stood by and laughed.

'It was the most humiliating thing,' Dustin said in that 1968 *Pageant* interview, 'until he did something that was worse.'

The gathered crowd were calling, 'Fight, Fight', when the aggressor got down on his knees, looked up at Dustin and said, 'Now I'm shorter than you.'

'That,' said Dustin, 'was the worst of all.'

In truth, he never looked anything like as bad as the teasing made out – teasing by a group of kids who grew up to boast that they were at school with Dustin Hoffman; who in turn has been able metaphorically to make an ungentlemanlike gesture whenever he hears about it.

But he tried dealing with the problem of making his mark in school. He was good at the sessions when pupils were encouraged to read out their work. In one lesson, he was asked to do a book review. He chose the autobiography of Jimmy Durante, *Schnozzola*, the story of the entertainer with the biggest nose in show business, the man who would sing, 'It's My Nose's Birthday Today' in which he said that the stork delivered the nose the day before the rest of him.

Reading Durante's pre-success agonies over his appearance, tears began to roll down Dustin's face. He was so affected that he ran out of the classroom. It didn't interfere with his other school work, however. Like Ronald, Dustin did well at school scoring As enough of the time to make them a commonplace and not something to boast about.

In the meantime, he was able to show certain talents of which both he and the family wholeheartedly approved. He was an extraordinarily good pianist. The senior Hoffmans thought that Mozart would be a way of introducing him to the finer things of life; perhaps he would be a doctor who was a concert pianist on the side, or even a concert pianist who was a doctor on the side?

He knew he would never be a serious pianist because, as he once mused, 'I was too crazy to be a pianist – sitting all day alone with a piano working out problems.'

But he kept at it for a time for totally other reasons. He thought that via his keyboard, he would finally have girls queuing up to sit with him on the piano stool. So in addition to Mozart at home, he played Gershwin at parties, and, as he later admitted, hoped that one day some attractive young lady would look down at the keyboard and say, 'My, what sensitive hands.' But no one ever did.

His main complaint in these years was that eligible girls thought him 'cute'. None called him 'sexy'. That was his big problem. He hadn't 'made it' with a girl since that dreadful experience in the school assembly to which his mind would constantly revert.

Other fellows told stories of getting into the backs of cars with girls who allowed them to undo their bras and fondle their breasts as they looked into their eyes. All anyone looking into Dustin's face could see was spots.

So he tried to drown his sorrows in other activities. He took a course at the Los Angeles Conservatory of Music and enjoyed it immensely. He plainly had talent and his teachers thought so as well. But was talent enough? As he was to show years later, unless he could one day be the best there was, he didn't see much point in continuing.

So he gave up the piano, because he was convinced it would soon give him up. Perhaps he did have to think about being a doctor . . .

Leaving school, Dustin gained a place at the Santa Monica College, which most certainly was not Ivy League and was not anything like UCLA or the University of Southern California. But – and this was no advantage either – the boys all looked as though they were taking part in Elvis Presley beach party movies and the girls as though they wouldn't be interested in short, spotty Dustin.

There was an additional difficulty which most other boys did not have. Lillian decided that she was younger than her years and started dressing like a very young woman indeed – and enrolled for a course at the same college at the same time as Dustin was there. It was all set to cramp the youngster's style even more than it had ever been cramped before. But fortunately for him, his father was even more appalled and Lillian withdrew before the problem reached crisis proportions. They had, however, approached one difficulty before she left: her marks were better than Dustin's. He himself was now certain that he could get nothing at all out of student life.

'I simply lacked the necessary concentration and discipline,' he recalled. 'Besides, my grades were bad.' He went into analysis at this time. But that didn't last long, either. Deciding that he didn't need it could have been a good thing. Dustin's reason was that he really couldn't be bothered with carrying on. His teachers had noted much the same thing.

What the college did give him, however, was a chance to act. He joined their dramatic course, 'Not for any positive reasons, but as a sheer negative reaction to the necessity of studying. I thought if I could become an actor, I could get away from all those responsibilities and that's what appealed to me.'

However there was more to it than that. Suddenly, being an actor really was important. 'Something clicked inside,' was how he explained it. But he had really never expected it to, even when he started acting at the college and enjoying it. 'I didn't want to be an actor.'

His drama teacher Barney Brown was one of those who helped him change his mind. He gave him a book of essays and letters called *The Creative Process*. The book, edited by Brewster Ghiselin, contained thirty-five examples of the writing of men who were undoubted geniuses. The one that stood out for him was a letter of Mozart's. Years later, Dustin remembered the reason for his being so influenced by the book, and by Mozart's contribution in particular. 'He tells how he was just walking home one evening and this melody came to him, all the different instruments. When he got home, he wrote it right out. There wasn't any work involved. The music just came to him. That's genius.' Dustin did not imagine for one moment that he was a genius, too. Perhaps that was why he determined to work so hard – and why he always has, frequently to the despair of those working with him.

At college, he kept his dramatic ambitions quiet. At first. For a year, he pretended that he was a pre-medical student. He took exams, and flunked them. He could have taken them again and his parents expected him to do so. But he hated the college and after a year abandoned it, and with it his notion (or rather his parents' notion) that he ever would become a doctor.

Instead, he intensified his acting plans. The nearby Pasadena Play-house took on fledgeling actors who thought that a career on the boards was for them and decided that Dustin could be among them. It was a spur-of-the-moment decision on his part. It was not something he had been thinking about quite as seriously as the people at Santa Monica College might have thought, and not very much more intensely than Aunt Pearl ever considered. Certainly he hadn't been talking about it for long. But he enrolled, took the lessons and started demonstrating his newfound prowess on the stage. He regarded the Pasadena Playhouse as an extension of his education; a college for junior actors in the way that interns spend their last years in training working in hospitals.

It was playing an elderly man in a sketch that can now be seen to be the opening shot that fired the Dustin Hoffman career. 'Dusty,' said one of his instructors (which was preferable to being called 'Dustbin' and what most of his closest friends now called him), 'it may take you a long time, ten or fifteen years, but you're going to have a life in the theatre.'

To the teenager, it was like an altar boy being told by his father confessor that he had received the call to the priesthood.

More important, he instinctively knew that if an acne-ridden kid who stubbornly refused to grow beyond five foot six inches in height could make that sort of impression with a theatrical professional, then perhaps he had a few things going for him.

As he was to remember: 'I'd be on stage, rehearsing a scene, saying to a girl, "I love you, I really care about you", things I'd wanted to say for years to girls. All my life I'd been writing and acting scenes in my mind where I'd be telling guys off and telling girls I loved them; all day long in class, that's what I'd been doing, transferring myself instead of listening. I felt a naked passion for acting; getting laid was the only thing I ever felt that way about – no, not just getting laid, getting to know a girl and sit in front of a fire with her and be loved and accepted.'

Now, for the first time, he *was* being accepted, although his love scenes were just words, and not actions. But in real life, things were getting much, much better. He had girls ready to provide him with the experience of getting laid, which he thought he needed so much. He had found a footing in a world where people did not tease and where anything that happened did not have to be explained away as part of a role he was playing at the college.

He worked at the small parts he was given at the Playhouse as enthusiastically as his parents would have loved to have seen him in a laboratory or sitting in at lectures at the Cedars of Lebanon hospital medical school's dissecting room.

At their best, their most indulgent and optimistic, the Hoffmans hoped that acting would be no more than a passing phase. They didn't say that going on the stage was no job for a Jewish boy – even for the son of a star-struck mother – but they surely felt and believed it.

Dustin meanwhile equally believed that he was going to be a great actor, if not the kind that was being bred in this first television generation.

He had a natural abhorrence of the idea that the kind of acting he would do would be the sort that might one day get him into Doris Day romantic comedies. It has been said that he was already the anti-star. Dustin Hoffman was only prepared to be anti anything if he couldn't achieve it.

He was not totally alone in that at Pasadena. There was one particular friend with whom he felt he had almost a soul-brother relationship, a slightly older young actor called Gene Hackman. Hackman wasn't quite as intense as Dustin, whom he remembers partly for his musical prowess, playing a bongo drum while wearing practically nothing but a sheepskin jacket. He also remembers his acting, although he only experienced it for four months. After that time, the future star of *The French Connection* decided to up sticks and make for New York. Dustin had similar ideas but thought he had better stick it out for the rest of the year.

He was more sure than ever that his aim was not Hollywood but the New York stage. As he said: 'I dreamed only of Broadway.' And he carried that dream into reality at the drop of a play script. People would ask him if he came from New York. It was the ultimate compliment. He always replied that yes, he was a New Yorker. Somehow, he did not even think he was lying. 'I always felt New York was home,' he said later.

But to be fair, the Pasadena Playhouse helped all they could. With the judgement that he would make it as an actor ringing in his ears and, unusually for someone of that age, prepared to wait until he had served his apprenticeship, he set about getting the experience of acting in the plays that he felt would help him.

Offered a part in the theatre's production of Arthur Miller's *A View From the Bridge*, Dustin grabbed it. He also grabbed the chance of a scholarship teaching drama at a dance camp for rich youngsters in Colorado. Two New York dancers teaching there, Daniel Nagrin and Helen Tamiris, were his strongest influences at that time and he remembered them in years to come. It was valuable training for a trade that had many forms and he was sensible enough not to despise any of them.

But again there was the problem of the atmosphere at the Playhouse, which seemed to him to be breeding a new generation of beautiful people who only wanted out of acting the chance to look attractive, have open Cadillacs to drive, beach houses at Malibu and thousands of requests for autographs.

This was no place for a budding character actor who already believed he was ready for the big break, and one that he did not want to happen on some local soap opera.

His fellow-actors were not so lofty in their ideals. Cowboys were the big thing then on TV and all the guys at the Playhouse would practise drawing on each other in the hallway. But not he.

The Playhouse had enabled the bug to get into his system. But he wanted a different strain for his own future. 'I had to get away from all that,' he recalled.

Again much to his parents' disappointment, getting away from all that meant getting away from California. The sunshine state might be the home of the film and television industry, but Dustin Hoffman wanted something more, a different kind of acting, the kind where you went on and did a different performance of the same part, night after night, applied your own make-up and actually felt as well as heard the reaction of people sitting out in front.

There was only one place where he felt sure that would happen and it wasn't Los Angeles. He had to get to New York, the place where those dirty-faced kids played on even dirtier streets and swam in the filthy East River.

It was 1958 and he took the conventional route eastwards. His parents were supportive, gave him enough money to keep him alive for the next few weeks and his mother probably made him sandwiches – as Jewish as they still were. He used the kind of transport hard-up students with knapsacks on their backs adopted as a matter of course – a Greyhound bus. It was not comfortable, but he didn't think it would be. What was more, he had few illusions about New York either. He was not looking for a city paved with gold. He thought he would have to struggle for a week or so. But before very long, one day, he would be taking a bow at the St James's Theatre as a stiff-shirted first-night audience called 'bravo', and a few hours later would be sitting surrounded by fawning admirers at a table at Sardi's, reading the first editions of *The New York Times*, the *Daily News* and the *Herald-Tribune* carrying rave reviews of his startling performance. The Greyhound was a wonderful means of dreaming. There was nowhere to go and if you wanted it that way, other people would leave you alone on the long country-wide journey east.

He was not alone in the city that seemed as different from Los Angeles as the moon was from earth. Other graduates of the Pasadena Playhouse had gone there before him and beaten a trail he thought would be as easy to follow as the ones trod by those gun-toting figures in the TV Westerns he abhorred so much.

Among them was Gene Hackman, who was just about the first person he called on arriving in what was for him the great unknown. Hackman told him to come on over to his fly-ridden apartment and there Dustin stayed for three weeks, refusing to venture outside, sleeping on the kitchen floor next to the refrigerator.

It could have been a scene from a Marx Brothers movie, Dustin lying on the floor next to a far-from-new fridge, making way for Gene and his wife every time they fancied a midnight snack. But there was more hilarious sound accompaniment to it all. Dustin remembered the exotic behaviour of the refrigerator: 'Every night at two and four in the morning it would have a heart attack. It went "brrr" and woke me up.'

In truth, he was paralyzed by fear – like a person in the midst of a mental breakdown who is frightened of getting up in the morning. Dustin put it like this: 'I was too afraid to go outside and become an actor.' And while he remained inside, there was no chance of getting a role on any stage, anywhere, least of all of being able to become the great actor he now planned to be, let alone a star. Stardom, actually, did not come into it. Young actors who know they are better than anyone else tend to disparage such ideas. It wasn't any notion of having to suffer before you make it, more a kind of inverse superiority. Any good-looking fellow with a decent voice could be a star. Being an *actor*, however, was something totally – but totally – different.

The problem was being able to prove it. After those first three weeks, he summoned up the courage, with Gene Hackman doing the required amount of pushing (after all, the kitchen floor had to be cleaned now and again) to go out.

He discovered what he had expected in the first place: Broadway wasn't exactly crying out for him. He haunted the agents' buildings and on a lucky day was told that his name would be put on file. Hadn't anyone said that he was not the first to go to New York looking for acting work? Didn't he know of all those waiters who were really stars simply awaiting the right opportunity? Hadn't he noticed the Santa Clauses ringing those bells in the weeks before Christmas?

Just occasionally, things looked a little better. He contacted the dancers Daniel Nagrin and Helen Tamiris again. The couple who had been so helpful in Colorado gave him one of his first jobs in the city that had not yet coined the name Big Apple for itself. He played piano for the lessons they gave at their dance studio. Dancers were always to be a big influence on Dustin. He appreciated the dramatic quality of what they were called on to do, but he came to the conclusion that the ones at the dance studio didn't know enough about acting. With that thought in mind, he decided there was only one sure way of making money – running a drama class for dancers. At the local Salvation Army hall he bought twenty-five chairs, which he kept in the little room he now rented. He gave lessons to his friends, too – for nothing. Those friends were mostly men and he didn't think it made much sense to have women-only classes. Nor did it make much sense to have an acting school for dancers – not enough sense to make him any money, certainly. So he gave it up and went looking for other work.

He wasn't sure he would ever be a star, but he knew he was going to be a serious actor. Off-Broadway was the place he was headed, with the hope of the occasional character part. When he couldn't land a job there, he went further afield to Bronxville, a leafy residential suburb that owed nothing to the Bronx nearby, and one of whose principal recommendations was that it had been the home of a number of celebrities, including Jerome Kern. There, the Sarah Lawrence College was putting on a Gertrude Stein play, *Yes, Is For A Very Young Man*, and perhaps he would care to have a small part?

Care? It was if he had been invited to have a meal after two months of scrounging from dustbins on the Bowery.

And there were women to meet. Sarah Lawrence was a very upmarket girls' school.

The play might not have advanced either his career or his bank balance – he was paid $30 for the experience and all but $3 of it went for his fares – but it did his ego a world of good, not least of all because to the students at Sarah Lawrence College, the sight of even 5 ft 6 inches Dustin Hoffman aroused emotions not altogether different from those he felt himself.

It also didn't look too bad on his curriculum vitae, or résumé as most aspiring youngsters in New York called it. And that in itself was important – having a résumé at all and considering himself a New Yorker. Even though the place seemed soulless and the taxi-drivers shouted at him as he jay-walked in their paths, crossing the street close to the George M. Cohan statue, avoiding the tramps and the dope addicts as he stepped off the kerbs.

No doubt it was not what either Harry or Lillian would have wanted for their boy, but the week that he was travelling to Bronxville, there were smiles creasing Dustin's face. It would have taken a great deal to drag him away from all that and, strangely enough, the one thing that threatened to do so was a possibility presented by a place that was much more hick territory than his part of California could ever have been.

He was offered a chance to *direct* a play in North Dakota. The one advantage of the job at Fargo – in addition to the fact that he would be working and earning money – was that it was a better place to spend the winter than snow-driven Manhattan. So he went – and thoroughly enjoyed the experience. His *Two For The Seesaw* was, he liked to think, the best the North Dakotans had ever seen. But he realized that this was not what running away from Los Angeles had been about. He had to get back to the grime and the truth was that he couldn't get work at the theatres he really cared about.

As Gene Hackman noted at the time, he could have taken the easy way out and gone back to Los Angeles, enjoyed the pool at his parents' home and got the odd job in television. But he really wanted much more.

In the end, he was convinced that his real problem was that nobody wanted a man who was only 5 ft 6 inches tall and who had for so long had those wretched spots. He was sure that incipient acne would still come to the surface whenever he wanted anything serious to happen.

There were days when he simply pushed an envelope containing his photograph under the agents' doors and ran. His depression was so deep that he could not bring himself to consider that that could do him no good whatsoever. When he did think about it, he either broke out in a cold sweat or burst into tears. Sometimes, he simply went to sleep. The old escape mechanism was still something of an answer. Not the real answer. Not the complete answer. But some sort of one.

When he did manage to get an audition, the chances were that he not only did not get the part, but would be rewarded with explanations like: 'You don't look right for it.' When that happened, he allowed pride to take over. Instead of sulking, he'd say: 'You're right.' Sulking came later.

The only consolation was that, as before, in adversity Dustin Hoffman the clown took over. He would stand on street corners insulting perfectly innocent and nice women as they passed by. They were infuriated, wagged fingers or umbrellas, and sometimes looked ready to slap him – until he assured them they were on television and this was just another episode of *Candid Camera*.

Anyone good enough to get that far would also be able to suggest to these passers-by that they should go home and enjoy the show; certainly not to call the nearest policeman. They would be satisfied – always, and they would never see themselves – ever. Fortunately, they never saw Dustin Hoffman again either, unless it was from a seat in some theatre.

Other women took to him more happily, particularly if they were young and beautiful. It was now apparent that the looks that attracted the attention of no agents and which all but repelled Dustin himself were having an effect on the opposite sex that few could have predicted.

He became the most popular figure in the crowd that Gene Hackman had assembled around them. And not just with other actors. The short, funny-looking Dustin Hoffman had no trouble whatever bedding the prettiest girls around.

One of the people with whom he mixed was another young actor named Robert Duvall, who later made his name as an intense artist in roles like that of the adopted son in *The Godfather*. Duvall was singularly impressed with the lack of difficulty faced by Dustin when he set about getting a young lady to take off her clothes and go to bed with him. He had a line standing outside his apartment, Duvall remembered.

Dustin also stood in line himself, trying to get jobs. When he realized he was not getting them on any stage, he found work where it lay – in a series of jobs that make very good reading for actors who subsequently become big, important international stars but which a failure never writes home about.

For a time he worked in a mental hospital as an attendant. He probably figured that he would have an opportunity to use the experience in some subsequent role, which indeed he did. Even so, at first he quite enjoyed the work. 'I've always been attracted to mental illness,' he said, without any malicious intent. 'In any event, the people were defence-less,' which has been another characteristic of many of the characters he was subsequently to play.

He at first gave all the signs of being well cut out for that sort of work. He actually did enjoy being with a number of patients, particularly those with whom he played volleyball. Dustin played the piano for them, and they showed all the signs of appreciating it. He played Scrabble as well – and they beat him. Signs of *Rain Man* there.

But he gave up the work when he started contemplating the futility of much that he was supposed to do, to say nothing of the sheer horror of it all, the human degradation he witnessed.

One of the patients, a doctor, had a 'call sign' that seemed to attach

him to life. He loved the song 'Goodnight Irene', and Dustin played it
for him. Only once did the man recognize the wife to whom he had
been happily married for years before being struck by his stroke. Dustin
saw him rush towards her crying: 'I can't help it! I can't help it! I'm
trying!' Then, within seconds, he turned away. He couldn't remember
anything. The man of science was a vegetable once again.

Another one of the patients fascinated Dustin in a way that was both
moving and horrific, to say nothing of frightening. This man had a habit
of charging down his wards, saying totally inconsequential things like:
'I'm getting out next Sunday, my wife's an old Dutch cleanser and
you've got nice teeth, sonny boy – are they yours?' All in one gulped
sentence. More interesting – particularly for an attendant who believed
in his heart that he was an actor and that this was a very interesting
acting school – was the way the man would suddenly take on the
'personalities' of the things with which he was dealing. Without saying
anything, he would 'become' the electric razor he was using. Suddenly,
he was shouting, 'Bzzzzzz . . .' Dustin thought about that. 'That's the
kind of thing you have to do in acting,' he told himself. 'I thought if
he can have this concentration, why can't I?'

He was to adopt the technique when he took acting lessons from the
respected Lonnie Chapman. 'Become the word, "life",' said Chapman.
Dustin thought of the human electric razor and decided he would act
out the role of a pinball in a machine at a fairground. He wrapped
himself into a ball and crashed into chairs and every other piece of
furniture around, shouting, 'Bonnnkkkk! Brrrr!' It might not have got
him a lot of work, but for a time, he felt like an actor.

But before he felt like an actor, he felt as if he were turning into one
of the patients himself, and before long would be committed.

'My dreams got so bad,' he said, 'I had to quit.'

The only thing young Dustin Hoffman was prepared to totally commit
himself to was an acting career. Easier said than done.

Another job required him to look after a human being with whom he
found it much easier to identify. At the age of 24, Dustin became a
companion and honorary uncle to the child of a 70-year-old multi-
millionaire and his much younger career-woman wife. Dustin later
recalled: 'The kid was a lonely little guy, wandering around in a twenty-
room town house. He was a creative challenge for me.'

Together, they made up scrapbooks and went on outings which Hoff-

man devised; the zoo one day, a trip to the top of the Empire State
Building the next, and then on the Statten Island Ferry.

He remembered: 'Of course, I knew I'd be leaving him and I worried
constantly that he would become too attached to me, becoming even
unhappier when I did go. So we'd have long talks about my one day
not being with him. He'd tell me he understood, but when the day
came that I actually had to go, both of us cried. I was determined that
when I did become a father, no child of mine would have to suffer for
lack of parental guidance.'

Other jobs were somewhat easier on the Hoffman psyche, even if not
always on the Hoffman feet. Like the time he worked in a dance studio,
not as a dancer or an instructor, it has to be said, but as a janitor.

Those feet were to be tested again when he reached the virtual peak
of achievement for any resting actor – being employed as a salesman at
Macy's department store. It is fascinating to contemplate the number
of future stars who at this very moment are walking up and down
Macy's sales floors, trying to talk unsuspecting men and women into
buying things that they don't need now and never will. Sadly, no one
at Macy's in 1959 realized that the 21-year-old selling a life-sized doll
sitting on a counter would one day be a double Oscar winner.

But he stayed there for two years. Not even Christopher Hackman
realized how fortunate he was to be served by Dustin Hoffman, although
he had got to know him well. He was just two years old at the time,
but his father Gene brought Christopher into Macy's to see Dustin at
work. The child was placed on top of the counter and told to keep
perfectly still. Remarkably he did, so still that a customer started search-
ing in her purse for the money to pay for the life-sized doll. That was
when Gene decided that Christopher was an even better actor than
Dustin and wanted no more of it.

It was not the end of Dustin's Macy's career. When they wanted him
to demonstrate their ice-hockey equipment, he put on a plaid lumber
jacket and a pair of earmuffs and addressed all the potential customers
in his interpretation of a French-Canadian accent.

That was as close as he got to acting for the time being. It unquestionably was preferable to washing up, which he seemed to do as frequently
as the machines now being advertised all the time on television and in
the newspapers and magazines. At Rudley's Restaurant in Manhattan
he worked serving the customers perched on stools in front of the
counter. One of the perks of the job – he needed it because the money
was derisory – was to be able to eat from stock all that he could down

at a single sitting. One lunchtime, he persuaded his stomach to consume six steaks. 'They were paper-thin,' he recalled later, as if to minimize the effect of what he was doing. Nothing, however, minimized it in the eyes of his employer, who decided that was carrying staff welfare much too far. He lost the job.

So the young Hoffman was looking for more work and finding it – as a typist, for instance. This was a skill he had learned at school and he was in as much demand sitting in front of a typewriter as he would have liked to have been standing in front of the footlights.

But his employer was Yellow Pages and so many people were ready to let their fingers do the walking that he could have stayed there for years, especially since he had a job working as a waiter in the evenings.

That waiting job did offer some kind of future. Or so he believed. Important, moneyed customers were the sort of people he had to get to know, people with influence, people who knew theatrical managements.

It was an opportunity to show what he could do and he was not the kind of fellow to turn down any opportunity that could advance his career. Although, to be fair, that was not necessarily the precise reason he did not merely serve dishes of hot roast beef, collect the cheques and then go home nursing a pair of sore feet.

There was an ever-present urge to be 'on', which is possibly the first requirement of anyone aiming at acting as a career. He affected a French accent, which he decided was as important for a waiter as his French-Canadian tones had been when he was trying to sell ice-hockey gear. That lasted until a customer spoke to him in French. M. Dustin, *le pauvre homme*, developed a vicious cough and had to be helped back into the kitchen. Because it was one of those places where show people gathered, Dustin had reason to hope that something would come out of it, despite all the problems and frustrations. But not, though, if Sam Spiegel had anything to do with it. Mr. Spiegel, flushed from his experiences of getting his production of *Lawrence of Arabia* under way, wanted nothing better than to relax at the restaurant – which he did, until a waiter spilled coffee all over him.

The waiter was, of course, Dustin. 'I'm not really a waiter,' said Dustin, 'actually I'm an actor.'

'No,' said the producer angrily, 'from now on, you're a waiter.'

After a time, the waiter had to reconcile himself to a job as dishwasher. Even so, he had his optimistic moments, especially when the place where he worked also provided – or so he thought – opportunities to impress.

The Premise club in Greenwich Village was frequented by the kind of people whose company he enjoyed, mainly artists and actors and producers and directors.

All his efforts bore fruit of a sort. Employees were expected to do a turn. The evening Dustin was on, a producer was in the audience. Joan Darling invited him to audition for her. It was an opportunity, if nothing else, for lessons, and possibly the most important lesson of all – that a performer should always be sure of his material. Dustin turned himself into a sort of Lenny Bruce that night – a real irony considering the movie role he would have a few years later. On this occasion, Miss Darling assessed that his particular form of vulgarity was not for her. So Dustin had to go back to looking for more work.

At times he tried to rationalise what he had done. It wasn't easy. In fact, it all came down to trying to find ways of escaping from the guilt that he felt at not doing anything well enough to receive the plaudits, not just of his family, but of the people he had known at places like Pasadena, who were showing evidence of doing a lot better than he ever thought he would. He knew that he could bluff his way around his parents' doubts in New York much more easily than he could in Los Angeles. 'It's easier to fail 3,000 miles away from your family,' he said, and he knew it was true.

He still gravitated back to theatres, doing jobs that he hoped the actors would not notice. At the Longacre Theater, he worked as a cloakroom attendant. It was one of his more memorable jobs. One of the people who handed him a coat was Mrs Eleanor Roosevelt. He sat looking at the former First Lady's garment all through the performance. He couldn't get over the fact that it was her coat, *her* coat.

Other jobs he picked up at this time were more challenging; to *Time* magazine, he seemed a valued employee, although no one was around in the morgue – the magazine's library where he worked – to recognize that within ten years he would be featured on the cover; perhaps the highest accolade available to anyone anywhere in public life.

He got work finally in another Broadway theatre – selling orange drinks. That was probably his lowest ebb. It is not true that an aspiring actor only has to be able to smell the greasepaint (or hear the roar of the crowd, but that's another title altogether) to be happy. The job was degrading and frustrating, but it did provide a few much-needed cents and there is no record of his telling patrons that the butler did it or that he could have played the part better.

Those who knew Dustin wondered how long he could carry it through. After all, there was a limit to all endurance tests and the months of looking for acting work had stretched into years; several years. How could a man who had turned down medicine as a career when he knew he wasn't getting anywhere, who had forsworn a life in music for the same reason, be so persistent? The dedication of some of his future film roles plainly had its roots in these heart-breaking years. He was going to do only what he wanted to do, what he knew he was going to be brilliant at. If nobody else knew it, that was their loss. He would prove himself to them. If only he had the chance.

Occasionally, he could see that what he was doing had some purpose to it – even if it was not showing much purpose for himself personally. For a time he raised money in aid of victims of muscular dystrophy. Useful, serving the community, but not likely to make him a fortune and certainly of no value at all for the career of the man whom he knew would before long be the most talked-about actor on Broadway.

And sometimes, just sometimes, things were much, much better. In a small summer-stock company in New Jersey in 1963, he thought he had got something out of his system: he directed a production of Arthur Miller's *Death of a Salesman*. It was a daunting prospect for any young director. For Dustin Hoffman, it was going to be not just an important theatrical landmark, but something of a catharsis. Willy Loman was always his own father, the Salesman. The story was that of his family, particularly now that Harry in his sixties had become a salesman who was suddenly laid off; a failure in his own eyes, just the way that Loman thought he was one. Rather than getting something out of his system, it had the opposite effect. Dustin didn't know that, before long, he would record a version of the play starring Lee J. Cobb, and later star in it too – playing, he was convinced, his own father, on both stage and film.

Dustin himself was actually rarely out of work, on the dole, although happen it did. In fact, he had a work ethic that was not always evident in other people of his age who couldn't make it in their chosen field. But his efforts hardly kept him above the breadline. For the first ten years of his working life, he never earned more than $3,000 a year, and people were still waiting for him to be that overnight sensation.

Did anyone else believe it? Hackman and Duvall gave every

impression that they did, as they sat in clubs with Dustin, listening to him holding court, usually with a pretty girl at his elbow.

Meanwhile, his parents sent him $200 a month, which they continued to do for two or three years. They couldn't afford it, but they also knew that Dustin couldn't afford to come back to California and give up his ambition to be a real actor. All the jobs he was doing were considered suitable enough for a young man determined on an acting career. The truth, nevertheless, was daunting: becoming an overnight sensation was taking a very long time indeed.

In the end, the only way the senior Hoffmans could really demonstrate their own displeasure at the way things were going was by cutting off their son's allowance. The $200 stopped and they hoped that the message would get across. It did not, even though the chances of Dustin's achieving any kind of success in the theatre were getting more remote, not less so.

But occasionally, he could show that, despite the reluctance of managements to put any money on it, he really was cut out for an acting career. The Modells Army and Navy story decided he was the right man to help them cash in on the misfortune of a newspaper industry caught up in a seemingly never-ending strike. They dressed him up in what looked like a British town crier's outfit and he walked the length and breadth of Times Square – home of *The New York Times* which, like the other papers in town, had been stifled by the strike – reading the news. He earned enough from this gainful occupation to buy himself a couple of items from the Army and Navy store.

When he discovered that a company needed someone to work weaving Hawaiian *leis*, he was there ready to offer his services. They were not quite as welcome by an employer as they were by the female population of the parts of Manhattan that he frequented. That seemed almost too much to expect, for the girls were still standing in line, not for a young man in the business suit he wore at Macy's or in the typing pool, but the one in the sheepskin vest – without a shirt – blue jeans and leather boots, who rode a fast motorcycle. Before the man at Macy's wanted it otherwise, his hair was virtually down to his shoulders. The girls flipped. Dustin Hoffman was making his point. Nothing that had been good enough for Harry and Lillian would be good enough for him.

But even for him, the frustrations were sometimes overpowering. He never again felt like having himself certified, but the temptation to sleep it all away was occasionally all he could think of.

He considered taking serious acting lessons and for a time managed

to gain entrance to Lee Strasberg's Actors' Studio which had influenced
so many people he admired – Marilyn Monroe had succumbed a short
time before – from Brando to James Dean. Mr Strasberg took a lot of
convincing, even though Dustin was highly recommended by two
former students, Robert Duvall and Gene Hackman. But after five
auditions, Dustin was finally accepted. That in itself was no mean
achievement. People came from all over America and from outside the
country, too, to audition for the great Strasberg, and people went back
home without getting further into the studio than the audition room.

Dustin may not have known it at the time, but young Jane Fonda
was having similar thoughts and taking private lessons from Mr Strasberg. But Jane had more money, and a great deal more influence, than
Dustin Hoffman, and in any case when Strasberg said something that
Hoffman did not like, the younger man kept nothing back. There was
no future in that sort of row.

Frankly, it seemed that there could be no future in acting for him
either. By 1962, he had been going through the routine of looking for
work and finding it only in a kitchen or a department store for almost
four years. He had to content himself with seeing other professionals at
work. One he admired more than most was the sometimes crazy actor
Zero Mostel who had not yet recovered from the shock of being black-
listed by Senator McCarthy, but was intriguing Standing Room Only
audiences as the lead in Ionesco's *Rhinoceros* (he was just a short time
away from his biggest successes of all, in *Fiddler On The Roof* and *The
Producers*). Dustin sneaked in for at least half a dozen performances of
Rhinoceros. He and Mostel spoke only once. 'Lewis Gilbert sends you
his best,' Dustin called as the much older star left the theatre. 'And
give it right back,' shouted Mostel. 'I melted into the concrete,' recalled
Dustin.

There was, however, one opportunity for him to express himself the
way he liked best. He started giving acting lessons again, suppressing
any notion of adopting the well-tried (unfortunately, all too well-tried)
notion that those who can, do, those who can't, teach.

His pupils at the East Harlem Boys' Club seemed to appreciate him
better than most of the managements he approached. He also appreciated them. As he was to say: 'It sounds a cliché to say this, I suppose,
but there was an awful lot of raw talent there.'

In 1962, he had what he thought would be the big break – a chance
to play *on stage* on Broadway. It was a small part in a small play that
had a small run of three weeks. He was one of a group of Army misfits

in *A Cook For Mr General*. Shades again of so much that was to follow. Although not straight away.

His role in that play was no more likely to get him noticed than anything else he had done. It was just a walk-on part and he had no more to say on stage than the critics had to write about him in their reviews. Was that all that Broadway was going to offer him? As he later said, his whole life seemed to be spent waiting for summer and the opportunities it would provide for stock productions. 'Only six months till June,' he kept telling himself. 'Only two months to June . . . only one . . .'

It has to be said that much of the fault for Dustin's lack of success in getting the jobs in the theatre for which he craved was entirely his own. The man who would endure washing-up, typing and baby-sitting, wouldn't accept roles that he did not think were suited to his talents. Other aspiring actors were delighted to accept jobs requiring them to do nothing more than walk on to a set carrying tennis racquets or trays of tea, but Dustin wouldn't. His mere refusal was enough to put doubt into the minds of producers and directors. The way that he refused them was sufficient to put him on to the pages of black books that would be opened every time his name came up – and were more likely to send him back to the dole queue than anything else. Give him a line to read that he thought ridiculous and he would say so. 'Instant slickness' was one of the kinder terms in his vocabulary. When a director criticized what he did, chances were that he would grow increasingly angry, to the point of tearing up the script and sprinkling the bits into the auditorium in the direction of a producer previously perfectly willing to give him a chance.

He couldn't live well, behaving like that. But Dustin had his way of saving money. He distributed what little cash he had in a series of jars; one for food, another for fares, a third for rent. One jar would never be used to come to the aid of another.

If he hadn't had offers to go into summer-stock, taking whatever came his way, he might even have been dispirited enough to pack up and go back to California. But when he knew that the season was about to start and someone, somewhere wanted him to play a part or two, he decided against going back. And he still went to auditions and he still lost jobs. He still said: 'Yes, you're right,' and he still meant it – although what he really meant was, 'I'm not right for doing the part the way you want it done.'

He was still in his twenties and if he couldn't be so sure of himself, or so determined at that age and with no commitments to anyone else, what the hell? He wasn't married and that was the way he wanted it too. Dustin did want sex, but not the ties of marriage. When he wanted a girl, they still seemed to be waiting in line for him. Could any man ask for more? Some would, but not Dustin. Only that part, which he could do his way.

He was still a popular fellow to be around. Robert Duvall said that he sometimes looked like Barbra Streisand in drag – and he picked up new friends constantly. Among them at this time was another struggling young actor who was as unlike Dustin as it seemed possible to be, a tall, good-looking, blond man named Jon Voight. He was as impressed with Dustin's romantic success as was everyone else. Actually, girls still mystified him. He knew they found him attractive, but could never understand why. And when he made advances that did not bring the required response, he couldn't understand that either. He aimed high. Never Jewish girls. They didn't appeal to him at all, as if encouraging a Jewish romance would bring back the life with his parents from which he had escaped.

He was introduced to Marisol, a fashionable sculptress. Never frightened of ridicule – although he always tended to expect it – he asked her for a date. He could not think why a woman who already had her own following would be interested in an out-of-work actor, but he was not prepared for the response as she turned him down flat. 'I won't go out with you,' she declared, 'because you're a creep.' It was as much as he thought of himself. That did not mean, however, that he was any the less hurt by her cutting riposte. It was an assault below the belt and that was not the way he liked to be treated by women.

So he went back to concentrate on work. He had an agent now. He had previously found himself in the Catch-22 situation of not being able to get work because he didn't have a full-time agent, and not being able to get a full-time agent because he didn't have the work. That, at least, was in the past. He might be answering jobs for washers-up between work, but he was not planning to sign for any more two-year stints at Macy's either. And that was something to give him pleasure, even if it did not give much satisfaction to his bank manager or accountant. Provided someone gave him the chance to work somewhere, he contemplated the opportunities that were beginning to come his way, and was content if not totally happy.

It was in a totally different frame of mind that he went to the clubs and entertained the assembled company with his stories of experiences and impressed them with his unconscionable optimism that one day he was going to be a success.

That was how at the Improvization Club in Greenwich Village he had struck up conversation with a tall, statuesque brunette, who had got his juices racing. Her name, she said, was Anne – Anne Byrne.

3

Anne Byrne would doubtless not take kindly to the suggestion that she was in any way a Dustin Hoffman groupie. This was, in any case, in the days when the expression was first being used and certainly long before his was a name anyone other than his own circle of friends and his legion of employers would recognize. Anne Byrne was not one of the girls who seemed to swarm round Dustin like iron filings to a magnet.

She was beautifully lithe, dark and with a smile he found enchanting. She was also a good three inches taller than he was. But, as he was to say, ' I always like them high.'

The night that she went to the Improvisation Club in Greenwich Village she was accompanied by a man who was of the Hoffman circle, his current room-mate. Dustin was at the club earning another meagre crust, this time playing the piano. By the end of the evening it was he in whom she was interested for all the reasons that other girls had been equally keen on the 26-year-old sometime actor. And for all the reasons that he himself had thought of, before the 3,000-mile trip East made him feel so inadequate.

'We were instantly drawn to each other,' she told me. 'I thought he was rather good-looking in his funny way. That was the initial attraction.' But there were more important reasons, or as she would put it, more serious reasons. 'My friend had spoken about Dustin, and I could see why people liked him. And he seemed to be very serious. Since I was the ripe old age of, I think, 19 at the time and was very serious about my dancing, we seemed to have a lot in common.'

They went out together, but she did not think, didn't hold any illusions then or now about knowing, that she was witnessing the burgeoning of a big star. 'I never thought about his being a star. It would have been a completely different world. Movies to me just didn't come into the life I lived.'

In truth, movies seemed a lot less serious (that word again which meant so much to her and she thought so important to him) business, the mere fripperies of acting.

However this was 1963 and a lot of changes were to occur to them both before long. They spent a lot of time together that summer. 'Then I joined the Pennsylvania Ballet and we lost touch with each other.' The Pennsylvania Ballet was a new company partly founded by George Balanchine and an invitation to join as a ballerina was too tempting for a girl for whom dancing was a way of life; the only life.

When she thought about Dustin, it was as a man 'with a single-minded purpose, and that was to be a very successful actor, but, again, I didn't for a moment associate it with stardom.'

To give some idea of how long ago 1963 is, Dustin bought a suit so that he could go out looking well-dressed on his first date with her.

He was to recall that he told her how much he liked the way she dressed. She said that the shirt that he particularly admired had been bought from a man running a pushcart on Orchard Street on New York's Lower East Side, the thoroughfare which became internationally celebrated when it was featured in the first talking picture, Al Jolson's *The Jazz Singer*. It had cost her $1.25.

Dustin took her to the beach for their second date. It was a happy, pleasant day, but until they were violently awoken from a sleep, nothing more. They both dozed lying on the sands – a good, respectable three feet away from each other. But suddenly a passing jet disturbed the idyllic setting. Instinctively, from the shock of the aircraft noise, they almost literally jumped into each other's arms.

Dustin didn't need any further convincing: he was in love, and Anne seemed to give him the impression that she felt much the same. But they were both convinced it was a youthful fling. There was no sign that it would blossom into anything more. Before long, they parted.

It was another five years before they saw each other again, during which time Anne joined the New York Ballet, Les Grandes Ballets Canadiens and was a guest dancer in Europe.

Dustin also advanced in those years. He worked in Boston for the eminent director Ulu Grosbard, earning $65 a week at the Theater Company of Boston, which produced the work of Ionesco, Sartre, Bertolt Brecht and Harold Pinter. It was with Grosbard that he starred as Pozzo, the slave-driver in *Waiting for Godot*. 'Until he did it, I never did understand the role,' Grosbard said.

For one night, Dustin was a New York star. Grosbard brought the play to the off-Broadway theatre, Circle In The Square, and Dustin was brilliant in his role. When Grosbard produced Arther Miller's *A View From The Bridge* in New York, he had a part for Dustin in that, too. But not acting. He would be his assistant director. At first, the Hoffman sensitivities were outraged. The play would feature his friend Robert Duvall. But before long, he revelled in it. Grosbard introduced him to the play's writer, the eminent Arther Miller. 'Hoffman might be someone to watch out for when you do a new production of *Death Of A Salesman*.' said Grosbard. Miller took note of the suggestion – and so did Dustin. And there was the excitement of what he was doing in *A View From The Bridge*. He thought that he wanted nothing more out of his professional life than to direct.

'I learned more from [Grosbard] than from anyone,' he would say. 'Acting is a tricky business – you're too dependent on all the neuroses around you. I want to be removed from all that pain. When you are an actor, you tune your violin the best you know how and then along comes someone and says, "No. I don't want it tuned that way". I just want to do my work and say the hell with everyone else. People say there aren't enough good actors. The fact is there are a hell of a lot of good actors around, but very few good directors.'

It would take a very good part indeed to persuade him off that course, Dustin liked to think. But he knew that when a part did come that offered 'important' work, he would grab it with all the enthusiasm that he could muster – and he didn't have to be the good actor he knew he was to assemble all the enthusiasm in the world. He did, however, in those dreams of his, think only of doing things his way. If he were given the best part in the world and he disagreed with the way the director wanted it done, he'd still pass it up. But now, strangely, he found he was in demand as an actor, too.

Quite suddenly, after all the time in which he secretly convinced himself that the nearest he would ever get to acting in New York was by using those accents in Macy's and the clubs, jobs that meant more started finding their way to him.

There were others who came to similar conclusions as Grosbard at this time. The writer Robert Ribman for one had seen some of Dustin's out-of-town work and had liked what he had seen.

When Dustin's agent suggested that among his list of auditions should be one for Ribman's play *Harry, Noon and Night*, Hoffman agreed. After all, at this stage, he had little to lose. Ribman, on the other hand, thought there was a great deal to gain and offered him the part of a hunchbacked German homosexual. George Morrison, the director, said after his audition that it was the most brilliant he had ever seen. 'It was incredible,' he said; he had never seen a performer start grabbing props and improvising the way that the young Hoffman was able to do.

Dustin liked auditions and was usually good at them. Rehearsals, though, were something else – both for Dustin and for Morrison. 'One day he disappeared in front of my eyes,' Morrison later remembered. 'He was unreachable. But the next day he came out of it. In the end his part was brilliantly realized. It was an incredible meeting between playwright and actor. It was like Tennessee Williams and Geraldine Page, Eugene O'Neill and Jason Robards, an actor finding his playwright and suddenly realizing his talent.'

Ribman himself was to tell *McCalls* magazine: 'Dustin has the ability to annihilate his own ego and become the character he is looking for.'

That was a generous statement and Ribman is just about the only person who has gone on record – or spoken off it – to claim that Hoffman would ever sublimate his ego, let alone annihilate it. It was a small role, but it got him noticed, certainly by Ribman, who earmarked him for his next play.

Even with that work and that reputation, Dustin was still existing below the poverty line – helped out by food parcels packed by Lillian when he wasn't actually getting money – but there was little poverty about his performances.

Quite unexpectedly, he was about to get recognition in New York, courtesy of the playwright Frank D. Gilroy. Gilroy was re-casting for his Pulitzer Prize-winning play *The Subject Was Roses*, which had been so successful in New York that most of the original cast were going to Los Angeles for a West Coast production, something that only happens to the shows that attract the best box offices. Would Dustin Hoffman be interested in being part of the second New York company? He would be playing a part created by Martin Sheen, who was among those going West in the play about an Irish family as different from Dustin's own as could possibly be imagined.

Would he be interested? It was a question that only those who didn't know Dustin Hoffman could possibly ask. Of course he was interested. The part on offer was not just a bit role. He was being given the chance of playing one of the leads as the son. And on Broadway.

They rehearsed and everything went very well indeed. Dustin was behaving himself. In fact, his behaviour seemed as angelic as the way in which he played the role.

Plainly, there was cause for celebration. And how does an actor who has spent most of his waking hours looking for work celebrate when that work finally comes? By doing the one thing that had always seemed so difficult – eating, and eating well. He was going to have a dinner party for his closest friends, conveniently at the home of his current girlfriend, for the people who would appreciate just how important a milestone this was for him, people who would understand that what they were eating and drinking was the closest they might come to edible gold.

It all seemed to have gone so well. At least, he hadn't thrown the script at the director; hadn't made impossible demands that the management regarded as the ultimate in *chutzpah*.

Dustin was in a good mood as he planned the main feature of the evening, a beef *fondue*. He knew how to cook it; the recipe was as ingrained on his mind as the lines he had read in the theatre that day. The meat was diced; the oil was hot. Too hot.

He knew how hot it was, which was why he didn't attempt merely to drop the beef gently into the couldron. Instead, he threw it in, which was roughly equivalent to pouring a fire-hose on the seething mass. It didn't just sizzle, it jumped out of the pot and on to the furniture around him. A small fire broke out, which he tried to smother with his bare hands. The pain was indescribable; the effect on his hands hardly less damaging than if he had tried to cook his fingers and his palms along with the diced beef. Later, he discovered that he had third-degree burns, although he couldn't know it for sure at the time.

He had to weigh up what to do about it. If he sought medical treatment, the doctors might force him to stay in hospital; they certainly would have said that he could not work. And even if they did not, the time he would have had to spend at the hospital as an out-patient would have cut into his rehearsal schedule. The company wouldn't like that. They might decide to give the part to someone else.

So he carried on rehearsing – until the moment that he collapsed on stage. Doctors took off the bandages he had applied (he didn't tell anyone how serious were his injuries) and found that the burns had become badly infected. Worse than that, the infection had entered his bloodstream. His chances of stardom, it seemed, had burnt away along with his rug and furniture and the charred mass that had started off as a beef *fondue*. So, too, it seemed, might his chances of a long life.

Indeed, he had lost the part. Mr Gilroy could not wait for a lead actor who had to be rushed off to hospital without anyone being able to tell him when he would recover. Indeed, *if* he would recover.

An urgent operation was prescribed by the doctor Dustin saw at the hospital. It was one of those judgements that could not be questioned. The burns had to be treated somehow if he were to stay alive. The blood-poisoning was on the verge of being fatal. It was at this point that the inner Hoffman self came to the fore. Just as he had at school or when the girls weren't responding in the way that he believed they should, he faced a crisis by becoming a clown. He knew that before long, the clown would be Pagliacci, but it didn't matter. It was his best weapon; a defence that was a kind of attack.

When the surgeon visited him before the operation, Dustin laughed. When he heard that there were inherent risks in the surgery, he told a joke. The joking continued as the trolley on which he was being wheeled into the operating room trundled along the corridors, in and out of the lift.

The anaesthetist took the necessary details. Blood pressure was checked. His heart-beat studied. He was asked whether he had eaten recently. He had. That was the danger signal. Everyone knows that anaesthetics are dangerous for someone whose stomach is full. There is an ever-present risk of vomiting. So he was told that a tube had to be inserted through his mouth. It would not be easy because one could never be certain that the tubing had reached the right place. 'How will I know when it's in the right place?' Dustin asked. 'You won't be able to talk,' the doctor replied.

The anaesthetist tried three times. On each occasion, both he and Dustin knew that it wasn't in the right place. The fourth time, the doctor shouted, 'That's it.' 'No it isn't,' shouted Dustin. 'I can still talk.'

And this time he wasn't joking. He insisted on being taken to his room for the anaesthetist to try again in the morning. 'You might die,' he was told. He muttered something about being certain he would die if the tube was not put in place properly. The anaesthetist by this time was sweating profusely and the general opinion in the operating theatre was that he was incapable of doing his job properly – in those circumstances at any rate.

Dustin did not exactly cure himself, but his heart continued to beat at something like the right pace. He stayed alive that night and early the next morning the operation was successfully performed. Which is more than can be said for Dustin's career in *The Subject Was Roses*.

There was another disturbing feature of his time in hospital: to try to stem the agonizing pain, he was given large doses of Demerol. Three or four times a day, the shots were administered. Before long, he realized what was happening: he had become addicted to the drug. As he later recalled: 'I said to myself, now I know what it feels like to be a junkie – because I couldn't wait for those shots. Every morning I'd get a beaut before they changed my bandages. And every few hours I'd get more shots. I felt I knew what addicts' lives are like and what they think they're getting from dope.

'My euphoria was almost complete. I had no sex drive, of course, because drugs take its place. In a sense, taking drugs is very sexual. Perhaps what I mean is that you have a powerful feeling of love, and while you're on drugs, you experience no hate or fear. Also, you don't eat because, even if you feel hungry when the tray comes, the effort of picking up a fork seems too much to handle.'

He remembered that he went into hospital weighing 140 pounds. By the time he left he weighed only 110. Weight was not the only thing he lost. With it had gone what was quite simply the will to live. He weaned himself off the Demerol and felt worse than he had ever felt before, even in his worst moments. 'I honestly didn't think I could stand it,' he told a writer from *Family Circle* magazine. 'My life was unbearable. I didn't feel pain from the burns any more, but that had been replaced by a pain 1,000 per cent worse. I felt as if hordes of people were constantly shaking me, shaking my whole insides, shaking me until I'd cry in anguish. But gradually I beat the craving for the drug.'

What he had not beaten was the craving to act, and for success. An understudy, Walter McGinn, took over the role and neither he nor the play made very much impact at all after that, despite its previous reputation. When Dustin came out of hospital three weeks later, he was allowed to be the understudy for the understudy, a kindly man who could see the effect it was all having. When he heard that Harry and Lillian Hoffman were in town for the day, Walter McGinn contacted them and suggested they get tickets for that evening's performance. Once he knew they had done so, the actor reported sick and Dustin went on in his place. It was just for that evening. But his parents had seen Dustin Hoffman acting on Broadway.

Dustin's luck for that night showed no sign of lasting, at least as far as his career was concerned. He did land another part in an off-Broadway production of *Sergeant Musgrave's Dance*, but this time he behaved like the Dustin Hoffman of old. There was a natural kink in his character that not only did not endear him to the people with whom he worked, but did little to help himself. It was almost as if there were a death-wish within him. He didn't like himself any the more for it and once again, this self-disdain would reveal itself on his analyst's couch.

On this occasion, his idea of what he wanted to make of the part of Sparky at the Theatre de Lys was distinctly different from that of the director who in despair, told him to take a day off. He then added: 'Take two days off . . . take a week.' Dustin knew what he meant. He was being asked not to come back at all. He took the hint and stayed away for good.

As Sally Kempton was to explain in a particularly incisive article in *Esquire* magazine: 'The problem he understood then and was to under-stand better later, was that he was an inner-directed actor who had to find his character, when it came to him. The directors who tried to force his performance to coalesce before he was ready sent him into a sort of catatomic trance, from which he would emerge shouting in rage and frustration.' He and the director decided that it was in everybody's best interests if they parted company. Permanently.

But Robert Ribman, as before, had more faith in him. He had a part which he believed was right up the Dustin Hoffman street. In 1967 he cast him in a role that would do more for his reputation than anything he had ever done before: that of Zolditch, a Russian clerk with no love for his fellow-man, which was not taken to be a judgement on Dustin himself at the time, although there were those who thought that it might. The part turned out to be the star feature of his coming production of *The Journey Of The Fifth Horse*, to be presented at the American Place Theater.

It gave Dustin an opportunity to be simply an actor, an opportunity that few things he had attempted to date could possibly have matched. Zolditch was at least ten years older than Dustin was himself, but Ribman thought he could do it. His faith would be rewarded – if only in terms of Dustin's performance. In that respect, it worked as well as his other attempts at success had failed.

In *The New York Times* Stanley Kauffmann wrote about Dustin's 'vitality', which he said he used as a new-born actor (obviously not knowing a great deal of what had gone before it), but with 'the fine control of a skilful one'. And he added: 'With sharp comedy techniques, he makes this unattractive man both funny and pathetic.'

The most revealing part of the review was the highly prescient statement: 'Perhaps – the insanities of the theatre world permitting – we will be allowed to watch an extraordinary career develop.' Few could possibly imagine by how much.

But the play itself ran for only three weeks. Even so, now Dustin really did believe he could forget Macy's. The critics thought so, too. He was awarded an Obie, roughly the equivalent of the on-Broadway Tony and the Hollywood Oscar, for the best off-Broadway performance of the year.

It certainly was a heady experience both for him and for the people who saw him. Naturally, as time and fame have made their impact, there are those who claim to have recognized in this early performance a great deal of the outstanding film actor to come. It would not have been a difficult thing to do. Suddenly, it seemed that a new actor was pulsating himself on the way to fame, if not fortune. Even so, if anyone was unsure of it all, it was Dustin himself.

He again found it difficult to find the performance he was looking for. His inner self was taking an age to come to the surface and once more a director was showing what Dustin would regard as a singular lack of patience. They squabbled until it seemed as though they were close to blows.

When the director Larry Arrick wanted to know when he was going to come up with the required performance, he got an answer that could be summed up as 'Dusty', in both senses of the word. 'I haven't given seven years of my life to give a summer-stock performance,' he replied.

Dustin was certainly close to dismissal and could have been excused for secretly wondering why it was taking so long in coming. He did not know that when he took his cue at the first preview performance, a substitute was about to be taken on.

But then he was on stage, speaking lines as a Russian manuscript editor on the verge of a hysteria that was not totally unlike his own, and using a voice that had not come to him in a single rehearsal. The voice was high-pitched and he wasn't sure how it came out, but come out it did and it stayed out. The eminent critic Walter Kerr noted: 'Dustin Hoffman has a sharp nasal bite that is frequently effective.'

He followed the stage play with a television version. People were noticing him all over.

Other members of the company wanted to know why he was so erratic; brilliant at his auditions; lousy in rehearsal; remarkable in performance. 'The purpose of the audition is to get the job,' he told them. 'You grab hold of everything you know, anything that stimulates you.

Then you get the job and they think you'll start with pulling out all the stops. But I go down to the basement and explore.'

He admitted he got 'pretty low' in that basement. 'So low they don't think I'm doing anything. I know when I'm on the right track. A tankful of directors couldn't sway me from that. But most directors say, "You gotta tie the character down. You gotta lock it in." The last thing I want to do is put the old locks on it.'

There were other ways in which he was able to put his keys in those locks. He played small parts in TV series, notably an episode of *The Naked City* which occasionally delights late-night addicts and shows a glimmer of what was to come. And he played another role as a crook in an episode of the popular series *The Defenders*, which also starred Robert Duvall. He got $500 for that. Big money indeed for him in the mid to late 1960s.

More significantly, he was given the chance to make a big-screen film. It was not exactly stardom, but he wasn't altogether prostituting his art either by succumbing to the temptations of the Hollywood that he had scorned so much. The mere thirty seconds in which he could be seen were in an Eli Wallach film, *The Tiger Makes Out*. It was shot on location in New York, which meant that he could work on stage at the same time.

'I got there at 10 a.m. and was done by 1 p.m.,' he said later. 'Then I phoned everybody and said, "Well, I just finished my first movie." '

An idea of the significance of that movie is given by Douglas Brode's remarkably comprehensive book, *The Films of Dustin Hoffman*, which has six pages and as many stills devoted to the picture – but not a single picture of Dustin, who played the boyfriend of the girl Wallach is trying to inveigle into his lair.

Dustin has since tried to buy up all copies of that picture in existance, for at least the thirty seconds that count for him. The film did, however, cement a friendship with the movie's writer Murray Schisgal, whom he had first met while working in a summer production at Stockbridge, Massachusetts where Dustin was featuring in three one-act Schisgal plays.

Schisgal was to say that he never found Dustin an 'easy guy to work with'. He explained: 'He is obsessed with his work.' He certainly had been that in Stockbridge, where the writer would like to take very early morning walks – and always found Dustin waiting for him as he left his hotel. Dustin had a copy of the script in his hands – 'And a million questions', like 'What's your thoughts here?' and, 'What do you want to do there?'

As Schisgal said: 'I had never worked with an actor like that. He is eternally dissatisfied with what he has achieved.'

Certainly there wasn't anything at all to be satisfied with in *The Tiger Makes Out*, apart from working with Schisgal, that is.

But better things were on the way for Dustin, in his new play. With the success of *The Journey Of The Fifth Horse* still ringing in his ears, he was offered and accepted an even better role, playing a cockney in *Eh?* by Henry Livings, at the Circle in the Square Theatre, as big as off-Broadway could get. Hoffman, a native of Los Angeles, a New Yorker by adoption who was so committed to the city that he could have formed a political party to pay tribute to it, playing a cockney?

The part of the schizophrenic night-watchman was an example of that most over-used of words, a challenge. He took it as eagerly as he had thrown the beef into the *fondue*, and as apprehensively too. But he was brilliant. Walter Kerr noted him again and said this time that he was a cross between Buster Keaton and Ringo Starr, which would have amused all the citizens of Liverpool who were used to being called names . . . but described as cockneys? Never. But Wilfred Sheed, writing in *Commonweal*, came to a similar conclusion and said that he was just like a Beatle.

Dustin said he enjoyed the role, because he liked playing eccentrics, a factor that remained in his professional psyche. He explained: 'It's so easy,' (There, he doesn't do himself justice. Even an easy role he would make hard, because anything easy couldn't be worth much to him). 'You're free to operate behind a mask.'

Two directors decided that if he were free to act in any way at all, they wanted no part of it and resigned. The third director appointed to run the show, anarchic comedy actor Alan Arkin, was also close to distraction and called a meeting on stage of the entire cast to warn Mr Hoffman that he for one was taking no nonsense.

Even so, once more, Dustin was described as giving the best off-Broadway performance of the year. He won the New York Drama Desk Award – which came at just the right time. Dustin was about to be sacked from the part, after yet another fight with the director. But now he felt no director could argue with him. And to a great extent he was right. Winning the prize meant that people would come to the theatre to see the performance by the one actor whose name everyone knew. Sack Dustin Hoffman and you sacked the whole play. Dustin stayed.

So did *Eh?* He was the best thing in it and constantly produced a sheaf of press cuttings to prove it. His head, never the smallest feature of his body, now seemed bigger than ever.

Dustin was noticeably happier when he went to his psychiatrist's office. But everything was still far from being in place. He lived on the Lower East Side, a part of the world that was intimately familiar to people like his own grandparents. Anne Byrne had disappeared over the horizon and there wasn't anyone else closer to hand for whom he felt anything like the same degree of emotion. As he said in one analysis session, all he wanted out of life was to be employed, married, have children and live in a town house in one of the better parts of Manhattan.

All that was on the way. His bank account had recently had the advantage of $5,000 – the proceeds of another movie he would dearly like to have bought up. *Madigan's Millions* was made for television, but had a brief theatrical opening that mercifully was almost completely ignored by critics and public alike. Ostensibly, the film starred Cesar Romero who actually only appeared in a cameo at the very start of the picture. (That was to have been a role for George Raft but he went sick before the crew could get to Rome, where it was being filmed. Raft was either giving honest medical reasons for his absence or was demonstrating more commercial sense than he had ever done in his professional life before). As for Dustin, he didn't think further than the proffered cheque, the free travel and five weeks' accommodation in Italy that he got for accepting the part of an inefficient US Treasury agent in search of a gangster's salted-away fortune. Most people seeing it would doubtless consider that he had no future at all, and in truth the trip was the only tempting part of the deal – apart, that is, from working with Elsa Martinelli, who looked totally delicious.

Fortunately, many more people thought of him in terms of his role in *Eh?*

One of those who sat in the audience at the Circle in the Square was a young film director named Mike Nichols.

4

Nobody could have had the remotest idea of what was going to result from Mike Nichols' buying his tickets for *Eh?* The director of *Who's Afraid Of Virginia Woolf?* was looking around for performers for his new movie, but he had no definite notion of who he was looking for and certainly he felt anything but sure that he was about to see his new star on the stage of the Circle in the Square.

Indeed, anyone knowing Charles Webb's hit novel *The Graduate*, would have been hard put to find a role for a member of the cast of this play, least of all Dustin. Unless it was a walk-on part as an usher in the wedding scene, or perhaps one of the passengers in the bus, or possibly – just possibly – as the student, who would be played by another young, short, Jewish actor named Richard Dreyfuss. The role of Benjamin Braddock, Dustin would say, was of a 'walking surfboard'. Compared with those who normally rode such boards, Dustin could hardly crawl, let alone walk or surf. He would have been the last person to think of himself for Benjamin. And what else was there?

But something about Dustin Hoffman playing the cockney night-watchman struck a chord with Nichols. Not an obvious one. Not one that would prevent his being laughed out of Hollywood in normal circumstances – but these were not normal circumstances; it wasn't normal to have a blockbuster called *Virginia Woolf*. So he was listened to.

As for Dustin, he had no intention of going back to Los Angeles, especially after those previous screen appearances, neither of which indicated an overwhelming desire to make the movies a career. The only people who would have been pleased about the idea would be Lillian and Harry and Dustin's bank manager – but none of them knew about the thought fermenting in Nichols's mind either. As far as Dustin's own world was concerned, it at last seemed to be taking shape.

He wanted to be a New York actor and he was finally being recognized as just that. What more could he ask?

Nichols *was*, however, prepared to ask just that little bit more. He rang Dustin from California, suggested that he make a trip and take a test for the part of Braddock – the lead in *The Graduate* which was almost ready to go into production. What was on Dustin's mind when he accepted the offer cannot now be easily imagined. Probably the most tempting part of the suggestion was the knowledge that he would be going from East Coast to West by air, and first-class, which was more than a little different from the old Greyhound bus on which he had initially made the journey in the opposite direction.

As it was, he had only one day in which to make the return trip. *Eh?* was still running and he had had enough difficulty in the first place in taking that time off.

But he agreed to come, and he had read the book – which left him no less dumbfounded than all the other people who saw him turn up at the studios rented by Embassy Pictures for the screen test. After all, he was not being looked at for another one of those eccentric roles which had seemed to fit him so well amid the hard chairs and peeling paint of the theatres off-Broadway. Certainly, Benjamin Braddock got into some fairly eccentric situations, like being seduced by a woman old enough to be his mother and then eloping with the woman's daughter in the midst of the ceremony marrying her to someone else. But he was a clean-living lad whose early scenes show him swimming in the family pool.

And quite a family it was. Not just Californian – don't all Californian families have swimming pools? – but one with more money than they really knew what to do with, but could get away with pretending that they did. Money sat as well on the head of Benjamin Braddock's mother as the hats that she bought in one of the smarter shops on Wilshire Boulevard.

Much more unlikely for him was the fact that the part of the son and heir of this family was written as if his natural habitat was the sand of Laguna Beach; a youngster who played softball with the beautiful girls of the neighbourhood and who took it for granted that they would swoon as soon as they looked at his rippling muscles, his blond good looks and the thought of his carrying them off in his Cadillac convertible. It was totally understood that he was an Episcopalian, or possibly a product of one of the more fashionable Methodist churches. It was unlikely the family would be Catholic – this wasn't Boston and their name wasn't Kennedy. Certainly, none of them would be Jewish. And, of course, he was 19 years old, 20 at the most – after all, the whole point of the operation was that he was unschooled in the ways of the world, that he was about to be sucked into an affair with the wife of his father's best friend, a woman who when she unhooked her suspenders in front of him in a hotel room would make him look as if he were crying for his mother. That bit, Nichols thought Dustin could handle – as easily as he was supposed to find if difficult to unfasten her bra. It was the reverse of the situation in *Journey of the Fifth Horse*. In that, he had played a man ten years older. Now he was portraying a man at least ten years younger than he actually was.

He had to try to think of it all as just another character part. 'I tried to remember how I felt when I was that age back in 1958. I made no attempt at all to give it a feeling of the Sixties,' he later explained.

The seeming impossibility of it all became apparent when Dustin went through the paces of the screen test. The 30-year-old dark-haired Hoffman resembled a nervous puppy – and that was what probably got him the part.

He did not think it at the time. He arrived at the studio not feeling a great deal different from his mood when he entered the operating theatre after he burnt his hands. 'I was feeling awful,' he admitted to *Time* magazine fairly soon afterwards, 'and paranoiac. I was sure the crew was asking, "Jesus Christ, where did they get him?" ' He wasn't totally wrong about that.

In fact, everything that could go wrong for him did so. He was to act with the beautiful Katherine Ross, who played the girl he went away with – daughter of the woman who had taken him to her bed and robbed him of his virginity. It was a strange situation for him. Not only was he making a screen test for his first important role, it was also the first time he had made love on a stage. 'I'd never asked a girl in an acting class to do a love scene,' he said at the time. 'And no girl asked me.' After the test, it seemed unlikely that the beautiful brunette Katherine Ross would ever again ask him to either. He didn't exactly make her comfortable. They were supposed to enact a love scene, sitting on a bed. To, as he put it, 'prod some life' into it, he grabbed her buttocks to bring her closer.

It was not something that even old friends often did when they were working together in a movie, and this was between strangers, and strangers on the set of a test at that. Miss Ross was not pleased. 'Don't you ever do that again,' she shouted. He later apologized both to her and to Mike Nichols. He tried to explain his motives. 'I was insecure. I just wanted to grab on to something.' It wasn't a joke she appreciated and he was sorry again. He felt even more need to apologize for his whole performance. It was, he thought, terrible.

Katherine herself said afterwards that she thought he looked about three feet tall, 'so dead serious, so humourless, so unkempt, this is going to be a disaster'.

Making the test, he said, seemed like a cruel joke, the kind he might have suffered at high school had he been made captain of the football team. No one in his right mind would have made him that and now he didn't feel any more suited to the role of Benjamin Braddock in *The Graduate*.

Looking towards Miss Ross, he remembers saying to himself: 'A girl like that would never go for a guy like me in a million years.' He knew it had all been a failure.

He said that it was the worst experience of his professional life, even worse than one of those auditions from which he had walked away, muttering that the director was perfectly right in rejecting him. Only this was worse, because he had taken the risk of embarking on a whole new career and had signally failed before he thought he had had a chance to succeed. Dustin actually *knew* that it was terrible – and so did the technicians around him.

He felt so dejected when he left the sound stage that he was almost frightened by the thought of having to report to his ever-eager parents when he saw them that evening. Leaving the huge shed-like building, he put on his jacket – and a New York subway token fell out of his pocket. A crew member picked it up. 'Here, kid,' he said, apparently kindly, 'you're gonna need this.' Dustin was certain that if there was a way of the studio cancelling the rest of his round-trip ticket back to New York and inventing some kind of subway train to take him there instead, they would have done so.

Six days later, he had a call from Nichols. 'We're in business,' said the director. 'You came up with just the kind of confused panic the character is supposed to have.' He wasn't immediately thrilled at the prospect and made the seemingly overwhelming error of telling Nichols so. 'A complete injustice would be done,' he told him. 'Clearly Ben Braddock isn't Jewish.'

'No,' said Nichols, 'but he's Jewish inside.' Whatever that meant was not explained, but it was enough to persuade Dustin to take the role after all.

It was five months before the cameras were ready to turn and Nichols was ready to shout 'Action' for the first time on the set of *The Graduate*. Five months in which Dustin kicked his heels, looked at the contract he had signed and pondered a future that had taken a new and perhaps disastrous turn.

But then the day came; the first-class ticket back to Los Angeles was in the mailbox. He made the trip, checked into his hotel and next day arrived on the set – feeling, if anything, worse than he had when he made the test. That, after all, could have been written off and forgotten. Few people need have known about it. But now he was committing himself to a performance which would be preserved for posterity. He couldn't get out of it. If he were bad, not only Mike Nichols and the studio would suffer – he would, too. The world would know, or at least every part of the world he cared about. An actor without a reputation has nothing.

The panic he felt was not totally different from the confusion either. Secretly, he wondered what he had let himself in for. He had absolutely no intention of giving up the theatre. After the experience of the screen test, he was certain that all he had thought about Hollywood was just about right. The only really tempting feature of starring in *The Graduate* was the money – all of $17,000, which even at the time, 1967, would have barely bought him one of those Californian swimming-pools.

There was one other who shared his doubts about it all . . .

Anne Byrne had come back to New York and back also into Dustin's life. Just before leaving for California, he had seen a photograph of the beautiful dancer in a Manhattan paper, written her a letter and they had met again. She told him that she had married a businessman, had had a daughter, Karina, by him, but was now divorced. They started seeing each other again, but more seriously than before.

She became his confidante in more ways than one. He talked to her of his worries and his ambitions. He told her how excited he was about *The Graduate*. She told him that she was not.

'I wasn't pleased about it at all,' she told me. Partly, she was not happy at the prospect of being separated from him for up to five months, the estimated filming schedule. But her concerns were even more serious than mere physical separation. 'I thought it would spoil his career,' she told me. 'He had finally become a serious actor who was recognized for his acting ability. I didn't want to see that spoiled. I really hadn't thought of him as a star even then.'

There was another factor, a more personal one. Dustin later recalled it: 'We knew that our lives would be changed. An experience like that could either solidify a relationship or explode it.'

She was, however, just about the only one. *Time* magazine would, within eighteen months of the movie's opening, feature Dustin (and Mia Farrow, his co-star in a film he was then making) on their cover under the heading, 'The Young Actors – Stars And Anti-stars'. Dustin, as we have seen , fitted into the latter category. But there was little that was 'anti' about the movie itself.

The Graduate was a highly sexual piece made before the cinema had really discovered sex, or rather the nudity which seemed to pervade every picture made after the following year, 1968. But because that was only a year away, there were inklings of things to come; the story itself, the suggestion of clothes removed and allowed to fall on to the floor; things that the Hays Office when it ran a morals squad in Hollywood – no double beds; no long lingering kisses; no décolleté, let alone nudity – would have balked at and had the Legion of Decency screaming its protests. Dustin was not asked to appear in a full-frontal, Katherine Ross was decorous in her appearance throughout. Anne Bancroft as the seducing and seductive Mrs Robinson did, it is true, show her thighs.

However it was every bit as much Miss Bancroft's picture as it was Dustin's – the beauty of which her husband, Mel Brooks, was the first to appreciate. At about the time that Mike Nichols was making overtures to Dustin to film *The Graduate*, he himself was planning to invite the 30-year-old actor to play the German homosexual playwright in his film *The Producers*, which was to star Zero Mostel and Gene Wilder. Dustin would have liked that part, considering how he had always felt about Mostel, but he now did have the consolation of working with Mr Brooks's wife instead. Actually, he might have had to make do with Susan Hayward, who would have been superb and very sexy casting, but she was already ill and rejected the part. In turn, Nichols had considered the French actress Jeanne Moreau. She would have offered a fiery Mrs Robinson, but one that would not have been quite Californian enough. So Anne Bancroft took the role and posterity – and Mr Hoffman, too – has reason to be glad that she did.

Most of the other performers were glad as well. Dustin struck up a close friendship with Elizabeth Wilson, the middle-aged actress who played Mrs Braddock, Benjamin's mother. They lived in the same apartment building and quite frequently they had dinner together. Suddenly, there were rumours that they were having an affair, not unlike that between Benjamin and Mrs Robinson. That was one thing Dustin learned very quickly: get a good part in a movie and you are instantly grist for the rumour-mill. People thought they knew all about him.

Joseph E. Levine, the head of Embassy Pictures, was however an exception. He was not quite so sure. And he pulled no punches in saying so. He noted that when he met Dustin, it was like coming face to face with a window-cleaner, and told him so. Dustin took the hint – fetched out his handkerchief and started cleaning the office windows. Levine later said that he could see why Nichols chose Dustin but the proof of the pudding had to be in the eating, and he could not be sure that early on that he fancied the meal.

When he was sure that the taste was to his satisfaction, he offered Dustin an option on his services for two pictures to follow it. Hoffman, ever cautious, said that he needed to consult his analyst first.

There were times when Nichols himself felt that perhaps he ought to have his own head examined in casting Dustin in the first place.

The Hoffman psyche did not exactly spare him from the traumas experienced by his off-Broadway directors and at one stage, Nichols was heard to say about his new star: 'Well, we'll never work together again, that's for sure. This is my most important new work and I'm going to get hit. I've done too many new things.'

The Graduate and Dustin Hoffman were certainly both new things and he decided to stick with them. But it did not make him pull his punches. Soon after that outburst he told him: 'This is the only day we're ever going to shoot this scene and no matter how exhausted or lousy you feel, I want you to remember that what you give me is going to be on celluloid for people to see for ever and ever. I know you're tired, but when you go to see this film, if you don't like your work in this scene, just remember always that this was the day you screwed up.'

In truth, Dustin knew he couldn't afford to screw up, that day or any other. It was good for all concerned that he did.

He tried to show that he had not changed much, that he was still one of the boys who fancied all the girls, not just those who had stars on their dressing-room doors or trailers to themselves. He lined up for his own coffee. When the girl asked him for his order, he could reply: 'Black with sugar – and a kiss.' He usually contented himself with the coffee.

However, later he said that he hated the way the studios operated.

Everyone called him 'Sir', so many times that he said he 'felt like a Kentucky Colonel', but nobody talked to the crew and the extras were 'treated like scum'. (In years to come, others said he thoroughly enjoyed being treated like a Kentucky Colonel and wasn't so nice to lesser bodies himself.) But he gave no evidence of not being totally content.

Dustin's father Harry enjoyed the filming even more than he did. The senior Hoffmans went down to the set as often as they could, which, since they were locals, was very often. Mike Nichols was not always as delighted to see them as they were to be there, especially after being congratulated by Harry on the way he had directed a very difficult scene. They were on location at the Taft Hotel and Harry and Lillian were standing behind the ropes forming a barrier between the public who were there to watch the action and the performers and crew. They had promised to behave. Dustin thought he knew what could happen and warned them both not only to keep behind the ropes, but to say nothing.

His real fear was that they would ask to be introduced and he told them on no account to ask, just stay quiet, don't talk to him, don't get in the way of another player's eyeline. Sometimes, Dustin would look in their direction and nod. They would nod back and smile. He was grateful that they didn't wave. When he thought they might do so, he buried his head in a copy of the script. The senior Hoffmans were extraordinarily well-behaved.

Harry, for one, was ecstatic at what he had seen and wanted to tell Nichols so. As the shooting of the scene was completed Harry approached the director and said, 'How do you do, I'm Dusty's father.' He then proceeded to tell him how very competent he thought Nichols had been. 'That's a good shot you got there,' he said, giving his thoroughly professional opinion. But he didn't leave it at that. It was at that moment he added: 'But you know, on the next one, I'd shoot it like this . . .'

A director who had threatened his star was not all that delighted with the lesson from the old hand from Columbia, ex-scenery designer – cum – prop man. But Nichols kept his cool, hoping that it would show in the final product. As time went on, however, he saw the funny side of it. He agreed with Dustin's judgement. His parents were 'nice people', especially since they made him laugh.

In fact, when Mike wasn't complaining about Dustin's prima donna behaviour, the younger Hoffman made him laugh, too. Once he laughed so much that he had to leave the set and shout 'Cut' from an adjoining stage.

Nichols was the first to admit that the picture wasn't all his own work. Or even that of the writers Buck Henry and Calder Willingham.

'Dusty keeps saying his success is all me and he didn't do anything. He's the actor he is and he's terribly funny and most of all he's Dusty. The fact that he's Dusty makes the picture. He takes all sorts of wild chances. He's so inventive.'

The trouble was that both star and director were unsure of themselves. In the live theatre, Dustin would blow up a disagreement into a huge explosive row. Here, he was more inclined to clam up. It got to the point when Nichols felt he had to confront him with it. 'I get to you sometimes, don't I?' asked Nichols. 'Yet you just kind of clam up when I do. Why don't you just tell me to go to hell?'

'I can't,' said Dustin.

'Why not?'

'Because you're the director.' He did not noticeably show such deference again. And slowly, he began to put more of himself into the role.

Indeed, Dustin did his share of improvisation, which predictably was what drove Nichols mad for so much of the time. There was, for instance the scene where the hotel receptionist rings his desk bell for a porter after Benjamin Braddock had whispered that he wanted a double room for himself and Mrs Robinson. At the sound of the ping, Dustin puts his hand over the instrument so that no one will notice. He thought that one out, on camera, because it seemed such a plausible thing a nervous youngster in his position would do. It reminded him of going into a drugstore for a packet of condoms and waiting anxiously for a male assistant to come to his aid.

On another occasion, he showed his frustration at the scathing comments made to Benjamin by Mrs Robinson by banging his head on the wall, just as he had after putting his hand on the girl's breast in his school assembly. 'I never meant it to convey that Benjamin was a virgin,' Dustin said, 'which is what a lot of people seemed to think. I was trying to show that he was a virgin in *that* situation, that Mrs Robinson made him *feel* like a virgin.' But, he said, he never knew what he was doing when he improvised actions in the film.

The Graduate was not only Dustin's first important picture, but the first on which he did just that, improvise. He did it on and off camera. He did it with a young man called Irwin, who acted as his stand-in on the movie.

Irwin brought his girlfriend to the set. Dustin looked at her. 'You still a virgin?' he asked.

'Sure, I'm still a virgin,' the girl replied, not sure whether to be offended at his directness or amused and not a little flattered that the star should spend time talking to her.

'Why?' Dustin pressed.

'Because I don't think people should sleep together before they get married,' the girl replied.

'Are you saving yourself for your husband?'

'Yes.'

'Do you think your parents ever did it before they were married?'

'Oh, no,' said the girl, by now outraged at Hoffman's audacity. But it was in character – in character for a character actor; it was no more than he tried to do in front of the camera. If he could shock his audience as he had shocked this girl, he was in.

But he had no desire to linger on the field of battle. As soon as the filming was complete, he kissed his parents goodbye, packed his bags and left for New York – feeling much, much more comfortable about it than on any previous occasion.

He knew he had done a good job. But he later added: 'I couldn't wait to get back.' One of the reasons, naturally enough, was Anne. But *The Graduate* and what he had done in it was uppermost in his thoughts.

He kept saying that he didn't think the picture would be a great success. 'I thought it was a good movie and at best that it might have a limited run in the art houses'.

It was not until the film actually came out that Dustin knew he had achieved what he had set out to do the moment he reported for work on *The Graduate* set. Nichols had given him no more encouragement at the end of the picture than he had at the beginning – or at least so Dustin claimed. 'I never had the feeling he was happy with what I was doing,' he said, even though occasionally he would 'throw out a cookie. But I always felt like a disappointment'.

On the other hand, despite his fraught relationship with the director, Dustin said that he would never have made the picture if Nichols had not been in charge of the product.

He was pleased with the result only when he sidled into a sneak preview, held in a cinema on New York's 86th Street. He sat in the balcony, wearing an old sports jacket and a shirt without a tie. No one sitting close to him recognized him, which was useful because he was able to garner some insight into what they were thinking, a check a great deal more reliable than studying the cards the audience were asked to fill in.

Some people did recognize him: the columnist Sheilah Graham said that he went into the theatre as an 'unknown boy beatnik' and came out 'mobbed by the crowd'. He resented both being called a boy and a beatnik and said it wasn't true that he was mobbed, either. He did hear, however, that people liked the movie. He liked it, too. In fact, by the time the cast list appeared on screen at the end of the picture, Dustin was a disappointment only to some of those struggling fellow off-Broadway actors who had hoped he would fall flat on his Jewish face.

The critics mostly approved of *The Graduate*. Bosley Crowther told his readers in *The New York Times* that they had an opportunity to see a film that was 'not only one of the best of the year, but also one of the best serio-comic social satires that we've had from Hollywood since Preston Sturges was making them'. Which was praise indeed. As for Dustin himself, well, it got even better. He was 'a new young actor who is nothing short of superb'.

Stanley Kauffmann confirmed that he liked what Dustin did. Writing in *The New Republic* he seemed to be recalling his earlier piece when he wrote: 'Dustin Hoffman, a young actor already known in the theatre as an exceptional talent . . . here increases his reputation.' It was good indeed after all those years to read about himself being 'already known in the theatre', and he might have added, 'You could have kidded me.' But Anne was pleased to read that, too. Mr Kauffmann also said that he recognized there were weaknesses in the picture itself, but added: 'In cinematic skill, in intent, in sheer connection with us, *The Graduate* is a milestone in American film history.'

There was praise too from the critic Renata Adler. 'Seeing *The Graduate* is a bit like having one's most brilliant friend to dinner, watching him become more witty and animated with every moment and then becoming aware that what one may really be witnessing is the onset of a nervous breakdown'.

Dustin may have taken that personally – especially after all that time working in the psychiatric hospital – but chose not to do so. To be associated with a film that drew such attention, let alone praise, for himself was what he really was glad to see most. In the *Saturday Review* Hollis Alpert was even more effusive than the others: 'Dustin Hoffman is the most delightful film hero of our generation. Slightly undersized, totally unsmiling, he stares his way through a series of horrendous, harrowing experiences.'

Anne accompanied him to the world première of *The Graduate* and looked a suitably adorned (and adored) companion for a new star, a man of 31 who, a few short months earlier, had been saving subway tokens and who could not be sure he would ever get an important part in a real Broadway play.

Anne travelled in the limo provided for Dustin by the studio, sitting next to her parents and Dustin's parents, too.

The papers made a lot of the fact that the new star had to rent a dinner jacket for the occasion. The very fact that they were interested in recording that important event in American history said something about the actor and the film he had made. It was his first example of being a publicity object. When they had got the hired jacket out of the way they turned to the fact that, yes Harry and Lillian were there. Wasn't it a bit odd that a star should want to be so close to his family? They couldn't understand that any more than they did his clothes. For his part, Dustin could not comprehend why anyone should find any of these facts interesting.

The true proof of the success that he had as Benjamin is simply the fact that it is now impossible to imagine the picture without him; to think of a tall, blond Benjamin Braddock instead of the short, dark Jewish youngster who lived up to all the insecurities he had demonstrated in the screen test, a gauche student who might have read a few dirty books, secreted the odd copy of *Playboy* in his bedside locker, but who was no more ready for sexual intercourse than was Andy Hardy. Did it show a Dustin Hoffman of promise? On the contrary, it was promises fulfilled.

Almost as suddenly as the suggestion of his overnight stardom came the announcement that he had been nominated for an Oscar. Anne would have preferred it if he had settled for Broadway. They were now virtually inseparable from each other.

There was an understanding that they would marry, which may have struck Mike Nichols and others who knew the inside story of the making of *The Graduate* as fairly ironic. Dustin was short and Jewish. Anne was tall, statuesque and from a middle-class Gentile family living in Westchester County, one of the more fashionable areas close to New York city, although she insisted to me that they were not wealthy. Her father was a librarian, her mother worked on behalf of deaf people.

When Anne and Dustin announced that they would wed, her parents raised no objection to the mixed marriage and, perhaps surprisingly, neither did the Hoffmans, even though the least religious Jewish families tend to object their children 'marrying out'. 'But his family weren't in the slightest bit religious,' she told me, 'after all neither of their boys had been bar mitzvah – and they found nothing to complain about.' In truth, they were probably so thrilled by the success of their boy, the star, that nothing would have fazed them at that stage. He had, after all, made the biggest impact of a youngster in a film since the very different James Dean, who had been killed on the day Dustin entered the Santa Monica college.

Dustin himself was the first to recognize that his success was mostly due to this film. He didn't say it, but had the picture been bad, he might have ended up with another *Madigan's Millions*. As it was, he acknowledged: 'I've made a film that exploded, but I'm not responsible.'

He did not mention that two other youngsters had something to do with the picture's success: Simon and Garfunkel, who sang Paul Simon's songs, most notably, 'Here's To You, Mrs Robinson', which became a big hit not just for them but for Frank Sinatra, too.

Dustin did acknowledge the help of another group, however – the Beatles, which may have seemed only reasonable after the comparisons made between him and them and the similarities noted by the critics. 'They sort of Europeanized us all,' Hoffman was to say. But in truth it wasn't necessary to think in such philosophical terms. The success as far as he was concerned really was all his.

When someone stopped him in the street and said: 'You know, you look just like Dustin Hoffman', he could say that he had made it.

On the other hand, there was the other time when he arrived at a function in the standard Hollywood limo, and was greeted with the unforgettable statement: 'You know who you are? You're . . . Whatshisname . . . You were in Whatdoyoucallit.' Whatshisnamefound that a salutary lesson. On the other hand, there were people who knew precisely who he was and how well he was doing.

His mother knew it – putting in her oar every bit as strongly as Harry had on the set – by ringing the theatres playing the film in her neighbourhood (she didn't exactly threaten the ones that were showing any other picture, but she showed her disdain at their lack of taste and threatened to boycott them ever after), and asking how good business was. If there weren't long queues outside the cinemas, she felt ill, sometimes lying awake all night worrying about whether her 'Dustalah' would make it after all. She herself had no doubts about his true vocation. She wasn't worried about his success in the theatre. It didn't matter and was no more a whim that her boy had indulged in his early days. Now he was going to take things a lot more seriously and have his name inscribed on a gold star on Hollywood Boulevard, along with the other people who, to her way of thinking, mattered – like Valentino and her beloved Ronald Colman.

That was what acting was all about, being a star. Dustin Hoffman was going to be the biggest star there had ever been. And by becoming so, she was justifying all the regrets she had secretly harboured over the years at producing sons who were small and not really her idea of good-looking. But now . . . who needed a new Ronald Colman when there was a new Dustin Hoffman?

If Lillian was totally delirious about Dustin's success, the other woman in his life was, despite it all, still not sure. He and Anne were having difficulties. Today, she says it was all quite predictable, right from the time she told him that she wished he wouldn't make *The Graduate*. 'I didn't want him to do it and I still think I was right,' she told me. 'Had he stayed a New York actor, I think he would have grown in professional stature. As it was, he stayed the same.'

That, of course, ignores the fundamental fact that 'staying the same' had brought him quite suddenly the kind of fame he had never known when working on stage in Manhattan. She appreciated what was quite dramatically happening to him, but that was not making life, and the prospect of life together, any easier. As she told me: 'It is very difficult with all the pressures of stardom, with people offering you praise all the time, to stay the same person. So we broke up.'

Dustin has never denied the difficulties that fame brought him. 'Success means something different to a New York actor than to a Hollywood actor,' he said two decades later. 'I've often thought that I missed out, that I got hoodwinked by this movie stardom because I was beginning to build a reputation for myself on the stage.'

But people were now beginning to identify with him. Lloyd Shearer noted in *Parade*: 'With his short stature, hook nose, beady eyes, unkempt hair, he looks like a loser and it is precisely because of that loser image that the younger generation have made him their winner.' But not Anne.

The notion of a marriage of the new star to the tall, beautiful ballerina seemed to be in peril. But not Dustin's career. The scripts piled up in his agent's office in California and all around the small apartment he still kept in Greenwich Village. The flat cost him $125 a month and he declared that he wanted to keep it 'for ever', or at least as long as the battered violin standing on a shelf. He had picked the instrument out

of a dustbin about five years before, at about the time when the bin
began to look like a fair receptacle for his career.

He said that he hated getting rid of things, anything – old socks and
underwear, books. He had been in the flat for two years and still had
not completed a set of bookshelves he had tried to install. But he still
would not get rid of the wood that was now very definitely warped.

'It's a fear of losing part of yourself,' he explained. His apartment –
'I need this place' – fitted into that category. His career certainly did.

He was not taking any of those offers of work even though he was
far from rich. Almost $10,000 from the $17,000 he made from *The
Graduate* was eaten up by tax and once he had settled his debts, he was
left with just $4,000, which didn't last long either. Soon, he was collect-
ing unemployment insurance again.

But this time, he didn't *have* to go on the dole. He said that he lined
up at the New York State Unemployment Office at 75 East 13th Street
because it helped him get a real perspective on life. How the munici-
pality, to say nothing of its local tax-payers, would have reacted to that
had they known his motives can only be imagined. But for a number
of weeks he collected his $55 cheque and hoped no one would notice
him.

It was just that his professional integrity told him he had to do so.
Almost any one of the scripts he was rejecting could have brought him
in $100,000 for the asking, but he wasn't asking, which might have
pleased Anne a little, but not enough to go back with him again.
Meanwhile he was subsisting on his unemployment pay and cashing in
on the offers he was getting to appear on TV chat shows, which were
very easy money indeed.

Above all, they made it obvious that what he had achieved was an
entirely new shift in his career. He was indeed a star. Stardom was his
and the world was talking about it. And sudden stardom, at that.
Suddenly? The word seems ridiculous, because it had taken so long; he
had been a small-time performer for ten years, an itinerant frequenter
of the staff canteen at Macy's and of the kitchens of clubs like The
Improvisation for even longer. But in terms of the time taken to leave
the studio set for the last time and for his international acclaim to be
heard, sudden it was.

He was more disturbed by all those suggestions of overnight success
than most would have thought necessary. 'The idea that they think I
am some guy off the street who happened to fit a role offends me,' he

said soon after the première and all the public reaction that followed. 'People don't realize I was 30 years old when I played that 20-year-old.'

It took, for instance, a considerable amount of forbearance to be able to accept this episode from the history of American radio broadcasting:

Broadcaster: Oh, it's so thrilling. And it happened overnight, didn't it?

Dustin: Not quite. It took about ten years.

B: How thrilling! You've been studying for ten years and you're only twenty.

D: Thirty.

B: Oh, you're not. Not really.

D: Really.

B: I'm disappointed.

D: So am I.

B: It's so exciting, that magic quality of yours on the screen and . . . and my goodness, we're out of time. This has been Getting To Know Dusty.

Dusty wasn't so sure he wanted to be known in this way, but he did not mind letting others know about it. For months afterwards, he would play a tape of that scintillating expression of the interviewer's art to guests and more welcome journalists.

Of course, people wondered what he was going to do next. He didn't know and he worried that he didn't know, and when he worried he reverted to the clown figure he had been at school. He said he had always been able to pick and choose what work he did. 'Of course,' he added, 'I've been unemployed for thirty years.'

Actually, he did have a part in mind. He had read a book called *Midnight Cowboy* that intrigued him. He thought there was a part in a filmed version of that book which appealed to him. It would be very different from *The Graduate*. Reporters were mostly anxious to know about his sex life and if he really made it a habit to go after older women. That, coupled with the rumours, seemed to be the main legacy that *The Graduate* had left him. He seemed to be the perfect definition of what twenty years later would be called a 'toy-boy'.

One woman journalist thought it was well worth putting to the test. She went to his apartment and made her encouragement very obvious. She fluttered her eyelashes, touched him affectionately. There was the promise of more to come. Before she could get either her own or his clothes off, she revealed all: her wiles were all in the cause of a good story. She had set herself the assignment of writing a piece that would have the title: 'I Seduced Dustin Hoffman'.

She was not exactly travelling a lonely road. For years afterwards, frustrated matrons and nymphomaniac wives of business executives would offer him further advice on the physical side of life and promise to reveal sections of the female anatomy that had been hidden beneath Miss Bancroft's undergarments.

Actors like to laugh at such suggestions or to tell of them at parties at which the champagne is flowing; Marlon Brando reputedly was offered as many bare breasts as autograph albums on which to sign his name. But the fact that it did happen is the surest guarantee that he had achieved all that he had set out to do. Dustin Hoffman was convincing all right. So much so that along with the letters from the nymphomaniacs came offers from other studios who wanted to make pictures about post-pubescent youths being seduced by older women. If imitation is the sincerest form of flattery, Dustin was being given all the flattery he could take. If truth were told, he enjoyed a great deal of it. At least, it had to be regarded as simply part of his day's work – which others might think was very nice work indeed if he could get it. And he could get it any time he wanted.

Because he still lived in the same apartment, he was prey to the whims of hundreds of girls who simply rang his doorbell and then ran away, once they had the satisfaction of knowing that he would come to the phone and ask who was there. For incoming telephone calls he would depend on his answering service, telling them that it was 'Hoffman' on the line and what messages did they have.

The number was a closely guarded secret. It was his agent's call asking him if he had yet changed his number that gave him the first indication that success had indeed come his way. He liked the sound of that. In a good mood, he would switch on his tape recorder and sing into it, sometimes quasi-operatic arias, at others just messages like 'I'm happy'. Most people would have said he had a great deal to be happy about.

He wasn't sure, though, how he should react to the way people treated him. He tended to think of his fame as 'notoriety'. It was not that he objected to being instantly recognized – that was what stardom was all about – but he did resent his loss of privacy. And when someone offered him an autograph album or a photograph to sign, he privately feared that what they were pulling out was as likely to be a gun as a ballpen.

Even so, it was nice when taxi-drivers stopped for him and refused to take a fare. He might be a big movie star, but he still did not own a car. He did not make this a problem when getting to the broadcasting studios, which was, notoriety apart, something he was going to have to tolerate. There were dozens of radio and TV producers lining up to have him on their programmes for entirely conventional interviews.

The studio publicists who organized the campaign for *The Graduate* certainly weren't helping him dispel either the image or the rumours that the picture had created, and publicizing the old film was taking more time than he could afford to spend on any new one. He was doing more interviews in the course of this one film's exploitation campaign than many other actors get through in a whole career.

They liked him, because he was a fresh new face making a fresh new kind of film. But much more significantly, he was intelligent and he could make the interviewers laugh. Most new actors and actresses were handsome or pretty – Dustin was neither of those things – and looked good on screen and had good voices. But deprive them of a script and there was nothing for them to say. Dustin Hoffman always seemed to have a lot to say. More remarkably, too, he did not seem to say things that would offend his bosses – which is the principal doubt that studios have about letting their stars loose on television.

Even so, Johnny Carson turned him down as a prospective participant in his late-night TV show. In a judgement he later came to regret, he said that he thought Hoffman was 'too normal'. It did not put off any of the other chat show hosts and he co-operated manfully. It was no more than he had been told to expect. His contract said that he had to do all the publicity interviews that came his way, which he thought was a more acceptable clause to have in the agreement than any paragraph that decreed Embassy would have an option on his services for later on. It demonstrated more than anything else that he had sufficient confidence in himself and his ability to make a Hollywood career, no matter what he said about his doubts about *The Graduate*.

He thought it wise to look for new media – and thought about it again. For three days he worked on a television pilot, but abandoned it when he realized that the small screen was not the best way to a film career. That was what he was aiming for and he would do nothing to spoil it.

Sometimes he even looked important, like the time he posed in evening dress next to a bust of himself which had just been sculpted, an old Hollywood tradition which indicated a degree of arrival. When he had important meetings – such as with Joe Levine – he could even be seen carrying a briefcase. This usually contained nothing more than a rain hat, a paperback and a packet of sandwiches, which brought him down to a level his old friends would have recognized. And yet he was now a friend with an Oscar nomination.

'Every actor thinks about winning an Oscar,' he said at the time. 'But I don't honestly believe I've earned it in *The Graduate*. It wasn't an important part anyhow.'

He himself was going to vote for Rod Steiger for his role in *In The Heat Of The Night*. That alone should have proved something about Dustin's instincts on good and bad films. Rod Steiger did win the Best Actor Award for his role of the racist police chief, and *In The Heat Of The Night* itself got the Best Picture Oscar.

Dustin showed what he really felt about the Awards on the night of the presentation. He might have gone to the trouble of renting a dinner jacket for the film's opening, but he had made no plans at all for this ceremony. Somehow or other, he managed to get a lift to the hall. But at one o'clock in the morning he phoned his friend, the actor Stanley Beck, and asked him to pick him up, and . . . could he stay for the night? He had neither a car nor anywhere to sleep. He was offered a bed in the living-room, but told to come by cab. As Beck later recalled: 'He came, slept, left without making the bed and I never saw him.'

Mike Nichols, meanwhile, was totally vindicated. He won the Award for Best Director. Dustin and Anne Bancroft had to make do with their nominations for best performances. It was, though, not a bad beginning for Hoffman.

He even said that he wasn't sorry that the Academy Award had not come his way. 'Thank God,' he said soon afterwards, 'that I didn't get the Oscar. After I got the nomination, I thought, "Okay. It's enough already for this one part." God help me if it had all happened at 18.'

Again, Anne would have echoed those sentiments and added that it was doing him no good at all that it had happened at 31, but they still weren't seeing much of each other, so her views were suppressed as far as he was concerned and what she believed was a matter that was fairly academic.

Finally, though, he was ready to say 'Yes' to a script and to a role that was as different from *The Graduate* as crispy bacon is from gefilte fish. The clean-looking Benjamin Braddock was going to become Ratso Rizzo, the sick and seedy pimp of *Midnight Cowboy*.

5

Everything Dustin Hoffman now did would have to be regarded as his post-*Graduate* period, although the definition required a certain degree of qualification. He might have graduated from the hard school of out-of-work actor, but he was yet to prove to himself or to anyone else that he could manage a full career as a film star. In the world of pop music, *The Graduate* had been his 'standard', as 'Mrs Robinson' had been for Simon and Garfunkel. Now he had to show that everything else he did would be a standard too or, perhaps even more important, that he could survive something that did not enter the charts.

Dustin was fond of quoting Arthur Miller's opening to *Death of a Salesman*, discussing the frailty of the ephemeral moment: 'Knowing that one has carefully inscribed one's name in a cake of ice on a hot July day . . .'

It was not just that *Salesman* was the greatest influence the theatre had had on Dustin's life to date; the lines seemed to fit everything he felt and thought. In many ways he was in limbo, professionally and personally. He had been the great new discovery of the cinema and yet to hold on to that reputation – to say nothing of trying to make the sort of money he was being offered – required fairly instant decision-making.

Joe Levine, for one, was amazed that he would not jump at the opportunity of cashing in on his appeal and accepting his offer, not just of options but of guaranteed work, perhaps for as much as $250,000.

'Dustin could make it with every kid, every boy and girl under 25 and 85 per cent of the world is under 25,' he declared. Where the somewhat dubious statistic came from is another matter, and if it was anywhere near accurate it took into account the young people in under-developed countries who had never even heard of a cinema, let alone been inside one. But the general idea of the point was well taken. And Levine rhapsodized about the Hoffman quality that surmounted most others. Sounding not a little like a movie mogul of a previous generation

– and mostly like Louis B. Mayer – he gushed: 'He's unlike any other movie star. That's his great appeal. He's the Boy Next Door.' But perhaps only if the lady next door wanted to take him to bed.

Yet you could not convince a gullible public that someone like Dustin could possibly have problems. 'It's the same old story,' he said at this time. 'Everyone says when you reach success, when you've got money and fame, you've won the battle. That's as much a cliché as when someone says, "Oh, I've got the money, I've got the fame, but I'm miserable." The only truth is that life is life. No matter where you are, you're kidding yourself if you say you're not struggling.'

And at that time, he still didn't have the money.

For all the worries, he was getting used to compliments. The ones he liked best came from fellow professionals, which, after all, is the great appeal of the Oscars; there is nothing like the praise of your peers. Elizabeth Wilson, Mrs Braddock – Benjamin's mother in *The Graduate* – went on record saying how outstanding she thought he was and, totally oblivious of the rumours of the year before, described him as having 'a quality that reaches out to the audience, a quality stronger than in any other leading man'.

He had to temper the praise with the worries and with the realities he would almost immediately have to face.

The cake of ice would before long start dripping. For the moment, the drips were merely showing that interest was still being excited. But if it began melting properly . . . and before long, it would . . . the notoriously short memories of international audiences could mean a lucky break being a thirty-second spot in a new Eli Wallach picture. So he had to act quickly.

Dustin had to think about his private life no less seriously. He was besieged by women as much as before. When he went out with a girl, he expected to take her to bed. He didn't believe in platonic love.'I've never been able to say of a girl, "Gee, we're great friends" and let it go at that,' he said. 'I've always had the urge to make love. I don't know any girl I've slept with about whom I can now say, "She's still a good friend".'

But he did want something more. He contacted Anne again. They agreed that they were in love, but what he couldn't accept was that they should marry. For the time being, he had to content himself with her picture on display in his apartment and her visiting him there almost daily, offering advice on what he should do next, helping him fend off unwelcome callers and interviewers.

She still believed that he had made a mistake in going to Hollywood, but accepted that that was what he wanted to do. It was also hard to resist the sort of money being spoken of. Two hundred thousand dollars was the sort of cash that, even if nothing followed, represented a fairly good insurance policy.

He spent about seven months wondering what to do next before taking up the offer of John Schlesinger to play in *Midnight Cowboy*.

He had spotted the potential he was offered at the time that he had read James Leo Herlihy's book. Now Schlesinger agreed that Hoffman was right for what he had in mind – which is itself a fair test of an actor's ability; once he knows what he is going to be good at doing, he is half-way to *being* good at it.

It was not an attractive role in terms of the kind of personality represented by Enrico Salvatore Rizzo – Ratso, for short. People for years after the film was completed would try to imitate the Ratso limp, which as played by Dustin sometimes took on the grace of a dance step, but apart from a few who felt sorry for a shivering unshaven cripple on the verge of death, the women were not going to want to take him to their hearts and their beds in the way that they did after *The Graduate*.

But it had attractions of a totally different kind, particularly for an actor who had already gone on record saying how much he enjoyed playing 'characters'. Ratso was one of those in spades.

Strangely, however, for an actor already decreed to be a star, *Midnight Cowboy* provided Dustin with only a supporting role, and one which his various advisers – Anne apart – couldn't understand him wanting to accept. The 'Midnight Cowboy' of the title would be played by Jon Voight. But Dustin, who had achieved his overwhelming success in *The Graduate* supporting (in more ways than one) Miss Bancroft, had no doubts about it. Why should this be any different in terms of satisfaction for himself and for his audiences? It was not.

He and Voight poured a lot of themselves into the story; Voight in his cowboy suit, Dustin the vagrant. They actually improvised about 75 per cent of the action and dialogue. The writers recorded on tape what they said and added it to an amended script for use on second, third and fourth takes. It was a useful compromise between what they wanted and what the writers and director had decreed.

Dustin admitted afterwards, however, that it took him time to get into his stride. He was better in some scenes than others. Anne said

that she spotted the point when it began to happen, where the real
character took over, most notably a scene in a hat shop. Dustin's voice
appeared to change. But you had to know him, perhaps to live with
him, to see it.

She frequently went to the location to see him work; this was not
difficult now since she had a baby-sitter and was spending a lot of her
time teaching blind children how to dance. She would just watch, wave
at a convenient moment or talk to him between takes. Sometimes he
shared a snack with her, like cutting up an apple and offering her a
slice. Dustin trusted her a great deal more than he had his father on
the set of the previous picture. She had the advantage of knowing that
Dustin wasn't a complete slob in real life, that he didn't smell and that
the decaying teeth had been applied by the make-up man over his own
healthy ones. When he finished shooting most evenings at seven – later,
of course, when they needed night shots, and there were a lot of those
– he had the comfort of knowing that she would be waiting for him.
They were now living together.

Midnight Cowboy was to prove to be the picture that confirmed Dustin
Hoffman as the real find of the late 1960s. It didn't do any harm to the
acknowledged star Jon Voight either. Voight, too, made a name for
himself after playing the 'Cowboy' of the title. But it was Dustin's
picture all the way through. He stood out in the way that a central
medallion stands out in a Chinese rug. Voight was the outer decoration,
but it is Dustin one sees and – much more important – remembers.

Some measure of that achievement can be gauged by the fact that
Voight appears in virtually every frame. Hoffman doesn't arrive until
twenty-five minutes into the picture and there are whole incidents in
which he does not appear.

He is the consumptive crippled Times Square hustler Voight meets
on his arrival in New York, the city he had determined to conquer in
the process of making love to all its women. In fact, he comes to the
conclusion that he can actually combine the two aims by charging those
women for the favour. Things are not too lucky for him. His first 'case'
ends up not only not paying him anything for his services, but fleecing
him of $20 for the taxi fare to meet her husband.

It is Rizzo who persuades him that he would do better by having a
business manager, a middle-man who can drum up the clients. It is no
good at all to 'pick up freight in the street'. Voight, dressed throughout
as a cowboy – Hoffman tries to tell him people are laughing at him, but
he thinks he looks good that way – naïvely puts his faith in the city boy

who plainly knows more about Manhattan then he himself will ever know. It doesn't bother him that Rizzo – who hates people calling him 'Ratso' – has a nagging cough as well as the eccentric dance, a movement that goes well with the brashness of the man in the white suit and long hair whom he plays at this stage of the film.

Before long, it is evident that Rizzo is dying of TB. But the cowboy still needs him, stays in the same condemned apartment he has established as his own, still takes his advice, still thinks that the unshaven, alternately sweating and shivering Rizzo – who soon loses the power to walk – can provide the management he needs.

Rizzo doesn't actually get him any clients, but he advises him to wash, take his clothes to the laundrette – Rizzo manages to push them into another customer's machine – and where to stand to pick up the clients. Eventually, he is picking up men, but never manages to get the promised money without a fight. Only once does he 'score' with a woman for the promised $20 fee, but then has to pack up business because Rizzo is dying and he promised to take him to Florida. A new twist on the whore with the heart of gold. Rizzo dies sitting next to him as the bus drives into Miami.

Yet it is the patient, not the nurse, with whom the audiences identify. They might have identified even more had Schlesinger allowed Dustin the opportunity to improvise the way Mike Nichols had in *The Graduate*.

In one scene, the two reprobates are sitting in a greasy-spoon café. Neither of them has ever looked or felt worse. It is at that moment of utter dejection that Dustin wanted to have a black man come and sit next to him. He wanted to be able to tell the black to move, to be able to say: 'I won't sit next to no nigger.' Schlesinger categorically refused. But Dustin thought he had a point: the irony of the filthy, stinking – because there couldn't be much doubt that he did stink – tramp telling a perfectly clean and respectable black man to move away from him. Dustin thought it would work, especially among other residents of the Bronx, where the mutual distrust between Italians and blacks was common knowledge. But even without that scene, the part worked.

And he *was* allowed his moments of spontaneity, the improvisation that provides a key to the naturalness of a part. Soon after his 'arrival' in *Midnight Cowboy*, the still outrageously optimistic and brash Rizzo, dressed in his white suit, walks across the road in the path of passing taxis. One of them almost knocks him over, 'I'm walkin' here,' he shouts at the driver. 'I'm walkin' here.' The driver answers with an obscenity. 'Up yours,' says Rizzo.

It was his own idea. The incident actually happened on a crowded street in Manhattan. It could not have been scripted. The thousands of extras and the hundreds of real cars in that one scene would have eaten up the entire budget of the picture. But Schlesinger had set up a hidden camera. Dustin was to say he thought it up after watching the way Marlon Brando picked up a woman's glove in a scene in *On The Waterfront*. It was between takes, but the director believed there would be mileage in keeping the camera rolling, focusing on his star in an unselfconscious moment. To Dustin, everything about Ratso – or Enrico – had to look unselfconscious, even though a clean-living actor born in Los Angeles needed to be a superman to forget how he dressed and looked.

Or how he behaved; like the time he put his finger in his mouth and then pulled his arm sharply to his side. It seems like an unnecessarily dramatic way of biting his nails, but he once saw a Times Square tramp do just that and he thought it fitted his character.

James Cagney, not renowned as a Dustin Hoffman idol, was known to observe and copy such characterizing, like the shoulder-shaking tough guy in *Angels With Dirty Faces* who used to greet all his friends with the same phrase: 'What da ya hear, what da ya say?'

Dustin's observation and use of that observation was pure Cagney. He, however, would have said it was merely getting into the part. As was the cough, which grew worse as the film progressed. Deeper, longer, louder. As Jon Voight was to say, it was hard to 'upstage a vomit'.

To play a part like that and have both men and women at the end sobbing into their handkerchiefs is an achievement not given to many, but then Rizzo was a very unusual character who had qualities of his own, even if, on reflection, ones which were not entirely different from those possessed by both the Russian in *Journey Of The Fifth Horse* and the cockney in *Eh?* All three were eccentrics and Dustin was good at playing eccentrics.

But he had the advantage of another superb movie – a picture which, like *The Graduate*, looked as if it was going to be good from the moment the first credits flashed on to the screen, accompanied once more by an outstanding song – in this case Fred Neil's 'Everybody's Talkin'.

He himself was dismissive of the 'proof', such as it was, that he had now really made it. That was why he was proving more difficult to interviewers, giving them flippant answers, like saying he had been unemployed for thirty years. 'What I am trying to do is keep myself on the ground. All of a sudden you get more press than Christian Barnard.

I was in perspective with myself before all this happened. I was doing pretty well off-Broadway before *The Graduate* came along. Well, this sudden stardom stuff completely knocks you out of perspective.'

Dustin would go out of his way to show that he had his feet on the ground. He was offered a chance to model suits for the Petrocelli company – somewhat ironical considering the way he was dressed now – and turned it down. He didn't actually need it. In fact, partly perhaps because of Anne's influence, he was trying to show that above all – to 'proclaim' it, was how he put it – he was an actor, and 'hope that some people will believe you and will stop trying to turn you into a fantasy figure'. And to demonstrate that he resented more than ever before the suggestion that until he went to Hollywood to work, he had done nothing at all. Sometimes, though, he would sound not a little conceited at what had happened to him. 'If I pass a group of people on the street, I can usually count three before I hear it – "eeeeh" '. He didn't give himself time to reflect on how preferable this might be to lining up in the dole queues or even to selling ice-hockey equipment in Macy's.

It was part of the job he had taken on in exchange for his salary cheque and the assorted perks that went with it. But there was a lot of what he said that needed to be understood. Values were changing and they were not his – and, to be fair, many of them he refused to accept.

If he were to be remembered for anything, he was thinking, it had to be for work like the *Fifth Horse*. As he told *Redbook* magazine in September 1968: 'I have tasted victory from work that I've done – moments of really tying into a character . . . I can tell you, there's just no taste like it. They can't take that away from you.'

He was asked about fame. Didn't he enjoy it? 'Sure, fame is nice. You can't say it isn't nice. You feel depressed and worthless and all you have to do is go out the front door and people ask for your autograph. But it's disturbing too . . .'

There was life for him before *The Graduate*, which was, after all, just 'a part in a movie, that's all'. And he added: 'I'd put in my years, begun to establish myself . . . done the work, sweated, got my award. I was pacing myself . . .'

There was real bitterness in him about this. 'I'm not doing anything that much different than I was ten years ago. You know, you really don't grow that much as an actor. Now . . . suddenly, I'm lauded. Is it because ten years ago, I wasn't any good? The truth is that now my timing is right. I'm not doing anything that much different. I'm just older. The enjoyment of it, the success is when you're in your apartment and you're able to say, "Well, I'm alone and not working, but I'm really not unemployed." '

Midnight Cowboy was shot on location, much of it around Broadway, a natural haunt for the kind of vagrants or hopeful ne'er-do-wells that Hoffman and Voight represented. It helped Dustin recall his early days in New York, the times when he was awakened twice a night by Gene Hackman's fridge.

'Anyone who comes to New York and isn't a millionaire feels as lonely as Ratso Rizzo did. This city is cold and lonely and terrifying.'

But it was not easy to keep the fans away – including the same women who yearned to take control of Dustin's life after he played Benjamin Braddock, and who this time peered beneath his make-up, established that his filthy-looking clothes didn't really smell as if he had just walked out from the nearest Salvation Army hostel and who now hoped for just a smile. They would have preferred a kiss but that was even more unlikely.

To him the most unlikely thing of all was that journalists still wanted to talk to him. At first, he admitted, he thoroughly enjoyed it. After a time, it began to pall.

Dustin knew when that was happening. He suddenly started smoking heavily, much more than before. That was a phenomenon he had not expected. Whether he had anticipated the other problem of giving interviews is a different matter. It was true that he was not sailing through the question-and-answer sessions the way that he thought he would or as the studio publicity people had told him would be the case.

He not only gave the same answers to what were inevitably the same questions, but he had heard those answers so often that he began to doubt them. Was he fabricating the truth? In the end, he reconciled himself to hoping that he wasn't believing his own publicity. 'What the hell,' he said at one stage. 'What they're writing is not Plato.'

Precisely what he told a teenage reporter is not on record. She said that she was endeavouring to get an interview to settle a bet with her friends. Would Mr Hoffman co-operate? And if he would, well . . . she'd be willing to share the profits. At least she wasn't offering to seduce him.

What had happened to Dustin was that he had become a star in spite of himself; not the anti-star that *Time* magazine had claimed, but a star who recognized and accepted the trappings of his new-found success, didn't either hate or enjoy them, but agreed that they were a very reasonable price indeed to pay for the kind of fame that had come his way.

And he did have Anne, who now wanted to teach full time. He was not sure about that, wondered whether it wouldn't be nicer if she spent more time just being his girl. On mulling that over, he concluded that, no, perhaps it wouldn't.

'I've never had a girlfriend who was devoted to me in the Victorian sense. Totally involved with me and caring for nothing else. I think that would be dangerous today.'

So he was happy to have Anne as she was – and their friends. As she told me: 'A lot of Dustin's friends were from his New York acting days and we still enjoyed their company. I must say I didn't terribly like the people who wanted to be with him just because of who he was.'

The old friends found it even more difficult than Anne did to accept his success. It was not that he moved away from them, but they could not relate to the Dusty they had lined up with in the unemployment queues 'suddenly' making it. To them it was almost like an illness. They put to him the strangest, though intended to be caring, questions, like: 'Is everything okay with you?' or 'How are you taking it?'

Dustin gave them the information that he thought and hoped they wanted to hear, yes, he was feeling fine. There were no problems in taking success. But that cake of ice continued to drip, even when he was working. What would happen next? He used to sit and contemplate his obituary notice. He was afraid it would say something like, 'Small-time actor who had brief moment of success in the 1960s.' What he really wanted it to say, he would tell friends was:'Died in his 90s. Started out to be an actor, went on to be a director and wound up doing . . .'

He resisted getting married, even though he and Anne were now so close. 'I just have to get over this period – that never in my life have I been so in love with myself . . . but marriage is one of the last things you do. That way you reduce the odds of a bad one. I'm still getting hairs on my chest. Now I have eighteen!'

That was the sort of statement that made the girls fall in love with him. And no matter how he felt about Anne, he was still not above teasing them.

Once he and his manager Walter Hyman saw a tall, leggy blonde in a drugstore. Later, they saw her again from their car, walking along the street. Dustin rolled down the window. 'Quick, get in,' he shouted at her. 'We'll give you a ride. We saw you in the drugstore.'

The girl didn't know what to make of it. But she jumped in. Neither Dustin nor his manager could quite understand why she accepted, but were happy that she did. He said that he had no ulterior motive and she appeared to have believed him. Once she realized she was riding with Dustin Hoffman she was possibly sorry that he didn't have one.

But any man in love with himself wouldn't worry about a girl like that. There was a childish simplicity about him. There was nothing that gave him more pleasure than a full mail-box, even if it only contained junk letters. These days, he was delirious. The box was always filled with a different kind of junk, the kind that keeps a big star alive – fan mail. Fans were constantly tearing the sign bearing the name 'Hoffman' from the top of the box. In 1968 he still wasn't sure exactly what his plans were, what his future would bring, but he was determined to make a success of it.

He wanted to reassure Anne about that, if no one else. She would always need reassuring. She didn't fancy his remaining a film star. He was capable of more important things than the shallowness of Hollywood.

She, like Dustin himself, could begin to take for granted the things that his new riches had brought. He still couldn't afford a Manhattan town house, but he was able to buy her a new washing machine. They both kept looking at it; a symbol of success.

She cared for him because of what he was, or maybe what he had been in his off-Broadway days. There was no doubt that now they had got back together again they were happy. Certainly, they looked good, in Dustin's apartment or walking in the street with Karina. His most obviously generous feature was that he did not allow the child, now two-and-a-half, to come between them.

Dustin not only liked being with Anne, he enjoyed being seen with her. Like all good ballet dancers she had poise. She was tall and he was happy with that. He still liked them high. And he had a name for her. She was his 'shiksa goddess'.

Harry and Lillian would still have loved the idea of 'Dustalah' and his 'shiksa goddess' getting married, but for the moment he wasn't promising anything to them or to her, or to those friends of his she disliked so much, the people whose motives she felt Dustin failed to appreciate. But he was far from simple himself.

Even a director of John Schlesinger's calibre had to reckon with a supporting player who demanded the deference accorded to a super-star. Judging by the critics' response, Dustin deserved it. Hoffman in

Midnight Cowboy, wrote Hollis Alpert in *The Saturday Review*, 'emerges with top honours, proving that his heady debut in *The Graduate* was no fluke'.

Stanley Kauffmann said the picture, starring the man who was now his favourite young actor, had 'A great deal besides cleverness, a great deal of good feeling and perception and purposeful dexterity.'

That, on the whole, was precisely what could be said of Dustin Hoffman, the actor. He had a great deal of purposeful dexterity. The purpose had been there for all to see for a long time. The dexterity was the element that had converted it into performances of a quality that was rare at that time and is hardly more plentiful over twenty years afterwards.

Dustin meanwhile was trying very hard to think of the future, and a more exciting one could not be imagined. What did he want to play now? Holden Caulfield, the central character of J. D. Salinger's *Catcher in the Rye*, and perhaps Che Guevara. But for the moment no one was asking him to do either.

His mind nevertheless was allowed to wander. He went from the ridiculous to the sublime, which in Hollywood was not all that unusual a journey, and from the possible to the highly unlikely.

He wanted to think of all options. And money was more important than he generally liked to say – it was nice and it was 'arty' for it to be thought that the play (or the film) was the thing and that money was secondary. Inwardly, and his financial advisers knew this only too well, he was interested in the big bucks. Five days a week, he was seeing his psychiatrist – the same man who four years earlier charged him $3.50 an hour and whose unpublished fees at this point were considerably greater.

'There'll come a day when a face like mine will not be able to get work,' he explained, apparently modestly. 'Ten years from now, they'll say, "I'll give half my kingdom for a walking surfboard." ' So he, therefore, was not being so prescient and clever after all. Twenty years later, there is no record of anyone saying any such thing. But neither has any producer – or even himself as an independent – allowed him to play the Dauphin in *St Joan* or, most bizarre of all, Adolf Hitler, which was another one of his allegedly serious ambitions. He wanted to portray Raskólnikov in a new production of *Crime and Punishment* and kicked himself that he missed the opportunity to be 'The Fixer' in a screen version of the Bernard Malamud story. Alas, he was beaten to that by the British actor, Alan Bates.

In fact, studios were still concerned about what to do with Dustin at all. Did he consider himself first a film or a stage actor? If he were the latter, when was he going back to the legitimate theatre? And if he did go, why didn't he do so between his two films? There was no ready answer to either of those questions.

Those in a position to do so wanted to exploit the asset that the name Dustin Hoffman now represented. He said that he appreciated the implications of that – and wondered if it could be turned to his advantage. 'I enjoy being tested,' he said about this time, and relished the challenge of being offered millions of dollars to play a dreadful part in an excruciatingly bad movie. 'I wouldn't do it, of course, but I should be tested.'

Dustin's brother Ron, who was achieving a totally different kind of success in accountancy, had already been called in to give advice on the predicament of Dustin Hoffman and money. 'If you ever hit it big,' said Ron before *The Graduate* changed everything, 'don't change your standard of living. If you do, you'll have to start accepting roles for the money, and then you're not your own man.'

Despite what Anne honestly believed, he was trying very hard indeed to stay his own man, and the same man. He was not intending to move from the Greenwich Village apartment and apart from the washing machine there were not many new acquisitions. The only one, in fact, was a $700 desk with which he had fallen in love.

The desk was bigger than anything he had ever considered he would own, far bigger than himself. It seemed to represent in his own mind what he had achieved to date.

Meanwhile American-International Pictures cashed in on Dustin Hoffman without paying him a cent for the privilege. The firm took the opportunity of re-releasing *Madigan's Millions*, which undoubtedly pleased its real stars Cesar Romero and Elsa Martinelli a great deal more than it pleased Dustin.

In fact, American-International did a great deal more than that. Looking at the exploitation campaign adopted for the movie, it seemed that the company were suggesting that the picture starred not just Dustin, but Jon Voight as well. For they released it as part of a double bill with a Voight quickie called *Fearless Frank*. The posters featured 'Dustin Hoffman, star of *The Graduate* and Jon Voight, star of *Midnight Cowboy*.' By billing the two films in that way, the company was

demonstrating whom they considered the bigger star while still paying
lip-service to the fact that Voight was the official lead in *Midnight
Cowboy*. American-International, needless to say, had had nothing to
do with either of the two hit movies.

The pictures were both ready to end their days profitably on
television, but the critics were a lot kinder to Dustin than he might
otherwise have thought. The role of the idiot agent was not going to be
such an albatross around the Hoffman neck as Dustin had feared. The
part had not only earned him $5,000 and a holiday in Italy, but also
comments like this one from *Film TV Daily*: 'No doubt about it, Dustin
Hoffman is talented. He is so naïve, nutty, clumsy and talented in
Madigan's Millions that he is the whole film. In fact, he saves the film.'

He wondered after all the excitement of making *Midnight Cowboy*
whether he would be needing someone to come and save him. The
Italian Anti-Defamation League realized that 'Ratso's' real name was
Enrico – Voight uses it only as the cripple dies in his arms – and took
offence.

'I had a little fantasy about this,' Dustin said. 'I imagined a couple
of Mafia guys coming up to me after the picture opened and saying,
"Don't you ever do a part like that again." '

How would he have reacted? He would have said, 'You're right,
absolutely right, definitely right. I'll do anything you say! Just don't hit
me.'

It could have been a line from any one of the pictures he made in the
years to come, the staccato sentences, the nod of the head, the sound
he utters that makes audiences wonder if he has stuffed his cheeks with
some kind of padding, even when he looks gaunt – like a Ratso Rizzo
who compulsively stops at every telephone box he passes in the hope
that there's some loose change to come spilling out.

What Dustin wanted to be hit with now was an exciting new film idea.
And that in itself was a compromise, just one of the compromises that
Anne believed she saw on the horizon. He couldn't adjust to the technique of filming, the mechanics of getting a part into the camera. Walter
Matthau once told me that playing in a film was 'retirement acting': one
line in the morning, then a break before reciting that same line again
the following afternoon. Dustin felt much the same. 'It must be terrific
to be like Doris Day and have it knocked, just work from nine to five.
Or like Sinatra. They shoot the whole film and then Sinatra comes in
for three weeks and does his scenes. Sinatra's a good actor. It's true

that I couldn't really work like that. What I don't understand is how anybody can *enjoy* film acting. I mean, it's great for the director, he's always cooking, but for an actor . . . there's so much time to sit around.'

It gave him time to discuss the world around him, to think about politics, although he was never the most political of people. He had supported the independent candidate Eugene McCarthy in the 1968 presidential election campaign, but did no electioneering, wasn't keen on addressing public meetings. He was far removed from the efforts of people like Shirley Maclaine and Jane Fonda – or, on the other side of the spectrum, Bob Hope or John Wayne.

'Maybe I'm cynical,' said Dustin, 'but I don't think it's particularly courageous for an actor to speak out politically today. I think it's fashionable now to be involved. People don't care whether you're for Eugene McCarthy or for whoever John Wayne is for.'

The right wing might not have agreed, but Dustin said that he was above all an American, a fact which he particularly felt when he went to Europe – one of the 'perks' his new wealth had brought him and something he had not done before. 'I saw the other side of being an American – the ones who get insulted because Frenchmen don't speak our language, for example – and I don't like that.' It was the time when students were in ferment all over the world, particularly in Paris, but in America, too.

'The youth outburst in this country is a good thing,' he declared. 'The kids are angry because the American leaders have made mistakes and refused to admit it.'

It was the time when Muhammad Ali was being stripped of his world heavyweight title after the comments he made about Vietnam. 'I really feel very bad about him,' said Dustin. 'I think it was absolutely wrong to strip him of his title just because of his feeling towards the draft and war. Politically I don't know whether I agree with him or not, but I do know he is a great athlete. I admire [him] very much for standing up for things in which he believes.'

As for what Dustin himself believed, this was more a question of contemplating new ideas. Not that any new idea was not going to be worth it, financially speaking. His agents had spread it around that Dustin's price had gone up – slightly. His services were being charged at the rate of $425,000 a picture, a figure that became apparent when it was realized that, once again, Dustin was being nominated for an Academy Award, for *Midnight Cowboy*. Once more, it was a nomination that never materialized into an actual award, but he was really no less happy about that than he had been the last time. He was concerned much more with what was going to come next.

He had decided that it had to be a new play, for which he was going to earn $4,500 a week.

Jimmy Shine opened on Broadway at the Brooks Atkinson Theatre before any member of the public saw *Midnight Cowboy*. The play, by Murray Schisgal – probably Dustin's best friend at the time – was no huge success. Dustin described it as a means by which the playwright could 'cut through to truth.'

But for Dustin it was an opportunity to have his first all-acting, all-dancing, all-singing role; an experience that was almost as frenetic to watch as it was for him to perform – especially in the scenes in which he danced with beer cans strapped to the soles of his feet. He would be centre stage throughout the time that the curtain was up. It was close to what London theatre-goers knew as farce; Dustin's trousers came off almost as frequently as did his best lines.

It had moderately good notices after a series of tremendous problems out of town; in Philadelphia he was heard to say that he hoped God was watching and would be kinder to him when it opened in New York, but that was no excuse for him not to be ready. There was good reason for his prayers; the prayers of a normally non-religious man somehow have greater poignancy than those of someone who prays as a matter of course: on stage in Philadelphia he cut his head on a garbage can and then felt as if he had broken his back when he jumped on to a bed and landed on a pointed helmet. He couldn't possibly do it to himself again when they got to New York.

But it happened in Baltimore, even worse, although that is not to talk about progress, or lack of it, of the play itself. In Philadelphia, this story of a painter had not really worked at all. The cast had had a hard job to persuade their audience that it was worth working on any play about that painter, let alone one in which Dustin has to say: 'I'm a painter. I have to paint. I have to do the one thing in my life that makes sense before I lie down and drop dead.'

It sounded not unlike the cry of Dustin Hoffman as he lined up in the staff cafeteria at Macy's. For painter, read actor.

If that was not sufficiently autobiographical, there was more. He was not just an artist, but the only one in Greenwich Village who wasn't scoring with the women he met.

Things were a lot better in Baltimore.

The laughs came in the right places. The audience liked the way he made love to a prostitute. He conveyed the right kind of sex, a very different kind from that in *The Graduate*.

The real trouble was in the scene where he had to vent his frustration by tearing into a canvas with a palette knife, a usually fairly inoffensive weapon. Except that on this night, a props man had sharpened the knife so that Dustin would have no problem getting through the canvas. He had, in fact, sharpened it so much that it sliced Dustin's right index finger as well as the canvas. His fingers were covered in blood and he had an hour's work on the play before he could get it attended to.

This was where he could see the difference between acting on stage and on film – and how much simpler it would have been to do those one-minute takes. What was more frustrating than anything else was that he had allowed the accident to happen and did not do anything about it. He simply put his hand in his pocket, which was slowly filling, it seemed, with sticky blood, and made no mention of it. Why didn't he improvise? Why didn't he make it seem like a legitimate part of the action? For days afterwards, he kicked himself about that. He could not understand why he broke that fundamental rule of good acting.

The Baltimore *Sun* did not mention the finger in their review, which was more complimentary about Dustin than about the production. 'A character in search of a play,' wrote its critic.

After the final curtain that first night, he went off to the local hospital and had to deal with nurses who were more interested in what it was like being a film star than tending his wound. The next night, there were notices in the programmes: Mr Hoffman would be appearing with a cut finger. A lot of people found that very amusing.

But the play was invaluable to him, more important than any critic or any member of the public who just liked to go to the theatre or gape at stars could possibly imagine. When it opened in New York in December 1968 it not only gave Dustin his Broadway debut as a star, and provided him with his first opportunity to sing on stage; it helped him exorcise a ghost.

He was able to convince himself that he could still work in the theatre, to say nothing of providing a ready-made answer to all those people who thought he had sold out, was demeaning himself in Hollywood.

Not that he was an easy star to work with. That was too much to ask. By that time, the play's director Donald Driver had walked out in protest at the way Dustin had taken over. It was the repeat of an old, old story. And he was unrepentant: 'I always knew I was right in the choices I was making and that they were simply wrong. But they get panicky when they don't know anything about you.'

Clive Barnes, the principal 'Butcher of Broadway', said in *The New York Times*: 'He has the strange ability to be himself on the stage. Or, at least, if that is not himself he is playing, then some aspect of himself. He must be so unnaturally talented that he is practically monstrous.'

Time magazine came to much the same sort of conclusion. The anonymous writer of its February 1969 cover story – shared with Mia Farrow under the heading (the almost inevitable heading now), 'The Moonchild and the Fifth Beatle' – declared the play to be 'a mere vaudeville of the absurd. But within it is the vortical power of Dustin, pulling in the laughs, the cast and the audience. He growls like Durante, drones like W. C. Fields, shambles like Groucho Marx and dances like a good-natured puppy.'

If all those statements were completely right, they were also completely wrong. Dustin was a star not because he was 'like' anyone, but because he had now established himself as his own man. His was a style and a personality all his own.

The *Time* writer seemed to be accepting that when he said: 'The elements are his own – so much so that other performers are already copying them. The surprise is Hoffman's secret: it is because no one expects him to be adequate that he excels. From the beginning, he has been the Chaplinesque figure who makes progress through a series of falls.'

The *Los Angeles Times*' Emily Genauer saw it and reported to her readers in the first week of January 1969: 'It remains the hilariously funny, ingratiating, even tender story of a boy who grows up with romantic dreams of becoming an artist. But what I think Schisgal intended to tell us was the story of an artist growing up. That absorbing, profound, mysterious, most challenging theme, the development and maturing of creativity, the consuming anger to make works of art, still waits its convincing expression in a play or novel or movie.'

Just about the toughest treatment was from *Newsweek*, whose critic, J.K., began his review with a warning: 'Watch out, Dustin Hoffman. The Baron von Frankensteins of Broadway are trying to turn you into a Hoffmonster. O.K., so you're this fiendishly talented little guy with a face like the cute mole in Disney's *The Wind In The Willows* . . .'

So *what*? J.K. plainly didn't think that that *what* was *Jimmy Shine*. He was quite merciless in his hatred for the piece, so much so that he felt impelled to throw good grammar to the wind in the process: 'One

of the baddest bad plays possible to conceive, a messy, incredibly hack-
neyed, shamelessly exploitative farrago of what the baron – composed
of author Murray Schisgal, producers Claire Nichtern and Zev Bufman
and their (maybe) willing audience – thinks are currently viable com-
modities. The play itself is a monster; it's got the far-out art scene, even
the rock music scene – John Sebastian, a first-rate rock composer,
supplies some acceptable but unassimilated songs which have the annoy-
ing non-virtue of turning this non-play into a non-musical.'

But to Dustin, the magazine was slightly kinder. 'The electrodes are
crackling, the baron is throwing switches like crazy, Dustin convulses
into all his routines . . . playing – with style and sensitivity beyond the
call of duty – unbelievably cornball scenes.'

His theatrical producers found him as difficult to deal with as had
those in Hollywood. He not only got his $4,500 a week, but once that
had been taken into account, also 10 per cent of the gross box-office
take, which was a huge percentage.

Producer Zev Bufman described him as 'a hard bargainer', especially
after Dustin walked off with half the profits of the dollar-a-time souvenir
programme sales. He made about $100 a week from that, a sum that
for most plays would have gone entirely to the producers.

To some people Dustin was as eccentric as the characters he played.
How else could one explain his determination to eat something yellow
every day? He was sure he would be taken seriously ill unless he had
three hard-boiled eggs and dry wheat toast for breakfast each morning.
You might laugh at that, but you couldn't hate him for it. Yet there
were people in New York whom he himself hated – people he didn't
even know, and when he thought about that he worried about it.

As he said at the time: 'One night I was watching the news on TV
and I saw two burly white guys kicking and rocking a car where there
were two little black kids whose parents were trying to drive them to
school safely. I was so outraged and full of hate I could smell it. But
then when I calmed down, I thought, "I really don't hate those two
guys. How can I hate people when I understand they are acting from
fear and stupidity." '

He was trying to steel himself to feel the same way about people who
not so much hated, but certainly envied, him. He remembered envying
the WASP children in Los Angeles during the time he was going to one
of the better schools there. 'Envy is something you have to experience
before you know how wasteful and useless it is.'

Dustin Hoffman the star found it difficult to get it out of his system. Starring in *Jimmy Shine*, there was the great joy of seeing his name on the marquee, every young actor's burning ambition. But he couldn't reconcile himself to such a change in his fortunes in the past eighteen months or so. 'I think, "How did *he* get his name up there while I'm down here looking for a job?" '

Dustin could have held on to the *Jimmy Shine* job for years, until, in fact, it had become a very comfortable rut. It was Broadway and it enabled him to live in New York, to mix with the kind of people on whom both he and Anne agreed and would have kept him going as the kind of actor she most wanted him to be. But he had to start worrying about that rut, because if he didn't, before very long he'd be worried about the dripping ice-cake once more.

And by now it was a very complicated time for him. While waiting for *Midnight Cowboy* to open, and performing in *Jimmy Shine* at night, Dustin had been making his third film, *John and Mary*, on location in New York. This was the picture he made with Mia Farrow that inspired the *Time* cover story.

Peter Yates, the film's director, had persuaded Dustin to do it when he went to Philadelphia to watch *Jimmy Shine* shaping up. He even gave some suggestions for the play, which must have pleased Murray Schisgal about as much as Harry Hoffman had thrilled Mike Nichols on the set of *The Graduate*, but said nothing, basically to keep Dustin happy.

Dustin was so overworked at this time that he couldn't worry about what people wrote about him – although he was to say that he hated the *Time* piece which took hours of interviews and then got him all wrong. Twentieth Century-Fox did their best not to get Dustin wrong, in fact to do all they could to get him feeling right.

They came to an arrangement with Zev Bufman to pay compensation rather than have to lose Dustin on matinée days, when he would not be able to film. So instead of turning up at the theatre, Dustin was working at Biograph, the old studios in New York which had been cleaned out for the *John and Mary* picture. Then the studio provided a limousine to meet him at Biograph and take him to Broadway for the evening performance, and then from the theatre back home again. In the morning, the limo would be on hand to take him back to the studio.

Such treatment had hardly been seen since the days when Ziegfeld girls would be taken by siren-blaring cars from the Folies to the late-night shows the impresario presented. It demonstrated just how indispensable Dustin Hoffman really was.

But it also showed how tough the schedule was getting. He could not go on doing two things at once. Neither could he continue with the sort of show that *Jimmy Shine* had become.

For him, it was more than just the usual problem with successful stage plays – even those on Broadway – an actor being tied to it for such a long period. A man who still wanted a film career, and Dustin did, had to move on. He left the cast and the play closed. It couldn't sustain itself without him.

But California said it needed him and he went, to discuss the progress on *John and Mary* and to think about the next picture, to be called *Little Big Man* – which was precisely what Dustin Hoffman really was. The *Los Angeles Times* ran a cartoon showing a group of hippies carrying placards, declaring: 'Prepare to meet thy doom.' One of the girls says: 'Oh, groovy. Dustin Hoffman's coming to town.'

But he had no intention of staying. He was still a New York actor. New York was still in his blood. It was still the place where he could smell the smoky, fume-filled air and feel as though it had a unique chemical reaction with his own blood. So he wasn't going to stay away long.

Soon he flew back into Manhattan. He had one overriding intention now – to marry Anne.

6

Dustin Hoffman married Anne Byrne on 4 May 1969. The 'shiksa goddess' agreed to a Reform Jewish wedding ceremony at Chappaqua, New York. Both families attended the proceedings.

The last sentence sums up the unusual event that the wedding really was. The Hoffmans were still not religious, but they wanted a Jewish ceremony for their younger son. The Byrnes remained as tolerant as they had been all the time that their daughter and Dustin had been close – for three out of the six years they had known each other. They had to have a Reform ceremony, because neither the Orthodox nor Conservative religious movements would tolerate a mixed marriage.

There was a beautiful reception at the Byrnes' home at Mount Kisco – 'middle class,' as Anne emphasizes – which could not have been more different from the one in *The Graduate* or the kind in *Goodbye Columbus*. Just thirty-five people attended the affair.

Religious authorities tend to think that such an event is a recipe for disaster. The new Mr and Mrs Hoffman didn't seem to think so. They gave every appearance of being certain they were on the way to a very happy experience together.

Would it really matter? Would it make any difference to make their living together official in a marriage ceremony? They seemed to think it would. Dustin still surprised people by being unconventional in show business circles saying how much he wanted to marry and have a family. It seemed less unconventional for Anne to say the same thing. To Dustin, in a somewhat obtuse statement, getting married was 'coming off the freeway'. Whether by that he meant that he would slow down or was simply accepting the fact that as a married man he would no longer be free was never fully explained.

They certainly knew what they were letting themselves in for. Dustin had always been very frank about that. In the years in which they had been together, they had 'loved, loathed and hurt each other'. But, he would add, neither had ever been bored.

Providing boredom didn't set in, the couple had no reason to believe that things would be very different in future. After all, they had had a rehearsal for their marriage in the time in which they had lived together. Whether that showed confidence that it could last is a different matter. Dustin knew that he could be selfish and self-centred, two descriptions he had given of his behaviour over the years.

They went on a short honeymoon to the Far East. That was one thing that success had brought him, the ability to write a cheque for a pair of first-class airline tickets and a hotel suite and not feel a gashing pain as a result.

One of the first changes to their lives that getting married brought was that Karina had a new father. Dustin officially adopted her, declaring that he would always treat her totally as his own. From that moment on, she was his daughter – a state of affairs four-year-old Karina accepted fully. She did not realize that matters had ever been different. Both Anne and Dustin were determined that so it would remain. They promised themselves that when they had their own children there would be absolutely no difference between them and Karina. She, like the others, would follow the religious sensibilities of the parents, which were then accepted to be non-existent. Karina had been baptized as a Roman Catholic, but now it was understood that she would not be practising this faith. There seemed no need. This was going to be a very happy family, with two very happy parents.

Certainly, Karina had the advantage of having a new father who did not go out drinking with the boys. In fact, Anne was known to complain that he stayed at home too much when he was not working, that he found solace in his pool table when he could have been doing more exciting things. He would much rather come home, get into his bathrobe and lie in bed. If she could survive that, she didn't have a great deal to worry about in what was going to happen in the years to come.

Both decided they were going to make a go of it.

Dustin and Anne became a team at roughly the same time as *John and Mary*. This was a mild sex romp revolving around a young, attractive New York couple's one-night stand, an event that was not only very common but was perfect material for what was described as a film comedy. Nobody, after all, had heard of AIDS in those days and it was an age of free spirits and spirited movies; which, alas *John and Mary* certainly was not.

The couple, Dustin and Mia Farrow, pick each other up in a bar – the fact that not just one of the pair does the picking up is highly relevant considering the period; just one of the reasons, as we shall see, for the period being so important – and then debate which place they go back to, his or hers. Before long, they are in bed.

It was not totally unlike the ways Dustin and the girls he had met had behaved in his 'freeway' years. But he didn't take the part simply because he related to John. In fact, he emphasized how very different they were at every interview he gave.

But Dustin had thought it worth doing – the excruciatingly hard schedule of working during the day, and doing the night scenes when his performances of *Jimmy Shine* were over. One of the reasons he did do it was because he had tremendous faith in the director Peter Yates, in whom he had implicit trust after the help he had given *Jimmy Shine*.

'It wasn't the script. I'm not even sure I understand the character,' he added, and in so doing put himself on roughly the same level as most of the people who later paid to see the movie.

He wasn't like John. Unlike him he isn't neat, isn't a fastidious dresser or designer of apartments, can't cook. But he thought that if the director of *Bullitt* could achieve some of his old magic it was worth going into. None of that would prove to be true. The only good thing to come out of it was a fairly accurate historical record of the period. For a time that would be seen as a weakness. Looking back on it now, it is, if nothing else (and there isn't very much else) a document of the times. It studies the morals of the late 1960s as much as the clothes (and lack of them) of the times.

And it made Dustin a great deal of money. Because of the date when it was made, less than two years after *The Graduate*, the sex is more open. Miss Farrow is seen nude. Dustin is naked from the back. Looking back on the Dustin Hoffman of 1969 it seems that it was a distinct attempt at showing that he could escape from the excesses of character-acting of which he had been so proud.

The role of John – rewritten to take account of height and Dustin's own lack of WASP good looks – could just as easily have been played by Robert Redford, Ryan O'Neill or a young actor Dustin particularly admired, Warren Beatty.

He justified climbing into the more conventional mould – or as he put it, being more 'normal' – by saying, 'I've begun to think playing eccentrics all the time is, for me, a cop-out. The tough thing for me is not to have a particular voice or gait for a part. I have this strong fear that if I am just myself, I'm going to be full.'

In fact, that was how a number of people regarded *John and Mary* and what he had done with it.

Not even the seeming magic of linking him with Mia Farrow really came off. The young, elfin former wife of Frank Sinatra – she had just been divorced and was soon to become Mrs André Previn – was not an ideal teaming, no matter how much *Time* rejoiced in the pairing. The girl who had made her name in *Peyton Place*, one of the first TV soaps, and had gone on to her outstanding role in *Rosemary's Baby*, was not about to indulge Dustin in the kind of support he considered necessary.

'All he wanted to do all day long was talk about his analysis sessions,' one of his fellow actors in the film told me, without wishing to be identified. It was not the time when Dustin Hoffman was at his greatest, and there remains a reluctance to be reminded of a share in moments of his which were not so glorious. People do not want to go on record, as I discovered in numerous instances, as being less than totally supportive of him.

Because they did not know each other well – and perhaps because what they did know convinced them how different they were – Dustin and Mia Farrow agreed to have a series of meetings. They met in a hotel room, with executives present so that no one should think (the *mores* of the late 1960s and the plot of the picture notwithstanding) they were doing more than talking shop. Since shop included getting to know each other it was perfectly all right.

They talked about love and marriage, Dustin saying – and considering what was happening to him and to Anne, hardly surprisingly – that he was just an old-fashioned boy at heart and how much he appreciated the values of a stable married life. 'I'm very Victorian. I'm clean-cut, use Wildroot'. Mia, with her Sinatra experiences so fresh in her mind, saying how great it would be if there could be marriage without vows.

Possibly to demonstrate how brave everyone was in getting this twosome together in a hotel room Dustin made it clear that although he did have those feelings on marriage, he had had his share of relationships. He made his point about loving and leaving women. Mia said that all her best friends were men.

Dustin said that he only had a handful of real friends. Mia thought she was luckier. 'Like, wow, I have so many friends.'

As reported in *Ladies Home Journal*, he told her: 'You probably open

Dustin Hoffman – the macho image

Dustin in the role of the artist in the 1968 production of *Jimmy Shine*, with Arnold Wilkerson and Gale Dixon

Fixing Mrs Robinson – with Anne Bancroft in *The Graduate*

The power of the visual – a furtive look from Rizzo in *Midnight Cowboy*

Jon Voight, the hustler, and Dustin Hoffman, the business brain *(Midnight Cowboy)*

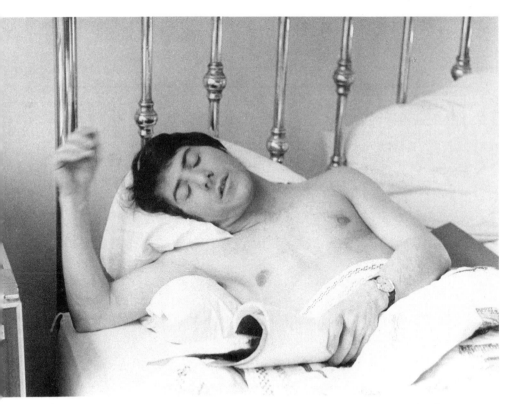

In *John and Mary*, Hoffman occasionally curled up with a script rather than Mia Farrow

Little Big Man – learning to ride was even harder than ageing to 121

Dustin the forger – *Papillon*

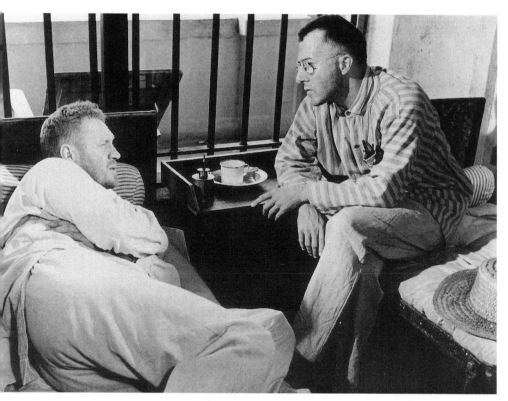

Steve McQueen *was* a different kind of actor, Dustin always made himself *look* different *(Papillon)*

Teaching Susan George a thing or two in *Straw Dogs*

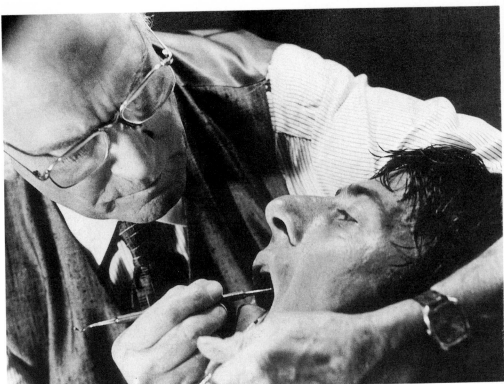

With Olivier in *Marathon Man* – Hoffman gave the veteran actor something to think about and the old man returned the pain in kind!

Off duty in Cannes at the time of *Lenny*, with his first wife Anne *(Associated Press)*

up a lot more than I do. I have pretty much the same friends I always had. I don't think I've made a new friend in ten years.' Anne would later wish that that was so. But for the moment, he was also saying: 'I don't put myself into situations where I'd make new ones. I don't go to parties, because I don't like them, and I've come to the point where I trust what I don't like.'

He thought that making a friend was no different from getting to know a girl. You needed to find someone who thought about life the same way.

It would have been even nearer to being ideal to find someone sitting in the audience at a performance of *John and Mary* who felt the same way about the film as the two stars had professed to feel about each other. Even Dustin's affection for Peter Yates had changed somewhat. It was one thing having him offer advice on someone else's product, but in this instance it was all his own work and not many people liked it.

Things did not go well during production. Dustin still wanted to improvize – and the best parts of the film were that improvization – and the director, not unnaturally, didn't care for a lot of it. Significantly, hours were spent discussing the best way Dustin should hand Mia a soufflé, or how they should discuss the diagrams in a sex manual. There wasn't a lot of time for much fun. Shooting was behind schedule for much of the time and Dustin was showing signs of exhaustion.

The story, by Mervyn Jones, was transferred from Britain to the United States, although the screenplay was by the eminent British writer/barrister John Mortimer. The one fascinating aspect of the entire story was that it was not until the final fade-out that the couple get to know each other's name.

They could not decide whether or not to continue the relationship and it is a measure of the picture that few actually cared.

The critic Judith Crist summed it up when she wrote: 'Despite all the "now" sets and surfaces, it's like an old comedy of the 30s – minus the comedy.'

Leslie Halliwell, the eminent film historian, saw little merit in the picture. It was, he decided, a 'slight, disappointing sex comedy vehicle for two stars who were very hot at the time'.

The point about such comments was that if Dustin was not careful the film could be seen as a watershed in his career. It was the first time since people had start noticing him enough to feature his performances in their reviews that he had received bad notices.

Another writer said that the film flopped because 'Hoffman simply lacked the confidence to be a calm lover or a strong self'.

That is uncharitable. Dustin Hoffman was not the cause of the film's failure. In fact, he was the only reasonable thing about it. But it wasn't good for him to be associated with failure, nevertheless. He had to start thinking about what was coming next. And he was the first to realize it.

It was time to move on to other things, while there were still directors who knew that he could act better than most and that in *John and Mary* there had really been very little wrong with his own performance. Certainly not enough to worry the fans. Girls still came up to him in the street and still found out where the house in Greenwich Village was situated. One of them threw her arms around him and begged him to go to bed with her.

He looked at her, appearing to size up the opportunity with which he had suddenly been presented, smiled and said: 'Okay . . . you want to come back to my apartment, right now?'

The girl froze – and ran.

Did Dustin have to run from his career now too? His contract said he couldn't, but the thought was with him. He either had to accept that *John and Mary* had not been a very good film and he was not going to make another like it or to think that he was almost half a million dollars richer as a result and be satisfied.

Fortunately for him he knew when had made a mistake. And even more fortunately, that other people knew it too. Robert Benton, a director of another Dustin film, was to say of him that he had an instinctive 'ability to smell when something is wrong'.

He was not wrong in smelling now that the time had come to go back into one of his eccentric roles. The character actor needed the make-up both cosmetically and mentally to succeed. He needed to be a character once again. He was going to have to go back to California. Even if only for the shortest possible stay.

7

Dustin once said: 'I've always had this fantasy – every actor has, I guess – that when I made it, I'd be able to do whatever I wanted.'

It could not be immediately assessed what he did really want as the 1960s – the decade that had begun so ominously for him but had ended so excitingly – ended and gave way to the 1970s.

It was fairly clear to those around him that Dustin was aware of his stardom and was taking advantage of it. He was much more self-assured and it was not difficult to make him upset. Directors and managers found him even harder to deal with. He wasn't suffering fools gladly, if at all.

Anne noted the changes only in as much as he seemed to be gravitating towards the friends she didn't like. She would have liked, above all, to see him changing as an actor. She couldn't. To her, now that fame decreed he could write his own contracts – to say nothing of his cheques – he had the opportunity to do so much more. He was wasting time not seeking Broadway roles that would have fulfilled and extended him. Instead, he had been bitten by the Hollywood bug at a time when he needn't have done. No big studio had him in its claws the way the moguls used to do in a previous generation and claim that without their benign dictatorship, the stars would never get work – and he did not need the money.

Dustin still said that he wanted to return to Broadway and that his real ambition was to direct, but he was taking few steps in that direction. But he wasn't about to accept another *John and Mary*-type role either. For his fourth picture, he was going to be a 'character' again – in fact, a character who is seen both as a youngster of 16 reminiscent of the innocent Benjamin Braddock and as a man of 121, which was a nice number to roll off the tongue.

In *Little Big Man* he plays the only survivor of the Americans who perished in Custer's Last Stand – who tells his story into the tape recorder of a credulous reporter. The audience is asked to be equally credulous. The fact that they are is a credit only to Dustin's acting, which survives the choice of vehicle – although the make-up man deserved a few credits, too. It wasn't easy to make the same man play a boy and a centenarian, but somehow it happened.

Anne went to California to be with him on the preliminary work and then out on location in Billings, Montana, close to the site of the battle that destroyed Custer's army and threatened to end the white man's domination of the Indians, who were known to have lived in the area of Little Big Horn for about 4,500 years.

Dustin was pleased he made the trip; he beat other members of the crew to eight dollars at poker on the flight out there. If his Great Dane, Murray, had not broken loose in the luggage compartment, it might all have been perfect, but the dog was sorted out before landing and most of the conversation when it was not on poker was on the work ahead.

In the wake of the film company's arrival at Billings, in the centre of the Yellowstone Valley, another battle was being enacted, for trade. The film people were expected to spend something like $1 million while working there.

There were as strong variations in climate during the making of the picture as Dustin himself experienced in age. The temperature in Billings was around 110°F. But, although the film took months to make, there was no way they could reproduce winter there – and a picture covering 121 years could not all be shot in summer. So the crew flew to Canada and temperatures closer to freezing. Wherever Dustin went, Anne went, too. 'I've never been a feminist and objected to doing that,' she told me.

They followed a procedure that became customary in the following years. They rented a house in the fashionable Los Angeles suburb of Brentwood, not as showy as Beverly Hills but with some of the costliest real estate in the United States. Film stars working temporarily in Hollywood provide the local estate agents with a staple kind of business that can keep them in their own homes and Cadillacs for life. The Hoffmans were plainly good catches, although neither of them could wait to leave.

They rented another house at Billings, a *nouveau riche* home owned by *nouveau riche* people who had gone on holiday. It even had fitted carpet in the kitchen, which Dustin found intriguing, but they weren't happy living there.

Whenever they could, they went back to New York. If there was a brief break in the shooting schedule, they got on a plane to take them back to Manhattan just as soon as the travel agent could deliver the tickets.

In New York, they would try to pretend that life was just a holiday. Anne had introduced Dustin to concerts and he was beginning to enjoy them, and together they went to art galleries, and to their favourite restaurants. At one, they received a message from the proprietor: another guest would like to meet them. It was Christiaan Barnard. 'Tell him to come over,' said Dustin, but Anne pointed out that of the two, Barnard was by far the more eminent, and it was incumbent upon Dustin to call on *him*. So the Hoffmans got up, went to Barnard's table and talked movies. The eminent surgeon who had pioneered the heart transplant knew more about *John and Mary* than Dustin would have believed. It was a stimulating evening, and also an opportunity to be in the place they loved best.

This time Anne had a particular reason for wanting to be home. As filming of *Little Big Man* drew to its close, she discovered she was pregnant for the second time – and for the first with Dustin as the father. A father who looked like an ancient or a boy, and would soon have to rush back to the other side of the country to demonstrate the fact.

The film had been an exciting experience for him.

Dustin was now 32, but he had beaten even his own *Graduate* record for having years taken off him for a picture. He was sometimes so tired that he couldn't help wondering which presented the harder job for the make-up man; making him 16 years younger or 89 years older.

Whatever it was, Dustin has been quoted as saying that the man responsible should have got a special Oscar. Anyone seeing the finished picture cannot but agree. Dick Smith achieved the virtually impossible; it had never been done so well before, to make Dustin not just age all those years, but look as if he had done it naturally. It was done with the aid of a rubber mask that Dustin wore for his scenes as the ancient. It was not, of course, just looks that had to be changed. In the best 'method' – or perhaps simply the best Dustin – tradition, he had to *feel* 121 – and to do that had to discover how a 121-year-old would feel and sound. Since there weren't that many 121-year-olds around, Dustin had to content himself with seeing much younger old people at a home on New York's Welfare Island. He wasn't satisfied. In the end, one of the technicians working on location came to his aid. He had a father of 104, and Dustin was welcome to come to observe him and listen to him.

In the end, there were three things about the man that were transferred to the personality of Jack Crabb, aged 121: his voice, the cigarette that seemingly never left his hand (a wonderful comment on all that medical science has been saying about smoking and early death for almost forty years) and the way he manipulated a table napkin.

If the results delighted the director Arthur Penn, they drove Anne to distraction. Suddenly, she was married to a man of 121 who coughed – differently from the way he did it in *Midnight Cowboy* – spoke with a voice that suggested he was suffering from terminal laryngitis (he had had a bout of the illness during part of the shooting) and played with a table napkin while he allowed a cigarette to dangle from his fingers.

'It was not so much that he deliberately took a part home with him,' she told me. 'He just allowed it to take over. Sometimes, he got immersed in his part. If things went wrong, he'd revert to the part, as he had as Rizzo. He wouldn't consciously go into it at home, making it real. He would say it was just a means of learning the part. But I think it was an excuse for letting out his frustrations.'

The voice itself took a time to mature. It was used only right at the very end of the picture when the scenes as an old man were finally shot. The hoarseness came in the most painful way, by Dustin shouting and screaming at the top of his voice on the way to the studio. He was to say: 'I screamed while I got dressed, I screamed leaving the room.' He doubtless would have done it much more at home, had he been not too concerned for the effect on Anne's health and the fright it might give Karina.

The scene as an old man was finally shot at a veterans' hospital, where Dustin met a 90-year-old patient who convinced himself he was the same age as Crabb, 121.

That turned out to be the key that finally opened a lock that had remained stiff and difficult to turn. To the old man's intonations, which Dustin studied like a Professor Higgins faced with an ancient male version of Eliza Doolittle, he added a Western twang which sufficed for the man he was playing in extreme old age.

If he had cured the problem of looking old, he still didn't properly feel it. But eventually he managed that, too. He wore contact lenses to make his eyes look as if they were covered with cataracts. The lenses were so good that his vision really was impaired. He had to be helped into the wheelchair in which he was sitting, narrating his 121-year-long story.

'It all helped my fantasy world,' he said at the time.

The earlier scenes had already been shot – including the one in a wind-blown tepee in which the 16-year-old Jack Crabb, adorned in war-paint, believed he was really an Indian, and not the white boy he actually was, the survivor of the Battle of Little Big Horn who had been rescued by the Cheyenne.

There was plenty of authenticity about the shots with the Indians once one had accepted that the tepee was being blown by a great wind and not by technicians vigorously shaking the skins of the tent. On the whole, there was no evidence of the white man making the picture speaking too much with forked tongue. There was also the invaluable advice of the real-life Indians on hand, notably Chief Dan George, playing the boy Crabb's grandfather Old Lodge Skins.

The picture was an obviously brilliant vehicle for Dustin Hoffman, the character actor. It was not so good for Dustin, the Western star – which he plainly was not. He might have invoked the name of Wild Bill Hickok in the picture – at one stage he works for the famous gun-toting medicine man – but Dustin Hoffman and horses were not natural companions. He had not done much riding and it showed. But because he was Dustin Hoffman he decided to try to learn, and he did. He also had to know how to use a pistol, but was not quick enough on the draw. He was constantly burned by the firing of even the blanks used in the picture. But he had to do it. Just as he had to do his own falling. Not for Dustin the luxury of having a stand-in to get dirty in dangerous situations, while all he himself had to do to camera was pick himself up, look injured and then dust himself off. All of a sudden there was a new meaning for his nickname, Dusty.

He also earned some dusty answers from members of the crew, particularly the man who did not terribly care for the sexy comments Dustin was making to the make-up woman. It was simply Mr Hoffman's own way of making people feel at home. He didn't bother to find out first if they were on his wavelength or not. He did not think it necessary, any more than performers taking part in a Friar's Roast ever thought it necessary to be polite before they handed out the insults. The differ-ence was that show people are supposed to be able to take it, and know what they are in for. With Dustin there was a suggestion of bullying techniques being used on people for the sake of his own sport; people who weren't able to answer back. They smiled and they laughed. How they felt inside was a different matter.

Ask him why he did all that, and he might have said that he was seeing the process of interviewing from a different angle. He went around with a tape recorder, asking people either totally inconsequential questions or personal ones like those to the make-up lady. On a plane, he took out his microphone and started questioning a fellow passenger on her parents. She took him seriously and replied with her innermost feelings. Should a star make fun of others in that way? Maybe it was just an attempt at making others feel comfortable. In this reported case it appears not to have succeeded. Or was it his old insecurity, the clown coming to the surface to take over from the doubter?

But he might have reflected on how he himself hated to be misquoted by professional interviewers. He fumed when he read that he was said to use words like 'groovy' which never entered his vocabulary at any time.

The film itself certainly worked, as did every minute of Dustin's portrayal. It is also, in the course of telling the story of the great swathe of American history represented by the white man's conquest of the West, a shocking indictment both of his treatment of the Indian and of his basic hypocrisy in claiming for him (and her)self standards that were never there.

It is in the course of making this point that the twin worlds of Dustin Hoffman's career and American sociological history meet. There were reasons to compare it with *The Graduate*. Once more, he is the innocent abroad who is seduced by an older woman as he makes his way across country from the Indian people who had adopted him as a child. This time the seductress is a minister's wife who tells him how much the Bible requires total cleanliness – while giving him a bath and plainly being turned on as she touches his firm young body.

The woman is played by Faye Dunaway, whom Penn had directed in *Bonnie and Clyde* and who expresses her sensuality almost exclusively in her eyes. If such things were possible, those eyes at this point deserved an X certificate. They were as sexy as another actress's breasts – and they brought Dustin hypnotically under her sway. Until, that is, he realizes it is all part of the hypocrisy of the world he is discovering.

It provided him with his best acting opportunities since *Midnight Cowboy* and enough of them for him to forget *John and Mary* while still enjoying the proceeds that the picture brought him. But it is as the old

man that the outstanding performer which is Dustin Hoffman is firmly
brought out.

The 1960s were now over and perhaps it was indicative of Dustin's
attitude to 1970 and all it represented that he chose a picture that looked
back so closely to his country's history, and asked so many questions.
Douglas Brode, in his superb study of Dustin's films, makes the point
that *Little Big Man* is in effect an allegory for Vietnam. It is more than
that. It is a study of humanity from a generation that was about to
proclaim that it had had enough of so much that had gone before – not
just Vietnam and all that was being spoken about that war, but colour
prejudice, the kind of society which in Britain, Prime Minister Harold
Macmillan had characterized with his immortal phrase that most people
had 'never had it so good', the society of Richard Nixon – on which
Dustin himself would be focusing before too long.

Meanwhile, the critics were happy enough to focus on their
impressions of the movie for the movie's sake, although the ubiquitous
Stanley Kauffmann was aware of the message. 'A tangy, and, I think,
unique film with American verve about some of the things that American
verve has done.'

The *New Yorker* would have preferred to see more film and less
import to it all. 'A hip epic with an amiable first hour,' the magazine
recorded. 'Then the massacres and the messages take over.'

They were going away on a short vacation once the film had been made,
Dustin, Anne and Karina. A trip had been booked to the Caribbean
and the best hotel suites organized for them. It was going to be a
necessary rest after the extraordinary pressure that ageing 89 years had
imposed. But the holiday had to be cancelled at the last minute. Karina
caught flu and neither of them thought it would be much fun going to
the Caribbean with a four-year-old flu victim, to say nothing of being
positively untherapeutic for the child.

Instead, they went back to New York – and barely escaped with their
lives for having done so.

8

New York had all its old pull on both Dustin and Anne. They flew back into Manhattan with the double satisfaction that a good job had been done, and that they were going home, ready to enjoy Greenwich Village precisely as it should be enjoyed – without too many cares.

They were planning for the new baby and thinking about their apartment in the way that people who are essentially home bodies do. The familiarity about it all was exciting at the same time as it was comfortable. Karina was delighted that they were all together again.

As a family they played games, they talked, they listened to music. As a pair, Dustin and Anne went round the antique shops and the art galleries. They went to concerts. Anne's influence was extremely strong in bringing the arts into the Hoffman household and Dustin not only went along with the process, but participated wholeheartedly. As Anne told me: 'My tastes became his tastes'.

He had more than made up for the lost time of the past.

They also all went shopping one morning. It was Karina's birthday and Anne, heavily pregnant, was buying candles for her cake. A lot has happened in the years since then, but every member of that household has reason to be extraordinarily grateful that on 5 March 1970, they did just that. Together. For by the time they returned to the house, there was not a lot of it there any more. A violent explosion had wrecked the building next door, set fire to the apartment, blown a huge hole in the wall where Dustin's desk stood – and left three people dead. If they had not gone out that morning, there could have been at least three more killed, Anne, Karina and Dustin Hoffman – whose last film, *Little Big Man*, would have been treated as his epitaph and would have probably won him a posthumous Oscar.

As it was, his wife, his adopted daughter and his unborn child went away with something much more valuable – their lives.

Two dead nude girls were found in the rubble. In the basement of the building was found the body of a man.

It took a certain time for the full implications of it all to be assessed. But it turned out to be one of those blessings in disguise that appears very disguised indeed until all the pieces of the jigsaw are fitted firmly into place.

In this case, it came in the form of an indecent assault on little Karina, which short of keeping her on a lead, could not have been avoided. She was walking in Washington Square Park one day, away from her parents who allowed her to play at a distance while still being watched. On that day they saw a man put his hand up Karina's dress. They vowed never to allow her out by herself again, and that they would move. They chose a new home closer to Central Park, which at the time was considered a lot safer place to walk and play in than Washington Square. People have since had reason to doubt whether that is so. But in early 1970, the Hoffmans thought that it was right to move from the apartment at 18 West 11th Street. Which was how they were out of the house that morning. They had gone looking for things for their new home.

Dustin himself had been sitting alone in the three-room flat (there were five other tenants in the house; he hadn't yet considered himself too big merely to rent an apartment) while the rest of the family had gone out. He was at that favourite $700 desk, which was wedged close to the wall dividing his apartment from the house next door.

The time had come, he had decided, to deal with one of those matters that had to be sorted out but which he could not fit in while making a film or acting in a stage play: he had to select the photographs taken at his wedding to Anne. Everyone else did it with their wedding pictures, why not the Hoffmans? The main reason had been that he had not had time, just as he had never had a moment to fix those book shelves. Well, now *was* that time. For the moment, there was no film to make, no play in which to perform. It was the conclusion of hours of going over scripts, and he thought a restful conclusion.

He left his desk to join Anne and Karina at 11.30. At 12, as he put it, the desk wasn't there any more. The rest of his burgeoning collection was consumed in the fire. Dustin did, however, manage to rescue a Tiffany lamp and another of his new loves, the pet turtle that had joined the family dogs (including a new Labrador pup he and Anne called 'Subway') in the Hoffman household.

'We lost a lot of photographs of ourselves and some books,' said Anne. 'The one thing we lost of any real value was a small drawing by an American painter. We didn't know who those kids were – not until after they were killed.'

The shock of hearing about the deaths – two other girls escaped with their lives and later evaded 'capture' by going on the run; they were embarrassed about being there – was considerable for Dustin.

The shock was all the greater because of the kind of lifestyle he had chosen for himself. He was not one who courted violence. Basically, he was the same devoutly unbrave person he had been at school. For all the bravado with his motorcycle in his unemployed years, he would now admit that he never rode it faster than 30 miles an hour, compared with friends who used to turn the public highway into a race-track. And he had some ideas about that, too.

'There's a theory that men who race are sexually inadequate. I don't believe that. What I do believe is that they're testing their immortality. They're testing God. They're saying, "Hey, You up there, look at me. See how fast I'm travelling. There's a good chance that I could die. But the fact that I don't, means I'm favoured." ' He was convinced that was why people climbed mountains – and not simply 'because they were there'. 'These men won't face the fact that they're only defying the inevitable, not beating the odds.'

Now, he realized that perhaps he himself had defied the same sort of inevitability.

What he didn't know was that he had been sitting teetering on the brink of an attempted revolution. The people next door who paid rent to the same landlord that he did were members of a radical group called the Weathermen.

He couldn't conceive how stormy they were going to make that weather – by manufacturing their own bombs. The Weathermen died along with the two nude girls and their boyfriend. Dustin was in turn angry and almost incredulous about the whole thing.

But he was full of admiration for some of the people who came out of the trouble, like his landlord James Wilkerson who remained so calm throughout that Dustin thought he would one day like to make a film about him. Wilkerson was the one who, in the midst of all the confusion, went fishing through the rubble and came out with a couple of the negatives Dustin thought he had been sorting out that morning. He also found a book that the Hoffmans had been studying. It was called *Looking for a New House*.

So Dustin tried to contemplate what he had so narrowly missed. As he said: 'I had no idea who my neighbours were, let alone what they were doing. I only know that I hadn't been out of the study more than half an hour before there was a terrible explosion. It sounded as if all of New York City had been bombed. I can't even think of the incident today without complete horror.'

It was more productive to think of his career and all its positive aspects. He may have recoiled in horror at the explosion: not many people were doing so about *Little Big Man*, although the *New Yorker*'s much respected Pauline Kael said it showed Arthur Penn to be rather 'smug'. The picture was not the biggest of Hoffman's hits, but it kept up the momentum of Dustin's career, and sufficient people paid their cash over the box office counters for it to make money.

Meanwhile, Dustin was having to wrestle with a problem that at first came to the surface with *John and Mary* and had not been resolved since. He was at his most outstanding best when he had a character to play. It wasn't that people only wanted to see Dustin Hoffman when he shuffled or had a hundred years of beard on his chin; but that was undoubtedly when he was 'different', and it was being different that people wanted to see him. The truth of the matter was that Dustin was becoming difficult to cast; not that people didn't try to tell him that what they were offering was a challenge, and not that he didn't in turn accept those challenges.

One of those he did take on should have been consigned to the garbage heap before the name of the film was appended to the contract. Since that film was called *Who's Afraid of Henry Kellerman and Why Is He Saying Those Things About Me*, the title occupied almost a whole page of the agreement on its own. It should have been long enough to give Dustin time to sit back and think about the whole thing.

There must have been *something* about this story of a pop music composer that attracted him, although looking back with the advantage of time it is difficult to imagine precisely what that could have been. He played a different character type, it is true, but the title was the only thing about the picture that was in the least bit memorable.

But Dustin took it seriously enough. For three months, he learned to play a guitar, which he ought to have found relaxing and not too difficult, since he was an accomplished pianist and he did see the connection.

He also trained his voice to sing, not well, but better than it had been with *Jimmy Shine* and well enough for it to have been left in the picture, although that doesn't really say very much. The great appeal to him was undoubtedly the fact that he had persuaded Ulu Grosbard to direct him, although he would have performed a kinder service by directing all concerned out of it. Dustin spent almost as much time as before researching the part, but those with him could tell something that for Dustin was very strange indeed – he didn't seem to have his whole heart in it.

He was called upon to age only a quarter of a century in the picture – from 17 to 42. After his experience in *Little Big Man* that should not have been too much of a problem, except that ageing 100 years provides a great deal of scope both for the character actor himself and for his make-up man. A mere 25 years requires an altogether different psychological change. It wasn't certain that Dustin made those changes at all satisfactorily, either to himself or to his audiences.

Grosbard confessed to doubts at the beginning of the exercise, but says he was persuaded by hearing Dustin reading the part of Georgie Soloway, a character like Hoffman himself who came from humble beginnings to make it very successfully in his own form of showbiz. In fact, Dustin was to say: 'The reason I chose this film was because it is about someone like myself. He was more multi-levelled than anything else I had done.'

So he worked at it and he rehearsed it, and as he said, he 'couldn't shed it. I took it home with me. I didn't enjoy playing the guy, and yet I enjoyed the experience more than any film I have ever done.' And Grosbard helped in that. 'Ulu reaches into people, tries to use the person and not a preconception.'

He was, however, as happy with the writer Herb Gardner – he had written the much acclaimed *A Thousand Clowns* – as he was with Grosbard. Or at least, so he said. Dustin was a great believer in believing his own publicity, or rather that of the very expensive, very well-trained PR organization that tried to sell the picture. There was no doubt, however, that he knew it should either have been done better or not done at all.

He needed to try to get shot of the project, mentally speaking, as quickly as he could.

Sometimes, he contemplated the wider international situation and, particularly, America's involvement in Vietnam. 'We have won a few wars and [the Vietnam] one, we didn't win it but we succeeded in bombing an entire country back to the Stone Age. We've lost our people but we've never been bombed; a foreign country has never gone over to us and dropped anything on us.'

Perhaps he should have taken as an omen the sound of another huge explosion – the second one in his life in a matter of months – while filming was going on. The Bank of Brazil's building on Fifth Avenue was attacked by terrorists at four o'clock one morning. 'That's twice they missed me,' Dustin told Anne.

Unfortunately, the picture itself did not miss him.

In short – and nothing was short about the picture with the longest title in Hollywood history – it was a sorry story of the composer who feels he is being persecuted, only to discover, thanks to help from his psychiatrist, that the one person who is persecuting him is himself. It gave full rein to both of what appeared to be America's prime preoccupations – Vietnam and drugs aside – in the early 1970s, psychiatry and pop. Fans of Dustin Hoffman would have been happier had it given more of a rein to their idol's talents. Everything about the picture was as wooden as Pinocchio.

Leslie Halliwell summed it up by saying it was a 'wild, shapeless, satirical psycho-comedy-melodrama. Not very good.' Dustin, however, has been sufficiently loyal to the other people involved in the picture (writer Herb Gardner, fellow performers Barbara Harris, who got an Oscar nomination, and Jack Warden, as the psychiatrist) and to himself not to say too much about it.

Besides, he probably thought that he had better things to look forward to.

The best part of all to come his way in 1970, he would probably have said, was that of being a father. On 15 October that year he was with Anne when she gave birth to their daughter, Jennifer – or, as she would always be from that moment on, Jenna.

He was to say that '*we* had natural childbirth'. And he meant it. He felt everything he was sure that Anne felt, even though he didn't claim any sympathy labour pains or morning sickness. But he did the same natural-childbirth exercises that she did, and felt involved in the whole process.

Yet he was rather like a supporting player in the whole affair. Worse than that. He said he was just a 'stage hand'.

He would ideally have loved a means by which the laws of nature were reversed and he himself could have produced the child from his own body and, most rewardingly of all, breast-fed Jenna, too.

That, in a way, was symptomatic of the way Dustin Hoffman was. It was as though – and this is not in any way to denigrate his love for his children, either of them – this was another production for him. Had

it happened in a film studio he would have found a way to give birth
on the table himself, to manipulate his nipples so that they produced
milk. He would have 'thought' his way into doing it. It might have
taken as many months as it took to 'find' the character in *Little Big
Man*, but in the end he would have done it.

There was almost some macho need in him to be the prime operator
in anything that deeply concerned him. To be second at anything that
was important in his life was to admit a kind of impotence, which was
something he had never allowed himself. Looking back on his life up
till then, he would have to admit that womanizing had played a considerable part in it. If he were going to abandon that – and he was – he had
to be sure of everything that touched him, and being in charge was part
of that.

As it was, he had to content himself with giving Jenna all the love
that he thought was available. 'I don't think it's possible to give a child
too much love,' he said after she was born.

And to prove it, he decided to spend as much time with her as
possible. For a year, he was going to read scripts and play with his two
daughters. He did not want to see a movie camera or climb on to a
stage. This was family time and he was determined to enjoy it.

Of course, it did not work out like that. Actors in their early thirties
should not take whole years off from their schedules and Dustin thought
he was sensible enough to know that, no matter how hard he had been
working.

But it was time for introspection. 'I'm not a bad father,' he said soon
after becoming one in his own right. 'When I'm working, I tend to
become remote and preoccupied. Call it selfish. Because I find it hard
to switch my mind from the role I'm creating to the demands of two
little girls who, naturally, have every right in the world to make demands
of their own.'

He did manage to get a holiday with them in Cannes and was able to
give them all Mr Hoffman's attention. But he still chose to work for as
long as was humanly possible. Vacations, he had decided, were a form
of hell to which he wanted as little exposure as could be managed. 'They
are grotesque. The most tiring thing I know,' was how he put it, giving
out his entire soul in the process. No, work was really everything and
he had to go on doing it, because that was the way he was.

Considering what he now undertook, however, it may not have been
a wise choice. Suddenly, Dustin was faced with a string of projects that

might have been better had he given himself a chance to sit back and think a bit harder.

But he and Anne did talk about the more personal things in life and, like a lot of other married couples, especially those who marry out of their respective faiths, they discussed religion.

Anne hadn't yet started to think about how good it would have been had Karina and Jenna been brought up to follow their religions. But both she and Dustin were disturbed by the inevitable questions that were already coming, questions about God that were every bit as inevitable as those on the facts of life.

Dustin himself became aware of the encroachment of that inevitability as he planned to take Anne and the two children to London, where he was to make his next film, *Straw Dogs*. Dustin tried to explain to Karina what it would be like to fly, particularly at night. 'We might see the moon,' he said.

Karina thought it necessary to take the matter a stage further. 'Maybe, we'll see God,' she said in her most matter-of-fact way, as though making a statement to the effect that it was raining or that there would be ice-cream before she went to bed.

Neither Anne nor Dustin knew how to deal with that one. They looked at each other, and those vacant, stunned looks indicated the beginning of some very familiar, very personal theological discussions that so many others in their place know so well.

'How do *you* know?' Dustin queried after his wife's insistence that, even though she no longer went to Mass, she still believed in the Deity. All Dustin could summon up for Karina's benefit was the statement, 'Some people know God and some people don't.'

Karina, listening to the theology, seemed satisfied by that. But today Anne really is convinced that life would have been easier if the children had been given some kind of religious identity; Karina brought up as a Catholic and, out of deference to what she firmly believes Dustin *should* have been, Jenna as Jewish.

To Hoffman all this was not nearly as important as *Straw Dogs*, a film that Anne told me she had virtually begged Dustin not to do. She didn't think it worthy of his talents or suitable for the man who had made *Midnight Cowboy*.

She still believed that he should have thought of himself as essentially a New York stage actor, perhaps one who was talented and successful enough to star in movies on the side, but a powerful stage actor before anything else.

The film industry would never have been convinced by that argument. No matter how many the doubts and how difficult it was to find just the right vehicle for Dustin, he was plainly the Big Star of the new decade. And that industry made their mark with him in the traditional way. In November 1970, more than five hundred leaders of the movie trade assembled at New York's Americana Hotel to pay him tribute. The Motion Picture and Entertainment Division of the American Jewish Committee had chosen that occasion to give him their William J. Germain Human Relations Award. Plainly, to them, making popular films was in itself a definition of human relations at their best.

Making *Straw Dogs*, however, was not.

It did little to promote human relations either within the industry – which is really only happy when fortunes are to be made – or with his public. For once, director Robert Benton's statement that Hoffman had the ability to smell when something went wrong . . . went . . . wrong.

He had no business playing the American university lecturer who finds himself in a small Cornish town and in the course of his visit ends up, in the space of twenty minutes, killing six people, the gang that had attacked him and raped his wife, played by the British *ingénue*, Susan George. It was not the image of a man whose film performances to date were in themselves courses in how to engage the sympathies of audiences.

Well, you didn't need a film critic to tell you that it should not have been his cup of tea at all.

The picture was based on a story called *The Siege of Trencher's Farm*, and Dustin was to say that he saw it as an opportunity to investigate how he would react in violent situations. He admitted that the picture was hard work and stressful, both physically and mentally.

Straw Dogs, directed by Sam Peckinpah – who shared the writing of the screenplay with David Zelag Goodman – has since achieved the dubious distinction of earning a moment in film history, as being the most frequently quoted example of a movie depending on gratuitous violence to bring people past the box office.

It was the perfect instance of what happens when chains are released, restrictions abandoned. Since American theatres now displayed codes, PG, R, and so on, in their movie advertising, no holds were barred.

It was the sight of the character played by Miss George walking through the Cornish street with plainly nothing between her blouse and her breasts that supposedly incited the local yokels to engage in a gang rape that she seemingly encouraged – right up to the moment that she attempted to fight them off. It was the thrill of Dustin spending so much time in bed with Susan that gave the picture one of the longest sex scenes in movie history to date.

American pictures had practically never before shown so much sex, nudity and violence. If the whole film had been shot through a red filter the image of spattered blood could not have been more overpowering.

What seemed to upset people most was that the mathematics professor whom Dustin played was so easily turned on by the attack on his wife, and appeared to so much enjoy his own violent reaction to it all.

But Susan George now looks back on the picture with all the affection of having come out very well from an experience that was one of the great influences of her life. She denied that it was gratuitous violence when I asked her about that charge.

'It was a wonderful memory, a wonderful experience,' she told me.

For her, it was the first important international role, one that became hers after ten readings for Peckinpah and plainly after gaining Hoffman's approval, too. She knew that she would have to read for him. That was the moment that Dustin Hoffman ceased to be merely the star she had seen in *The Graduate*. 'I didn't know very much about him, except that he was a very big name.'

She was to discover more, particularly that he had a very good sense of humour. 'It was, in fact, the first thing that I became aware of. He was lovely to read with. He always had a real twinkle in his eye. My whole existence with him was an example of his sense of humour at work.'

Five girls were tested for the role. Susan George's winning it was the result of a kind of endurance test not unfamiliar to army officers seeking promotion. Like the time she was called to a meeting with Peckinpah: 'I remember waiting outside the room and not being called in as I expected. Peckinpah's secretary Katie was sitting outside.'

Normally, Katie would have shown Susan straight in or had a friendly chat with her. This time, it was different. She was on the phone and nothing was going to distract her. 'She was ignoring me, which was something that had never happened before.

'I wanted to ask, "Should I go in?", but she continued to ignore me.'

Finally, Susan took the initiative and walked towards the director's door, which was ajar. She heard a voice call, 'Come in'.

'I didn't know if I should,' she recalled to me. Katie was still ignoring her. 'It was a set up,' she now realizes. She did not know it at the time, but she did risk going in, her eyeline obviously focusing on the faces of three men in front of her. One was Peckinpah himself, the second Daniel Melnick, the producer, and the third Dustin.

She still wasn't sure that she should be there, since she was being totally ignored. Not as obviously ignored as she had been by Katie, but now by three men who were in the middle of an extremely heated discussion, arms flailing as each made his point.

If discretion really were the better part of valour, Susan George decided for herself now to be very discreet indeed. There was only one thing to do, to leave. As she did so, she allowed her eyes to drop – to discover all three men were standing with their trousers around their ankles.

'I backed towards the door. I was in a terrible fluster.'

That was when Peckinpah broke from his conversation. 'Welcome Amy,' he said. The part of Amy, the girl around whom all the fuss was being made, was hers.

The way of giving her the news, the argument by three trouserless men, was all Dustin's. 'It was his sense of humour personified,' she told me. And it was just the first of a whole series of examples of it. Barely a day went by without a joke, some comedy business he had thought up either for the script or simply to keep Susan George amused.

It was the beginning of the film that was both 'joyous and tempestuous'. As she said, 'There was enormous excitement. Hoffman's personality was tremendous. He brought me tears and laughter.'

I asked her if the nude scenes had caused her considerable embarrassment. 'You have to be a very extraordinary person not to mind unclothing yourself in front of a camera. But it was an integral part of the story. Amy couldn't have been raped with her clothes on.'

That fear she felt of being a rape victim in the story was partly duplicated by the anxiety she felt at playing it before the cameras.

There was also a love scene with Dustin, which was a different experience. I asked her how she felt about that.

'Dustin was very gentle, very kind, very considerate and, I thought, a little shy.'

Shy? Dustin Hoffman, the man who discussed sex with complete strangers, who had first placed his hand on a girl's breasts at high school? 'Yes, he seemed shy, as indeed I was. It was really a very shy moment. He didn't crack any jokes or do anything funny the day we shot that scene.'

She now recalls: 'It's the one film I still dream about, as though it had just happened.'

And about that violence? Was she never afraid that people might imitate the action in the movie? No, she said. She was in the entertainment business and didn't expect people to imitate what she did on screen. 'After all, *Mary Poppins* was one of my favourite films of all time and I've never tried to jump out of a window carrying an umbrella.'

Dustin's kindness was one of the factors that helped her. 'He is one of the most generous actors I've ever worked with,' she said. 'He was very special. We are very different people as actors and work in very different ways. He is much more Method-oriented and I'm much more instinctive, but the combination was great and the chemistry worked.'

For three weeks Susan, Dustin and David Z. Goodman were in St Ives, Cornwall, together, just getting to know one another. Dustin and Susan to talk about their picture and what they planned to do with it. David simply observed: 'We needed to know how to make one another react. How to make each other laugh, how to make each other cry.

'There was one time when we were sitting talking, while I was chewing gum. Dustin watched the rhythm of my chewing and chewed in the same rhythm, too. When I chewed fast, he chewed even faster. Before long, we were chewing together. That scene was later incorporated into the picture.'

Moments like that are important in an actor-actress relationship. So were the times they spent off-duty together, with Dustin playing the piano in their evenings at the Tregenna Castle Hotel at St Ives and Susan enjoying every moment of it.

The critics were not so enthusiastic. Pauline Kael did not like the *Straw Dogs* image of Dustin Hoffman and the man she had come to think of as 'notoriously a cerebral actor . . . a cartoon of an intellectual'.

But other magazines seemed to like him more than most of the people who saw the picture.

To *Newsweek*, the picture provided a Hoffman performance that was 'all the more remarkable for the handicaps under which he labours'. And the magazine added: 'A superb character actor, he is called upon to play the kind of timid, repressed figure who requires a restrained, interiorized approach, depriving Hoffman of the bravura style at which he excels.'

In other words, Dustin was better than his picture.

It was not the first time that that had happened, nor would it be the last. What would have been rare would have been to have his own acting criticized. It almost never was. That was partly what had made him a star. But an unusual one – since acting was rarely the chief requirement for stardom. In his case, it undoubtedly was.

As usual, Anne went with him to England.

Now, she was about to accompany him for his next film to Italy. It was an exciting life for her – or it had been at first. Soon, however, the travelling, the living in hotels or in rented houses would pall on her. As she told me: 'There comes a time when you realize there are just so many different places in which you can go shopping.'

9

Precisely why Dustin Hoffman agreed to make a picture called *Alfredo, Alfredo* cannot be fully explained. It can't even be partly explained, except perhaps that the film provided him with a couple of months in Italy with the family and the cheque was extraordinarily large. In fact, the writing on that cheque was the best in the whole project.

But again, the question worth asking is 'Why?' If he had needed both the money and the vacation when he had made his last professional entry into Italy, certainly neither was the case now. Much more significantly, he was a man of reputation. Why risk all on what was not just a low-budget movie, but a low-intelligence script?

The kindest thing to say about the venture is perhaps that Dustin allowed himself the luxury of a brain-storm – the least damaging part of which was that he assumed *Alfredo, Alfredo* would escape unnoticed and he would still be remembered essentially for *Midnight Cowboy* and *Little Big Man*. In that, he was right – except that he was still also remembered for *The Graduate*. And when comparisons were made with other pictures after *Alfredo, Alfredo* was released, frequently *The Graduate* was the one referred to. Always, the comparison was unflattering.

Once more, Dustin appeared as a clean-cut young man (looking much younger than his 35 years) without the aid of excessive make-up or growth of beard.

It was not the sort of story that appeared to have any attraction for either him or his audiences at all. Just imagine this: Dustin is a bank clerk who falls madly in love with a girl who is so beautiful that he knows that she won't fancy him. Somehow or other, though, she does. They marry – and then he falls for another girl. There was not a lot more to be said about it. Dustin seemed to need all the long hair, pancake make-up and growth of beard that he could muster. A nice little case of TB in the script would not have gone amiss.

There was, however, a voice that made it all a little different. Not

Dustin's voice. An Italian voice. The picture was shot in Italian and Dustin expected to be able to learn enough Italian to do what he always did: speak his own lines. The research that he was accustomed to doing in preparation for a film was devoted almost exclusively this time to learning the language. Then came disappointment number one: the director Pietro Germi decreed that he wanted Dustin to speak English while everyone else spoke Italian. That way, American and British audiences would understand him better and relate to him more sympathetically. So his first real European film had him speaking English? Well, not quite. When Germi saw the rushes, he could see that it plainly wouldn't work that way. So he had his voice dubbed, by someone else, speaking Italian to Dustin's English language lip movements. Couldn't Germi have taken advantage of his star's Italian lessons? Not then, he couldn't. By the time he had decided to go that way, Dustin was already firmly back in the United States, resting and nursing a talent as well as an ego that had been deeply bruised by the affair.

The language mix-up was all Germi's fault. Dustin did not know that even if he had learned enough Italian to get by – which he was convinced he had (after all, they were not his own lines he was learning, so it was mostly a question of memory) the director planned to dub it just the same. He wanted all his Italians to sound like *real* Italians. But he had resigned himself to Dustin speaking in English at first because of the 'stupidity' of American audiences in particular, who refused to accept dubbed movies.

Someone in the Paramount office plainly thought that audiences weren't so stupid after all, which was, whichever way one looks at it, in the end a pretty stupid situation.

To say the least, the dubbing exercise did not exactly improve a pretty dreadful picture. Only audiences in art houses and die-hard Hoffman fans bothered to go to see it.

Alfredo, Alfredo was originally to be called *Till Divorce Do Us Part*, an obvious attempt at trying to con audiences into thinking it was probably going to be a sequel to the epics, *Marriage Italian Style* and Germi's own *Divorce Italian Style*. That was thought to be a means of getting American audiences to buy the picture. Perhaps the wisest thing of all that was done with this film was to abandon any such idea.

As usual, Dustin managed to overcome many of the handicaps of a picture that was not just dubbed badly, but written badly, directed badly and acted badly by almost everyone else. (The cast included

Stefania Sandrelli, Clara Colosino and Carla Gravina, not one of whom was guaranteed to entice people into a movie theatre.)

There were compensations of a sort. Dustin said he found the whole procedure very leisurely, compared with Hollywood. The director cut as he went along, fewer takes were shot.

If he was thinking that his own performance would always be good enough to get him by and that no one would worry about everything around him, it was dangerous thinking indeed. He was lucky that it was not so much his acting getting him by but the picture slipping by that really saved his reputation.

All the critics took the dubbed voice as their principal reason for attacking the picture. As *Time* magazine's Jay Cocks put it – the publication had just taken to abandoning the anonymity of its critics – removing a serious actor's voice was like depriving an acrobat of his legs. He didn't say so, but Dustin wobbled along in the role, giving every sign of not enjoying being parted from the rest of the company by having to use a different language from everyone else.

Only one thing helped *Alfredo, Alfredo* – a deft piece of box-office manipulation on the part of Paramount, who allowed it to slip in on precisely the same week as Dustin's next picture opened. This was *Papillon*, which had been made with everything that *Alfredo, Alfredo* had not.

It was again a time for introspection; for Dustin to start thinking about the way that career of his was heading. He could coast for just so long, he now had to realize, on what had happened before. It would not be long before someone, somewhere would be asking the question that dogs everybody in show business who has seemingly had a meteoric start (all right; in his case it hadn't been meteoric, but to almost everybody who hadn't kept Dustin Hoffman scrapbooks since his days in summer-stock it looked that way) – people were going to start asking, 'So what has he done recently?'

Once more, therefore, there was the issue of choice of work to be taken into account. If Dustin was now seriously becoming difficult to cast, there were signs of panic setting in. Why else would he make *Papillon*? It was not a bad picture – not bad at all when taken into consideration along with *Alfredo, Alfredo* which must really be regarded as a holiday in Italy partly financed by the few people who bothered to go to see it. *Papillon* gave Dustin some marvellous opportunities to show how well he could act in difficult, unpleasant circumstances. But it was all very, very reminiscent.

Papillon, based on the novel by Henri Charrière and directed by Franklin Schaffner, a man who specialized in making big productions (*Patton*, *The Boys From Brazil* etc), was *Midnight Cowboy* transferred from the seedier parts of Manhattan to the hotter, dustier terrain of Devil's Island. Once again, Dustin plays a pitifully sick individual, living on the coat-tails of a taller, fresher-looking blond man who nevertheless depends on Dustin's brain-power. Once again, Dustin took second billing to the tall blond man, this time played by Steve McQueen.

Papillon was remarkable in that for the first time Dustin was, in effect, his own boss – as indeed was Steve McQueen.

A short time earlier McQueen had joined in business three people who between them had a drawing power at the box office roughly worth a measurable fraction of the national debt. With Paul Newman, Barbra Streisand and Sidney Poitier, McQueen became part of First Artists. By 1972, Dustin had become a First Artist, too.

In fact, it had been while discussing the work planned by the company – plainly a 1970s heir to the United Artists organization of Charles Chaplin, D. W. Griffith, Mary Pickford and her husband Douglas Fairbanks, Senr – that Dustin started talking about *Papillon*. He was so fascinated by the story that several characters in the Charrière novel were amalgamated to form the role of Louis Dega, the counterfeiter.

This was just part of the reason why *Papillon* was earmarked for Dustin. Another was that it was something of a family affair. Anne played his wife in the picture – but, as she said, unless you read the credits at the end of the film, you wouldn't have known it. All she did was walk to and from that car. 'But I have to say that Dustin encouraged me in my acting ambitions,' she added. 'At the time, I was a dancer, but I've taken acting lessons since.'

The film has been dismissed as overlong, overpowering and overexpensive to make. But it did provide excellent glimpses into the degradation of prisoners on France's tropical penal colony, perhaps never more graphically shown than when the prisoners were allowed to wash – by being hosed down like cattle ready for the slaughter-yard.

Unquestionably, Dustin was good playing what people in his grandmother's home town would have described in the Yiddish word, *nebbech* – like many Yiddish words translating, in this case as 'pitiful', the word only says half of what it is all about. Suffice to say that Dustin's Dega, who joins McQueen to embark on an escape from Devil's Island, was the *nebbech* personified. Dustin *was* undoubtedly good at playing *neb-bechs*, but in effect playing Ratso Rizzo again was a questionable strategy.

What was more questionable was teaming up with McQueen as 'Papillon' – French for the butterfly he had tattooed on his arm and which gave him the nickname with which he is saddled throughout the story. They stay together because Papillon believes Dega is wealthy – with a fortune stored up his rectum. That was the sort of premise that had to carry the movie along.

A lot of footage was shot in French Guiana, where the humid climate and vegetation (what there is of it) was thought to resemble that of Devil's Island. One of the perks of stardom was that Dustin and McQueen shot their own scenes only in Jamaica.

To his credit, Dustin never denied that. He was never made to feel a prisoner when making that film. 'I was a movie star,' he declared honestly. The trailer was always at his disposal. The best food was there for his enjoyment along with the assistants and the luxurious hotel suite for him and Anne.

On the other hand, he had a hang-up or two. Unlike the situation with Jon Voight in *Midnight Cowboy*, with Steve McQueen he was having to take second place in the deferential stakes.

Dustin looked terrible in his glasses, his growth of beard (this was long before 'designer stubble' became *de rigueur*) and his striped uniform. Steve McQueen, dressed the same way, looked every inch the star. Worse, he *felt* every inch the star – or the super-star. McQueen was a super-star, Hoffman recognized, and demanded to be treated like one. Dustin was always made to feel that he was in his wake. Soon afterwards, he said: 'Well, I don't have to be too candid. He's fine. It was a workmanlike experience . . . I dunno.'

The late George Coulouris, who played Dr Chatal, told me: 'That really was an experience – McQueen and Hoffman. Neither was easy to get on with, but I could see Hoffman smarting at the way McQueen could get his own way all the time and not caring if he took the scenes from Dustin. I could see why he was peeved.'

The two stars agreed on practically nothing. McQueen said he was physically worn out from the production. Dustin said that the strain was all mental. 'It's always the mental aspect rather than the physical that is difficult for me. I had to exhaust myself mentally to look and act like the old man I play,' he said.

On the other hand, there are those who say that the pairing was a lot more satisfactory. In her excellent biography, *Steve McQueen*, Penina Spiegel writes: 'He admired Dustin Hoffman to the point of discomfort in his presence; Hoffman was a highly trained New York stage actor; he had succeeded where Steve had failed and he had credentials to prove it. Hoffman was Tony Franciosa and James Dean and Ben Gazzara all rolled into one.' Putting things into McQueen's métier, she was not wrong, even though Miss Spiegel did add – probably not so accurately – that Dustin was unhappy because Steve in the end gave a better performance. She was wrong because once again, it is Dustin's perform-ance that one remembers. The pebble glasses, the awkward walk, the screechy voice of Dega, those are the things that remain in the memory.

That this is so is a tribute to Dustin that should rank among the greatest of the plaudits that have come to him. The *Papillon* story is a true one, even if Dega was a fictional composite character. Nevertheless, Dustin felt, as usual, that he had to know a great deal about the man he was playing. He tried a psychological approach by looking at paint-ings by people who supposedly were as tortured as Dega was expected to be. It didn't work for him. In fact, he admitted to his fruitless search. Dustin was to say that there were a lot of lessons in *Papillon*. 'I learned from that experience. You can't create more than there is on paper – in the script.'

The picture was not nearly as bad as a great many people now think it fashionable to say. It was an adventure film of the sort Humphrey Bogart and Peter Lorre might have made in black and white a generation before. Perhaps it would have been better had it not had the wide, wide screen and the colour and the stereophonic sound. But it did have a wholly creditable Hoffman performance, one that he should not be so ready to deride.

Perhaps what really irked Dustin was that McQueen got $2 million for his role. Dustin's salary was the biggest he had ever earned, $1,250,000, which was huge by most standards, but was still $750,000 less than McQueen's.

There were physical problems, too. The thick glasses he had to wear as Dega throughout the picture caused a great deal of eye-strain. It took weeks after the film was completed for his eyes to adjust to normal usage again.

For him, one of the most frustrating aspects of it all was really how little control he had over the finished product. He didn't see the finished film for quite six months after it had been made. 'I don't know what they're going to do to me in the cutting room,' he declared. And he

added: 'This is the least interesting time for an actor.' The actor who
had tried to find his character in a painting kept the metaphor going.
'It's like being a painter. You decide on all the colours you're going to
use and you do all your sketches and you get ready to put it on canvas.
Someone comes up to you and says, "Oops. Thank you very much.
These are the colours. These are the sketches. See you later on," and
they proceed to do the painting. In a sense, that's what happens on the
cutting room floor. I'd like to get in there and at least say what I think.
"That little take there – because I set something up that I wanted to
do twenty minutes later. Please don't leave it on the cutting room
floor." ' That was one reason why what Dustin really wanted was to
direct himself.

Few of the critics thought that the movie was worth dwelling on. As
Paul D. Zimmermann wrote: '*Papillon* offers torture as entertainment
but winds up making entertainment a form of torture . . . a tournament
of brutality unrelieved by imagination.'

The always respected Pauline Kael put it like this: 'I was grateful
each time Dustin Hoffman turned up, simply because he tries to do
something for his characterization.'

And to *Sight and Sound* it was a 'two-and-a-half-hour epic trampling
the corn growing round the theme of man's inhumanity to man'.

Dustin himself was getting the message, but misinterpreting it. He
was taking personally everything written about his pictures. He was
angry at the snide remarks. 'Joe Nebish [an Anglicization of *nebbech*],
Mr Loser that. I read it and I think, "Jesus, what a jerk!" Lately,
though, it's been the way some of the articles are written. For the first
five minutes after *The Graduate* it was fine, because everyone wrote how
I'd worked up slowly off-Broadway. "He earned it," they said. "He
deserves it." Then suddenly I was the Establishment, the Enemy.
People started to write, "Who is this guy? How dare he?" In five
minutes, respect and admiration turned into – I don't know – envy and
ugliness.'

He had the sense to realize that the time had most certainly come to
do something about his career. He knew that he was best of all in
character parts, but the writing was getting very clear on the cinema
walls. Good character parts only worked when he had something very
different to offer. Perhaps there was also another lesson: next time he
himself had to be the star.

The only people who were really satisfied in subsidiary roles were
members of a double act. But Dustin Hoffman was no Stan Laurel or

Oliver Hardy, certainly neither Dean Martin nor Jerry Lewis. He wasn't even a Walter Matthau or a Jack Lemmon. He was brilliant playing second fiddle and turning out first violin. But he always had a different partner and it was not good for his own self-esteem.

So he had to do something that was unequivocal as far as status was concerned. He would be the star – by playing a star.

Lenny did not prove to be a great film, but it was a good one and Dustin was great in it. Once more, he played a character, but a real one, whom he felt to be real, and whom he felt to be himself and took home with him (much to Anne's disgust, as will soon become obvious).

It was a courageous part to play, if only because it was the story of a real live character. But it was all the more dangerous a venture since that character was exceedingly well-known (in fact to some, by reputation to many) and because he had died just eight years before.

Lenny Bruce was the best-known product of an age of stand-up comedian-satirists who flourished in the era when America decided it had sufficiently matured to stop taking itself too seriously.

In the 1930s, Will Rogers had talked about the political affairs of the day from the stage of America's most prestigious theatres, as he twirled a rope and spoke of his optimism. After him, Bob Hope, with the aid of his celebrated joke factory, had told topical stories, all of which endeared him to the solid Republican Establishment of the United States that had made him a multi-billionaire. But the McCarthy era which had dictated the premise that there were reds under too many Hollywood beds had put a stop to a great deal of that. When the country began to come to its senses, the comedians changed. Suddenly, a more vitriolic, intellectual breed was at work in a small group of clubs and, when the political climate became easier, branched out on to television and the bigger theatres. Mort Sahl was one of these. Lenny Bruce was too clever, too vitriolic, too outspoken to escape the club milieu.

People who went to a Lenny Bruce performance went to be shocked – which was perhaps a strange phenomenon. If you expected to be shocked, you were instantly anaesthetized from the effect of that shock. But people went just the same, sometimes brought in by a thirty-foot poster showing Hitler giving the Nazi salute. The poster carried the legend in big type: 'OPENING THURSDAY NIGHT. ADOLF HITLER'. Underneath in small type, 'With Lenny Bruce'. Even joking about Adolf Hitler was a shocking thing to do.

But Lenny's reputation was immense; his following huge in terms of what the clubs to which he was confined were used to. He was a product of what had become known as the drug culture and eventually it would be drugs that killed him. But what had killed his chances of ever really leaving the club circuit had he wanted to was the way he talked. The world he described said what its inhabitants felt. They didn't merely call a spade a spade. They were people who thought that life was shit. They fucked. The more outrageous the language, the bigger the following, although that was not the Lenny Bruce genius. It is one of the travesties of contemporary history that the outer shells of personalities are all too often all that is remembered. The language is recalled, the genius of the mind that produced the thoughts coated in that language is forgotten.

But the law only heard that, too. Bruce had been convicted at Manhattan Criminal Court in December 1964 – just two years before his death – of conducting a performance that was 'obscene, indecent, immoral and impure'. In the end he was banned from even appearing in the clubs where he managed to make a living.

That, then, was the challenge Dustin adopted for himself in making *Lenny*. He not only had to make himself feel like Lenny Bruce, he had to *be* Lenny Bruce. Anne suddenly found herself married to a man who never used a sentence without the word 'fuck' in it. 'His attitude became very trying for me,' she told me. 'No more than he had as Rizzo, he wouldn't consciously go into the part and he would again say it was a means for him to learn it. But I think that was an excuse, too.'

As must be fairly obvious by now, Dustin loved to shock. But he was not, on the whole, a compulsive swearer, until, that is, Lenny Bruce entered his life. Even so, Anne thought that *Lenny* showed a Dustin closer to his real self than almost anything he had done before.

'She thinks I used more parts of myself in that than anything else until now. Lenny had been the toughest by far, the hardest, because the screenplay was like the sharp lines, like the way Matisse sometimes puts together the whole piece of a woman, though there are no more than a dozen lines there. But I tried to do a full character.'

Again the painting metaphor. Anne's influence was plainly showing itself through artistic reference. Dustin, though, did admire great art and this gave him a perfect means of explaining what he felt.

Anne was happy to be at home for much of the time that the picture was shot on location in New York, although it moved to Miami before the final scenes and post-production work in Los Angeles. The locations were important: they were part of the task of making the picture real, despite the opposition the company received from vestiges of the Establishment who thought it was not a subject suitable for filming. Some theatre owners let it be known that they would not show the film. United Artists – not wrongly – took the view that when these people saw other owners making money out of it they would not argue.

Dustin never met Bruce nor saw him at work. But he could relate to him. 'Lenny was up against a wall,' he said. 'And I've felt up against a wall now for a while. I feel I haven't been putting it together the way I want in my work.'

After the experiences of *Alfredo, Alfredo* and *Papillon*, he was merely stating the obvious to some people. So Lenny Bruce held a key he had to find a way of putting into a lock. But not seeing Bruce at work was a problem, although Dustin's performance would not be influenced by memories that might subconsciously mean he provided a totally imitative performance.

'I never made the night-club scene, because I didn't have the money,' he explained. But in the early 1960s a girl had given him a record of Bruce's to listen to. 'That turned me on to him,' he said.

But playing him in a film didn't just mean 'feeling' he was Bruce, any more than it would have been enough to learn his lines and directions. Dustin did his own research as though he were planning a definitive work of his own, instead of something based on the book by William Goldman. He read all he could about Lenny Bruce, interviewed about fifty of Bruce's friends and spoke to his mother and his daughter. He came to his own conclusions about the comedian.

'Bruce was very naïve. His friends I talked to were full of contradictions about him, but concurred on his naïvety. At the same time he was very serious. He really felt he could talk to a judge who had spent thirty years in the National Guard, that he could get through to him. He believed it almost as a child.' Asking this judge to reason with Lenny Bruce was like asking a priest to think seriously of taking a wife.

And for an actor to play another actor or at least another performer was also asking a great deal. Dustin thought that painters were the real artists, not actors. 'There's the cliché – that as an actor you can pretend to be the opera singer, the boxer – but don't kid yourself. Don't ever think it's the same thing.' For someone who did the sort of research that Hoffman did that was quite a statement.

Most people Dustin had spoken to had, apparently, liked Bruce. Some, though, had not. 'But that was not the point,' Dustin said. 'He was not there to turn the audience on. He was angry. He was a social satirist – history had proved that – he was more than a comedian.'

Finally, the key to the part lay in a tape that came Dustin's way, the last that Bruce had made. In fact, he recorded it just three hours before he died. Hoffman worried about that. 'I really didn't know what I was getting into, playing someone this real for the first time.'

He was looking for a new insight into Bruce, who had been maligned, partly because of his own masochistic approach to life. 'The whole point of the movie [is] that Lenny was a man who loved his country,' said Dustin, in an attempt to show just how far patriotism had gone since the days when Eisenhower was President. 'Lenny believed in the Constitution, in the right to freedom of speech. He didn't use those four-letter words to make the audience horny; he was just saying, "Why can't we use the language on stage that we use in our daily lives?" '

Which is why Dustin used it too and why Anne wished that he did not. The project fascinated Dustin from the outset. 'What makes the thing really interesting is the period in which he lived and fought,' he said.

It was not difficult now to say that one opposed Senator McCarthy, which for all the shock and the obscenity was what made the whole film acceptable. They tried hard to get as close to the real story as possible. Some of the picture was shot outside Bruce's New York home at Livingston Street in Brooklyn Heights – or at least it was once they found where that home was. Bruce's manager, Marvin Worth, had given the company the wrong address and for much of the time it was somebody else's old house that had the cameras played on it.

Lenny had been a moderate success as a stage play starring Cliff Gorman, who looked a lot less like Lenny than Dustin did. Dustin had, however, seen Gorman at work and thought him brilliant in the part. When he was asked to play the role, he actually asked: 'Why don't you get Gorman?' The answer was obvious: Cliff Gorman would not have sold any seats away from Broadway. Dustin Hoffman would.

But he was not sure he could do it. 'I've never played someone who really existed, especially someone who lived to 1966,' he said. 'It feels tough. I don't have the freedom to do what I want. There is a fidelity you feel bound to. You can't be a mimic. I'm not a mimic anyway.'

Bob Fosse was the director of the picture, proving that he knew how to stand behind a camera when the girls weren't expected to dance extravagant routines he had designed for them and when leading men didn't suddenly start singing about the moon and June.

What came out of Dustin Hoffman's mouth in *Lenny* would have had the denizens of the MGM musicals reaching out for their heart pills.

While Dustin may have been a brilliant choice for the part, it was anything but a happy experience for him.

'I have never seen an actor go into the sheer depths of a part the way Dustin did,' Fosse told me. 'He was perhaps the most difficult actor with whom I have ever worked. Everything he did had to mean something to him in a way that showed absolutely no patience or feeling for anyone else. He always said that he knew how to improve the picture. I was never convinced.'

Dustin himself was to say of Fosse: 'Fosse is a dedicated man whose only vice is that he overworks himself.' Which possibly explains why he had open-heart surgery after the film was completed. Perhaps he was put off by having to have the sweat that poured off Bruce's brow when he was in the thick of his routines sprayed on to his actor's cheeks and forehead. Bob Fosse was actually heard at one stage to ask the make-up girl, 'Is Dustin's sweat in place?'

Sometimes, Dustin sweated for real – when he fought to get his own improvisations on to the screen. What he had done in *Midnight Cowboy* did not work this time. He remembered what a sports coach had once shouted at a referee: 'Why do you have to keep fucking up a perfectly good game?' In a scene where Lenny is on trial, Dustin turns to the judge and says: 'Why do you have to keep fucking up a perfectly good trial?'

It was one of those things that Bob Fosse didn't like. The line was excised from the picture.

That did tend to dent the powers of conviction, especially for an actor who knew he had to *be* Lenny Bruce. Some of the extras needed convincing, too. Fosse frequently had to interrupt the patter that Dustin was giving from the night-club platform, to tell them, 'Laugh, people, laugh.' It wasn't that Dustin was not being good as Lenny Bruce. The truth was that the extras were not the sort of people who would have gone to a Bruce performance. Several of them, in any case, were too wound up in their own 'roles' as extras to take that much notice of what was going on in front of them.

If they had been, they would have heard Dustin as Lenny call out to a woman in his audience,'You've got nice tits, lady. Pity they can't print them in the newspapers instead of those pictures they are eager to print of naked napalmed bodies of Vietnamese.'

It was hard, raunchy stuff and was just what Bruce would have said, mixing his outrageous language with what he considered to be his own bitter but totally justified, political sentiments.

It got close to one's feelings, that sort of thing. So did having a routine interrupted by a policeman telling the night-clubbers that their entertainer was being put under arrest. The fact that people sitting in theatre seats shuddered when that happened, showed that imperfect though *Lenny* might have been, it worked. The only trouble was that, although it made a fair amount of money in the theatres (enough to take it firmly into profit) the language and the situations made it off limits to network television in the United States.

Perhaps, on the other hand, it needed the 'feel' of being in a theatre to have any real impact, especially as the lights go down to reveal a blindingly white screen which then focuses on Dustin playing Lenny gripping the microphone (as Lenny himself might have noted, using less polite language) like a phallus.

Pauline Kael in the *New Yorker* complained that the picture sanitized Bruce and his intentions. She said that the picture was essentially 'for audiences who want to believe that Lenny Bruce was a saintly gadfly who was martyred for having lived before his time'.

Be that as it may, *Lenny* was a *tour-de-force* of the kind for which Dustin Hoffman had been waiting since *Midnight Cowboy*. It was a brilliant idea to cast him in the role of the Jewish youngster who goes out to beat both his poverty and convention on his own terms. It was an equally brilliant idea for Dustin to accept Fosse's invitation to take the part.

For all that, Dustin himself has always been less satisfied with his performance as the bearded Bruce than with almost anything worthwhile he has done. Plainly he is not including it in the same class as *John and Mary*, to say nothing of *Henry Kellerman* or *Alfredo, Alfredo*, and to do so would be as insulting to Bob Fosse as to himself, but he regards what he did in it as 'flawed'. As he said, 'it was certainly not Lenny Bruce'.

That was one of the reasons Dustin was angry with critics who said that the picture failed principally because it was so different from the book by Goldman. The book was different from Lenny Bruce, said Dustin. 'I understand that it's far from the truth,' he would say. 'Goldman met Lenny for five minutes in his dressing room and Bruce didn't like him and turned him away. I do not respect a reviewer who compares our film to that book.'

People did, however, respect Dustin Hoffman for what he had done with the film. His performance earned him a Best Actor Oscar nomination, which should have contented him and reassured him about capturing the 'real' Lenny Bruce. He did not win the Award, nevertheless.

Dustin decided that it was not worth winning in any case, which endeared him to Hollywood no more than the things Lenny Bruce said had made him popular with most of America. The man who played an entertainer accused of obscenity was quoted himself as saying that the Academy Award was 'obscene'. He immediately denied saying anything of the kind. But the charge stuck.

'It's a word I'd never use,' he said. What he insisted he said was that it should not be regarded as something achieved in a competitive way. 'I liked it when the Award went to John Wayne because it proved the point that it was an honour, not a contest.'

Frank Sinatra took up what he believed was a Hoffman challenge. He repeated the charge that Dustin had said the Oscars were obscene. Dustin had no right to call something as hallowed as an Academy Award obscene. Again, Dustin denied it. He had described the bronze statuettes as 'ugly and grotesque', but that's all. Neither was he following Marlon Brando and George C. Scott in refusing to accept an Oscar. He had not been offered one, but he did not endear himself to anyone when he said that he was refusing to go to the ceremony. What upset him was use of that one word. 'The only thing that disturbs me,' he said, 'is that I was misquoted by Mr Sinatra. I never used the word "obscene". It is his word. Interesting, that he uses it.'

As Anne had noted, it was at moments like this that he used words that Lenny Bruce might have found more acceptable than most people. As his new manager Jarvis Astaire told me, 'He was swearing all the time now.'

But when the next Oscar ceremony was held in 1975, the 'obscene' word was the one that was quoted against him.

By then, he was thinking of his next role. If that won him an Oscar, he would not spurn it.

But first, he was going back to the stage.

10

Despite all Anne's reservations, Dustin still felt in his heart that he was above all a New York stage actor. All right, so he made a fortune bigger than anyone else who worked for a living between the wings of a proscenium arch and received fan mail far in excess of any, too. But the contrast that Steve McQueen seems to have noted between himself and Dustin was very real.

Had he not made *Alfredo, Alfredo* and perhaps had he steered away from *Papillon*, he would have had an answer to his wife's charge to me that she thought he had stood still and would continue to do so. Experience has shown this not to be true.

Certainly, all the time he was in Hollywood or making movies in other places, there was a yearning to get back to the stage, to the 'real world', to the place where he could live in his own home and commute to the theatre daily for rehearsals and then performances.

Anne was right in one respect, however. His various forays on to the stage offered little that was rewarding. With *Jimmy Shine*, there was always the feeling that it only got into a theatre (including those places where it had its out-of-town trials, and trials is the appropriate word) because of who Dustin Hoffman was and not because of his talents as an actor or because of the brilliance of the play. Proof of this came in abundance when the play closed after he left it.

In 1975, Dustin was back on stage again, but this time as a director. He was finally doing what he thought he wanted to do most. He even had an office, decorated in avocado green, on Madison Avenue to show that he was perhaps also essentially a businessman, for business was very much what he was now in. Even directing a play called *All Over Town* which was yet another work by Murray Schisgal, the only writer who apparently could inveigle Dustin back on to a stage.

It wasn't very much of a play. But he thought he had a great deal in common with Schisgal after all the years in which they had worked together. 'I know where Murray lives,' he said, not intending to provide a guide to his address. Mixing the metaphors he added: 'I'm in the same ballpark.'

Schisgal was equally effusive about Dustin. In an interview in *Esquire* magazine in April 1975, which described Hoffman as a 'worrier, a nagger, a bouncing Tiger, a dog with a bone who never lets go until the bone is thrashed to pieces', the writer said about him: 'He never quits. He can drive you up the wall sometimes, but, Christ, he's got guts.' To which Dustin added that Murray was 'crazy. He's also the funniest and the bravest man I know.'

They were both brave to work on a show when neither knew whether or not it would ever recoup its $300,000 investment. Dustin would do all he could to try to get that money back, knowing that when he gave interviews, the show was merely a peg on which a writer could hang yet another celebrity piece about Dustin Hoffman. It would not be true to say that they worked totally amicably together, agreeing with each other every step of the way. 'A director alters a writer's work,' he admitted. 'And then the actor alters it from the way the director and writer saw it.' But he had hoped that it would work out well enough. 'It's an unco-operative art form.' he conceded. Was the play itself art? It was a farce and even Dustin dismissed it as 'all nonsense and puff', but it was by a man who had two sayings, 'life stinks', and 'money's honey'. He felt he could relate to some one like that. Money, after all, was important.

So important that it threatened to stop the play before it got on to the boards. Dustin was sure that he had backing from Roger L. Stevens who headed the Kennedy Center for the Performing Arts in Washington – only to have Stevens withdraw six days before rehearsals were due to begin in October 1974. At least, that was what Dustin said. Stevens maintained that he had not been the producer at any time.

As he put it, the play was a 'virgin' on Broadway, without the track record of a long run in London, for instance, to help it on its way. Dustin decided that he had to call in old friendships, or certainly old acquaintanceships. So he went to see the man who really got it all going for him, Joseph E. Levine, as he was having his breakfast.

Dustin was to say that Levine was one of his few lucky shots on what turned out to be something of a 'crap table'.

It was a very trusting Levine indeed. Afterwards, he said to Dustin: 'Imagine that! I put down $100,000 and I don't even know the name of the play.'

Perhaps he was hoping that before long his name would be all over town as a result.

But the luck didn't last. Levine, who had once thought Dustin was a window-cleaner, was less than impressed with the way the play was going and withdrew his money. There was, however, a guardian among the angels who had been persuaded to lay out money for the production. Mrs Adela Holzer, a leading New York commodity investor, decided to back the play and become its producer.

It was an unexpected situation. Not only was Dustin Hoffman's name as director anything but an automatic opener of doors, it couldn't attract attention from the public any more easily than it could bring in the investors.

Despite Dustin's name, that was not the only trouble. The play opened at the Booth Theater to virtually no advance sales, but was saved at the last minute by the closing of a musical that could not survive the onslaught of the critics. Thirteen theatre parties that were going to the show transferred to *All Over Town* instead.

Dustin interviewed 1,500 actors for roles in the play. 'I love actors,' he said.

So, apparently, did Schisgal. 'He's terrific, he's terrific,' said the writer about one young man who came to audition.

'You're getting very horny,' interrupted Dustin. 'Next you'll be wanting a dwarf here.'

It was one of the lessons of directing a play – when things get tough, get a laugh. Dustin had a very good sense of humour indeed.

Directing offered him the sort of scope he had wanted for a long time. It was a different sphere from acting, which he tended to regard as 'minor league'. That, too, was one of the reasons for problems with Anne. She couldn't accept that being an actor, and a great one, was not being somebody exceedingly special.

It took three years from conception for Schisgal to get his play on to the stage. He described it as 'a contemporary comedy about city life with eighteen characters of diverse and multifarious ethnic and social backgrounds'. If that didn't tell you all about it, he added for luck: 'It is a spectrum of our country encapsulated on a single stage during an evening's performance, my first microcosm. Before, they were macrocosms.'

Of course, he said he loved the challenge. He seemed to enjoy being a director, saying the same things to his actors that he had said to the coffee girl on a dozen film sets and to the fiancées of the make-up men.

To one girl, he said: 'You have a lovely bosom', and then thoroughly enjoying the sight of the woman looking down at her breasts and running off blushing.

'Do you enjoy sex?' he asked another, relishing an answer that might or might not be forthcoming. In this case, it was not. To one actor, he said, 'It's as though you can suddenly see through all these women's clothes – X-ray vision – and it's terrific, rejuvenating.'

One of his auditionees was not, however, amused by his talk and didn't find him at all rejuvenating. She was strong enough to walk away in disgust, muttering, 'The creep.'

As he interviewed this somewhat haughty-looking actress with the looks of a Scandinavian tennis player, he placed a hand firmly on her right breast. 'I thought, "What an obnoxious pig",' she said later, recalling that she did not get the job. The actress would live to fight Dustin another time. Her name was Meryl Streep.

In a way, this was all just symptomatic of his feelings for the theatre in general. He needed to feel it close to him, but on his own terms. He said that at one time he and Murray Schisgal – now more than ever his closest companion – thought they could both very easily chuck it all in and open an antiques shop somewhere. Of course they couldn't, but it made interesting conversation in the midst of a humorous chat. But Dustin did admit: 'The theatre is a killer. I tell all my playwright friends, "Write screenplays." When they say, "But I'm a playwright," I say, "Wait until something changes. You write a great play and you can't get it on. The odds must be a thousand to one." '

Actually, Dustin seemed to enjoy the role of a director dispensing advice, not all of which was businesslike any more than it was all sexual. To an actor, he suggested that he smoke a pipe. 'Clench it,' he advised, like John Mitchell (the Watergate Attorney-General, about whom Dustin was thinking a great deal now for reasons that soon will become apparent) at his trial. 'Now concentrate entirely on making the words travel down the stem [of the pipe] and out of the bowl. Everything else will happen automatically for you.'

He did his best with the show. Others were not so pleased. Dustin was not happy with his reviews that were in some cases less than charitable. But some were good enough and the association with the Hoffman name didn't hurt. Mostly, he resented the fact that they did not say that the audience was laughing. 'I'll never understand a critic who doesn't say that the audience laughed. How can a critic just say that he thinks a show is dumb or terrible and not include the information that the audience was laughing all the time? In a farce of this kind, the actors – the whole cast – have to act as if their problems are so big that they just don't have time for the audience. They have got to behave, to go about their business, as if they are wearing horse blinkers.'

A not untypical critique was that of Charles Ryweck, reporting back to the West Coast for the *Hollywood Reporter*. He wrote that Schisgal had 'pulled out all the stops and come up with a frenetic comedy that is artfully, if mechanically, constructed. *All Over Town* is overloaded with such comedy ballast as mistaken identity (which is a key to the play's working) so that it never really soars. It has been directed by Dustin Hoffman, his first effort at piloting a theatrical vehicle' – (the critic plainly knew nothing of Dustin's work before his starring days) – 'and while it won't win any prizes it has enough laughs to win the approval of not-too-demanding audiences.' Charles Ryweck particularly liked the star Cleavon Little who gave a 'dapper performance' as a con-man who takes over the home of a psychiatrist pretending to be a sex maniac. He thought that Dustin's direction 'might have profited by being a little firmer'.

Before long the play had to be written down to experience and Dustin could not allow himself to mind. Besides which, there were always diversions, like the wild rumours which started circulating that he and Anne were on the point of divorce. Even worse – and less likely – that Dustin himself was living in a commune in Oakland and was engaged to a student by the name of Patty. That would not have been too bad had Dustin not been told by a man he met at a party that he was going to be his father-in-law.

Fortunately, he didn't take these rumours more seriously than some of the jokes that went the rounds at the parties which he was reluctantly obliged to attend. Besides which, he was telling everyone at the slightest opportunity that the most important factors in his life were his wife and children.

The experience in *Papillon* had sparked Anne's continuing interest in her career – which was why she took the acting lessons and why she went abroad as a ballerina. But it was not something that was going to dominate her life. 'I was never a feminist,' she told me, 'and I didn't mind sacrificing my career. But after a time, I did get fed up. You're treated wonderfully on location, but . . .' as she had already said, there were just so many places she could go shopping.

When they did go shopping together, it was to buy more antiques, more Impressionist paintings, more of the things they had grown to like together in each other's company.

As has now become obvious, Dustin was always a hard worker. But the work was not merely acting alone, or direction alone, not even reading scripts alone. A great deal of it was simply thinking. It was James Thurber, the American humorist, who once said that his hardest job was convincing his wife that when he was looking out of the window, he was working. Dustin's work consisted of a great deal of looking out of windows, if only in a metaphorical sense.

He read a lot of books, not so much for the pleasure of reading them as because he thought they would make good movie subjects. One of these was part of a series with titles that had two things in common, the word 'Rabbi' and a day of the week – like *Friday, The Rabbi Slept Late* or *Saturday, The Rabbi Went Hungry*.

The central character in these stories was Rabbi David Small, a sort of Jewish Father Brown, a rabbi who seemed to spend his time divided into two distinct roles: as a pastor dispensing religious law and advice and as a private detective, solving crimes that were unconscionably frequent in his community, but which he accepted with the same equanimity that he greeted a wedding or a funeral following the death of an aged congregant peacefully in his own bed.

The stories were eventually made into a short and not terribly distinguished TV series, but, by then, Dustin's interest had waned, even though he had got as far as deciding that *Friday, the Rabbi Slept Late* would be the first story to be filmed, would be directed by his much-admired mentor Ulu Grosbard and would be in the hands of Wagner/International Productions. But even that extent of detail was not enough to save it for him.

Nor did another of Dustin's yearnings reach fruition, although he might have argued that this was one that came right from the heart. He wanted to play Harpo Marx in a film based on the life of the silent member of the Marx Brothers, whom even Groucho believed to be the funniest and perhaps the cleverest of them all. Dustin saw it all as a farce. 'I don't want any funny lines,' he explained going over and over in his mind how he would play Harpo. 'I just want to keep leaping after the girls and squeezing that horn,' he said, remembering the trademarks which, in addition to playing the harp, made Harpo also the most lovable of the Marx Brothers. Like all the best comedy ideas, this was something to take very seriously indeed; just as he had taken the playing of Lenny Bruce. 'I know I have a lot of nutsiness in me,' he said at the time, making up words in the nuttiest of ways. But maybe, Harpo was too serious a subject for farce. That picture, too, died on a drawing-board somewhere in Hollywood.

Of course, some people had occasionally noticed the nutsiness, which was how they explained his determination to put his own stamp on whatever he did, how he improvised, how he, in fact, now wanted to direct his own films as well as his plays.

'I have never done a picture of my own vision,' he said in 1975. 'It is always the director's vision and his feeling for life and it is never quite complemetary with my own.'

He thought that dream might come true as a result of something else he had read. He had been going over a book about the Watergate scandal and it seemed made to measure for an important new movie. The trouble for Dustin's directing and even producing ambitions was that Robert Redford had been reading it too. In fact, Redford had done more than that – he had suggested the book in the first place, so that he could then turn it into a film starring himself.

Redford had been intrigued by the work of Bob Woodward and Carl Bernstein, the two young reporters on the *Washington Post* who had told the news of the scandal from the first break-in at the Democrat headquarters at the Watergate building in Washington to all the revel-ations of the cover-up by Richard Nixon and his henchmen. Woodward and Bernstein took him up on his idea and the result was a thumping best-seller, *All The President's Men*. By the time the book was rocketing up the charts, Robert Redford had bought the rights.

Redford had also set himself up as the star, playing Woodward, like himself a blond tall, good-looking WASP, who voted Republican. That was wheeler-dealer dedication worthy of a Sam Goldwyn. When he heard that Dustin had been several steps behind him, but nevertheless moving in the same direction, he offered him the part of Bernstein – to all intents and purposes, a carbon copy of Dustin, small, dark, Jewish, hook-nosed, who very definitely did not vote Republican. Dustin's response to Redford's offer: 'I thought you'd never ask.'

The idea had a lot going for it – most of all, topicality. It was just two years after the scandal which ended with the resignation of Richard Milhous Nixon – the first President to resign while in office – and the audacity of such freshness in dealing with an issue on film made it compelling.

All The President's Men detailed how Woodward and Bernstein – dubbed 'Woodstein' to emphasize that they were a team – dug into the affair while everyone else was prepared to let it glide by, and as a result two hitherto junior and fairly undistinguished reporters became stars and millionaires.

There had, of course, been newspaper stories on film before. *The Front Page* in most of its guises – and there were at least four of them – is the one usually set up as the perfect example of reporters' quests for their stories above everything else getting to the screen. But this was different from the word go. Not only was the *Washington Post* a real newspaper (Dustin later suggested that a fictional title be substituted when the picture seemed about to disintegrate in a pile of petty squabbles) and the story about it perfectly true, but it was all part of history. What that newspaper had revealed, and what had been revealed in the book, affected the whole of America and ultimately much of the world, too. It had to be done effectively and responsibly.

That being the case, it was a picture without a love interest, hitherto almost unheard of, and where the only romance was that of getting the story that would topple the President. And yet somehow the drama had to be got across, while not ignoring or even playing down the drudgery of the phone calls, the searches through index files, the plodding detective work.

All these were the techniques, the stock-in-trade of investigative journalism, yet it was an investigative journalism of a kind that had never been known before. Was one man really implicated? Could he really be the President of the United States? The Leader of the Free World?

Bernstein-Hoffman was not getting any simple answers. He would count to ten and if his contact did not hang up, he knew that he had confirmation. Or did that mean that the story was *not* confirmed?

And there were the supporting players who were as important as the foundations of Watergate itself or indeed any other building. Jack Warden and Martin Balsam as editors on the newspaper, the superb Jason Robards Jnr., better than he had ever been before as the editor of the *Washington Post*.

Robards would receive an Oscar for his work in the picture. Dustin would not.

By now, people knew that Dustin Hoffman researched his parts as though he were embarking on some esoteric, scientific experiment. For four months, he 'worked' at the *Washington Post* himself, sitting in on news conferences, watching reporters go out on stories and following one man in particular, Fred Barbash, who happened to be investigating a corruption scandal of his own at the time. It was not of Watergate, international, dimensions, but the procedures were remarkably the same – a fact confirmed several times by Woodstein when Hoffman and Redford rang them from the Warner Bros. studios in Burbank, Los Angeles, to ask if they were getting things right.

But it was Bernstein whom Dustin shadowed – some say he was like a leech who attached himself to the reporter's body without showing any signs of allowing himself to be pulled off. Just like a good reporter on to a great story. 'He was glued to Carl Bernstein for six weeks,' says Jarvis Astaire. 'By the time the film was finished, he was more Carl Bernstein than Carl Bernstein was.' Bernstein, for his part, says Astaire, was extraordinary flattered to be played by an actor of Dustin Hoffman's calibre.

By the time they were ready to go before the cameras, Hoffman and Redford knew the whole process of getting a news story in place, from the initial phone calls to seeing the story set in type on the *Post*'s pages.

Warner Bros. were no less assiduous in their own quest for perfection. The *Washington Post* city room was recreated on the Warner lot by pushing two soundstages together, and it looked right to the last stapling machine. The set alone cost half a million dollars. The concealed lights shone through the same sort of ceiling for the same sort of distance. The same sort of typewriters – this was 1976, and the computer-input age had not yet caught up with the *Post* – tapped on the same sort of paper as used by *Post* reporters. So that there could be no doubt about that authenticity, real *Washington Post* wastepaper baskets were flown in from the paper's office.

The work on research began before the fine details of the story itself were hammered out. Once having agreed to make a picture about a *cause célèbre* without sex, there had to be inquiries made about its chances of bringing people to the box offices. Dustin conducted his own opinion poll on people's reactions to the subject-matter. It was not encouraging. Remember, this was less than two years after Nixon's resignation, but already in their spot checks, Dustin and the Warner team of pollsters discovered that there were people walking along the streets in a part of the United States who could not recall what Watergate was. And that was in Washington, D.C.

This sent warning notes vibrating through a team that was investing millions of dollars in the project. 'I thought we must be box-office poison,' Dustin confided at the time.

What ultimately convinced him otherwise was those four months he spent at the *Washington Post*. 'I wanted to be able to believe in myself, not just get in front of the cameras, loosen my tie, put my feet on the desk and play reporter.'

And it showed. You saw the film and you witnessed a journalist doing the things journalists did, and with none of the howlers that frequently made hardened newsmen cry into their beer. The hardest thing that a professional actor can have to do – although laughing to order can sometimes be no joke either – is simply to be on show, listening, and not to make it seem as though he is trivializing what he is listening to, not interfering; simply listening. Dustin Hoffman did a lot of listening in *All The President's Men*, which is why it became such a compelling movie.

There was another example of his acting that was as difficult as it was unusual. He and Redford played two men who were extremely junior in the *Post* hierarchy. Woodward had only been with the paper for seven months. Bernstein was a hard-nosed veteran of some sixteen months. In the presence of Jason Robards, alias Ben Bradlee, they both had to look determined to get their stories across while almost cowering in front of him. You watched the film, knowing full well that he was the boss and that they felt as well as knew it.

What was more, and which no critics seem to have picked up on, was that it was exclusively a drama-documentary. It was exclusively the story of the Watergate chase and the people involved in the chase, more true to life than anything of the kind had ever been before. And it wasn't just the absence of a love interest, there was virtually no time spent on scenic effects. There were no sweeps over the White House and no helicopters flying in between skyscrapers. That would never have happened in an earlier generation.

None of this, however, was obtained easily. After a time, the staff at the *Post* made it abundantly clear that they had had enough. The paper's publisher, Katherine Graham, didn't like it from the beginning. There were disputes over the writing as well. Carl Bernstein thought that William Goldman had written a script that was too witty, too funny for the everyday experiences of reporters hunting the root of a massive scandal. Not that there weren't laughs and excessive use of language that one would not normally demonstrate in the presence of ladies.

For a time, Bernstein himself and his wife-to-be Nora Ephron (their story and their subsequent break-up would before long become a film, too, starring Jack Nicholson and, ironically? Meryl Streep). The director, Alan Pakula, rejected this second version and ultimately stuck by Goldman, although allowing Bernstein to have an occasional input. In the end, it was an amalgam seemingly of everyone's ideas, not least of all, Dustin's.

According to Jarvis Astaire, Dustin delayed things continually by insisting on going over every line of dialogue, discussing every scene between takes. As a result there were more takes than Alan Pakula felt necessary.

To *Newsweek* magazine, Dustin was a 'mixture of cajolery and clumsiness'. How Jack Kroll came to that conclusion is far from obvious watching the film, one of the most intelligent newspaper – to say nothing of political – dramas ever filmed.

The experience was useful if for no other reason than that – the experience. As Dustin said at about the time *All The President's Men* was released, 'an actor's always working. In the back of your mind, you're thinking, even when you have your own sense of grief, "This is something I can use at some point." It's as if you're recording it, watching it, like a writer recording dialogue.' James Thurber would have been glad to hear Dustin Hoffman say that.

There was a lot of dialogue coming Dustin's way now. Not all of it was going to make his life easy.

11

It is popular mythology to believe that every successful man needs someone in his shadow, sometimes manipulating the strings that hide the fact that he is really only a puppet; sometimes just being there to offer the necessary support, to provide an occasional brake, to slow down a fast-moving train that has been carried on simply by its own momentum.

Anne was certainly in the second of these categories. No one at all filled the first role. Dustin was nobody's puppet. He did, however, need a guiding hand and, for four years, that hand belonged to Jarvis Astaire – no relation to Fred but a man who acknowledges his debt to the great dancer for all the wonderful restaurant tables he has been able to glide into with the grace of a man about to dance the Continental.

Jarvis Astaire is one of those people who sees the amount of money he is going to make at the end of a deal before the first discussions are held, before a single penny has been invested.

Astaire is a self-made man who rose from humble origins in a London family to success beyond his parents' dreams in the world of property – from which he branched out into show business. He produced films in Hollywood and Britain with various degrees of success. He was at one time Chief Barker of the Variety Club of Great Britain, an honour he cherishes more than many that have come his way. His elegant office in the heart of London's West End is replete with letters from members of the Royal Family, photographs with personages like the Duke of Edinburgh. And in 1974, he became Dustin Hoffman's manager.

Dustin was working on the campaign to sell *Lenny* at the time and Astaire, who had met Dustin socially in both London and California when their wives became friendly, helped with that. He set up the business side of the movies that were to follow, starting with *All The President's Men*. A year later, he got Dustin's signature on the papers for Dustin's next film, *Marathon Man*.

It did not take long, Astaire told me, for him to get the measure of Dustin Hoffman from his own perspective, in which the financial aspect is so crucial.

'He never had any sense of proportion about money,' he said. 'He would readily agree to forgo hundreds of thousands of dollars for something he wanted to do – yet he would argue about the poor quality of the suits he had to wear in his pictures. He would go through the motions of knowing about money and talk about it. But there was no sense of proportion.'

There was perhaps a more serious consequence of his disregard for money. He didn't think enough of the degree of professional and financial commitments of other people with whom he came into contact.

By now, even though uniquely in the world of show business he was generally only the actor with the second billing, he was a great star. Great stars are always being courted and flattered in the singular hope that before long they will make pictures which make a great deal of money for the flatterer concerned. Dustin was no exception. Astaire did not always like the way he treated those flatterers, those people who fawned at the greatness of actors.

'He would have four or five people on a string at one time, telling them that he probably planned to make their films. He can be totally relentless about wasting a year of a man's time, but after that year, he drops them.

Astaire charges lack of consideration on Dustin's part, rather than malice. 'He'd never say, "Give that guy $20,000 for his trouble", or anything like that. He just decided that he won't do it. It's not as though he breaks his word. He does not give his word in the first place. He just doesn't give people a thought.'

Marathon Man was one picture that did come off and most of the people concerned have reason to be glad that it did.

This was yet another picture in which Dustin shared the limelight, but never before had he done so with an actor like Laurence Olivier.

Marathon Man was a combination of two themes that in the middle 1970s were unbeatable: a thriller about part of the aftermath of the Holocaust.

Dustin's was a powerful performance as the marathon man – a mature student at Columbia University, New York, who spends his spare time running around Central Park, in the course of which he is captured by a Nazi cell, led by the former head of a concentration camp (Olivier). The Nazi, Szell, thinks that Hoffman knows the whereabouts of a horde of diamonds that Szell had smuggled out of Europe where he had stolen them from Jews.

Szell was a dentist by profession, which gives him every opportunity to indulge in a form of torture that was particularly nasty – using his dental drill. Dustin's obvious fear of that drill is something to savour in remembering that picture. So, too, is the acting of Roy Scheider, playing Dustin's brother, a businessman who, when he is murdered, turns out to have been a Government agent engaged in secret work.

The story is convoluted and confused, but it comes together in the joy of watching the way the screenplay by William Goldman – again – is put together by the director, John Schlesinger again, and complemented by the consummate performances of Olivier and Hoffman.

Dustin himself was none too comfortable having Olivier there with him. 'He was extraordinarily flustered at having to work with him,' Jarvis Astaire remembered for me. 'He kept blowing his lines on the first day on the set – which was extremely unlike him.'

In fact, Dustin apologized to the older man for each fluff. Olivier could sense what was going on. He tried his best to put Dustin at ease. 'Never try too hard, dear boy,' he advised. 'Just do it.'

As usual, Dustin thought he had the answer to his problems with Olivier. 'Why don't we just do what we think is right?' he suggested to the man who had first worked in Hollywood forty years earlier and who had earned the title of the English-speaking world's greatest actor. 'Dear boy,' replied Lord Olivier, using the term of which he was most fond in its most cutting way, 'I don't improvise.'

No, Dustin might have reflected, no, of course, you don't.

But he had to find some way of making contact with the distinguished actor who still inhibited him so much; some way of assuring he would not feel second-best, even a child alongside his teacher.

Dustin needed to get out into the fresh air to think. He invited Olivier out to join him, an invitation that was readily accepted by a man who soon had cause to regret it. They would talk it over, the younger man suggested.

Dustin, already in perfect trim from all the running around Central Park that he had done in training for the finished picture, decided he had to walk up and down as he spoke. Olivier had no option but to follow him.

People have since heard that story and criticized Dustin's lack of concern for Olivier's health in order to do the scenes the way he,

Hoffman, wanted them done. A simpler explanation could be that he wanted to overcome the cause of his own anxiety.

Jarvis Astaire, who witnessed the event, assured me that he thought neither was really true, even though the actual reason was no less flattering to Dustin himself. 'He was not being sadistic in doing that,' he said. 'He would simply disregard the fact that this man was old and ill. He would be impervious to it. It wouldn't have occurred to him that he shouldn't have done that.'

In a kinder explanation, he added, 'His aim is to do great work. Merely good work is not enough.' Olivier, for his part, seemed to recognize it, appreciate it and respond to it.

Dustin was now 40 years old. Olivier seemed to think he was much younger. 'Olivier recognized Dustin's ability,' said Astaire. 'I can't imagine for one moment that he did not.'

He could, though, have known virtually nothing about him. John Schlesinger really did not want Dustin in the role. He at least knew how old Hoffman really was – a 40-year-old university student (albeit a graduate student) called 'Babe' seemed to him to stretch the imagination somewhat. He had another intense, hard, dark-haired actor in mind for the part, another actor who looked destined for the kind of part and reputation that had come to Dustin Hoffman over the years, Al Pacino. But he was overruled by the producers, Robert Evans and Sidney Beckerman.

Jarvis Astaire, for his part, maintains that Schlesinger also had Keith Carradine in mind for the part of Babe, but it was Paramount this time who called the shots and insisted on Dustin. Whatever the reason, going with Hoffman was a sound decision in the end. No small consideration was the fact that Dustin so much wanted to do it himself, ironically because he knew Schlesinger was going to direct it.

The picture gave Dustin a whole string of opportunities to show what he could do and he took every one of them. One of the problems with *Marathon Man* concerned a flashlight. 'Babe' had one by his bed. Dustin didn't think that was right. He would not have one there. John Schlesinger appealed for him to get on with other things and deal with that little matter later on. Dustin insisted that it had to go – or he wouldn't go on with the rehearsal. The flashlight went.

Looking back on that picture now, Jarvis Astaire says: 'He is extremely creative. He is probably over-creative when you consider that John Schlesinger had told me that Dustin would come out with a dozen ideas of which only one or two were any good, but that those one or two were very, very good. He's also a pain in the arse. He's relentless to the extent that, as with Olivier, he is totally, obliviously, impervious to the wants of others. He can be very disruptive. But the end product is extremely wonderful.'

But not necessarily the end product of his business arrangements. Dustin was, in fact, beginning to justify those suggestions that he really thought he knew more about money and the manipulation of it then he actually did. This was being made clear by the sort of relationship he had with his business partners. He liked them as people, but he needed to realize that being a great actor did not guarantee equal dexterity with balance sheets.

Dustin was, in fact, entering a difficult phase in his professional life. He was making his debut as a First Artist star and he and First Artists were not getting on at all well in terms of their personal relationships, with him as actor, they as his employers.

He had embarked on two pictures for the organization, for both of which it seemed he would have little love for, even though he gave his all – and in the giving some might have detected a wish not to have offered it at the start.

The first of these pictures was called *Straight Time*, in which he played a robber. Naturally enough, a robber who knew what he was doing. Was he, though, merely robbing himself of his career?

12

Dustin was plainly becoming embroiled in situations from which he would have wanted to find ways of extricating himself.

He was as strong-willed and determined as ever; such as when he and Anne entered the New York marathon; nothing in the world would have allowed him – allowed either of them – to quit before the course was completed.

He still tried to use his sense of humour, still played the outrageous extrovert he never really was – like regaling a lady from Boston whom he and Jarvis Astaire were entertaining in the Oak Room of New York's Plaza Hotel with the story about the time his wife was in hospital. She was there having Jenna when, he said, a man was brought in after having got his penis caught up in his wife's birth-control coil. The lady from Boston was not amused.

To that outrageous image, however, was being added what was for him a totally different and new dimension. He was becoming conscious of his roots as never before. On his shelves was a growing collection of books on Judaism. He still was not what one would call religious – not by any definition of the term, but there were volumes on the Torah and the Prophets and he appeared to treasure them.

He had become an avid Zionist and gave a great deal of money to Israel. He was particularly keen on the impressive new Israel tennis centre at Ramat Hasharon and was exceedingly generous in his donations. Tennis was important to him. He played well, but that was all. What he really wanted was to be a player who was nothing less than great. The fact that he was not of, say, Wimbledon standard, irked him. Just as he wanted to be nothing but a great actor, there could be no other way of playing on a tennis court.

He used to play the game with his father. 'But I remember him being scared of his father,' Jarvis Astaire told me. 'He was very nervous about being with him; just couldn't deal with the man.'

The senior Hoffman would admit that he had never got close either to Dustin or to his older son, Ronald. 'I was too busy trying to make it,' he told an interviewer. When Dustin heard that, he was more determined than ever one day to make an impressive new version of *Death of a Salesman*. He found great difficulty in dealing with the business brains behind First Artists, too. And it all came bursting to the surface with his second film for the organization.

It has to be said that *Straight Time* did not always look as though it was going to be the kind of film Dustin would wish he had never made. He had started out with the idea that he could make an impressive impact with a story of an ex-con who takes up crime again only when society refuses to forget its prejudices against him. It was a tired old theme, but he imagined that playing the part of Max Dembo in the 1978 picture would give his acting talents enough scope to make *Straight Time* exceptional.

He had read Edward Bunker's novel *No Beast So Fierce* and desperately wanted to make a film based on it. It was a perfect vehicle for First Artists. And there was another factor: this picture he was going to direct himself. Could there be a more satisfying experience? He certainly did not think that there could.

But it was different from directing a play. This time the cards were all in his hands. Somehow, they all got confused in the shuffle.

Work began. Dustin was satisfied with nothing. He shot on and on. As Jarvis Astaire put it to me: 'He always expected directors to shoot on and on, regardless of the consequences.' He expected nothing less of himself.

In this case, the man who was so naïve with money finally saw the production grind to a halt after more than a million dollars had been spent. Even Dustin Hoffman had to admit he was beaten. He was not a film director. Not yet anyway.

He was also not a business executive. His rows with the money heads of First Artists – it wasn't a company merely operated by the artists concerned; its real boss was Phil Feldman, as hard-nosed a studio head as Hollywood had known since the era of the moguls – were phenomenal.

It seemed that they had reached their peak as *Straight Time* was being made. Experience later on would prove that not to be so. But his relationship with Howard Pine, the executive producer, was taut, to say the least.

Astaire remembers being on the set during the shooting of the film.

'Pine and other executives hated Hoffman with a passion. I heard one executive describe him as an animal.'

One day, Jarvis Astaire recalls, Pine met Hoffman on the set and the result was a scene that was not only better than anything in *Straight Time*, it was worthy of *The Big Knife*, *The Last Tycoon* or any other movie about the studio system.

As Dustin's manager recalls it, the scene went like this: 'Pine went up to Hoffman and said, "Hello, Dustin, how are you?"

' "I'm all right," said Dustin. "I hope you're not".'

Later Pine would say that his disputes with Hoffman were only because the star was a perfectionist. Astaire's philosophy about that is revealing: 'In this world, if you are rich, you are eccentric. If you're poor, you're crazy. If you're a star, you're a perfectionist. If you're not a star, you're a pain in the arse.'

It was the second time Astaire had used that phrase when discussing his former client. Yet again he found a need to modify it, especially when thinking about Dustin's acting in *Straight Time*. 'He's so good at his work and he delivers, so people are usually prepared to bear with it. Sometimes, though, you have the feeling that he's the dummy who takes over from the ventriloquist. But when you employ Dustin you usually get terrific value. He's hugely industrious. When it comes to work, he becomes a machine.'

The machine plainly did not function as a director, as much as any other reason because it had not been oiled by previous directing experience. Ultimately, Ulu Grosbard was called in. But even two such close and caring friends allowed the magnitude of the task to get the better of them. Grosbard who had been among the first to spot the huge talent that Dustin Hoffman represented, had only come on to the scene because Dustin badly wanted him to do so. Dustin respected him whereas other directors who allowed some of the best Hoffman scenes to fall on to the cutting room floor were merely tolerated. Now, though, they had rows the like of which neither of them had known.

They even spoke out in the open about each other. To *The New York Times's* Tony Schwartz, Grosbard said angrily: 'He had the project for five years and he controlled it completely. By the time he called me he had gone through four or five writers and six or seven drafts and he had some of the best people in the field working for him. If he's so meticulous and such a perfectionist,' he asked, 'why did he create such an enormous mess?'

Grosbard offered a possible reason: 'Dustin is a professional victim and when you put yourself in that position, you can make pre-emptive strikes against everyone and feel morally righteous. I think he does care about quality, but that's not a licence for his behaviour.'

He embroidered that remark a few years later by saying: 'He's very bright and very charming, but he can turn it on when he needs something from you and turn it off when he no longer needs anything.'

Things got so bad at one stage that the much-respected Grosbard asked Dustin which came first, their friendship or the movie. 'The movie,' he replied without having to think. It was the end of that friendship.

Dustin wasn't taking any of the blame. None of it had been his fault. In a statement echoing that of a general recently relieved of his command, he retorted: 'I was doing the best work I'd ever done. And I knew the film wasn't supporting the performance.'

There are other testimonies that he was, indeed, doing good work, if not necessarily his best. He did all the research that any other actor would do, plus all the additional activity that was so customary with a Hoffman vehicle. He went to San Quentin jail and watched how prisoners in Californian penitentiaries coped with life behind bars. Real former prison inmates were put on the payroll to give him advice. That was Dustin's idea.

A co-performer, Harry Dean Stanton, who played another ex-convict who joins Dustin in planning a new robbery, told me he was astounded by the extent to which Hoffman's meticulous dedication to his work manifested itself.

It was Dustin who had chosen him for the part in the first place. 'We sort of hung out together and I didn't think any more of it. We had some drinks together and then I realized that he was looking to see if I was right for the part.'

Dustin was, he said, a 'fanatical, obsessive worker'.

So fanatical that he needed to 'feel' not only how a prisoner felt behind bars, but how it was to be really guilty of a crime. Stanton claims that once Dustin sneaked out of the back of a restaurant without paying the bill – just to know the 'buzz' of failing to adhere to the *mores* of society. It wouldn't have been an easy thing for someone as well-known as Dustin Hoffman to do and he doubtless paid the bill later on, but it does fit into the picture of obsessiveness he displays. 'He can be temperamental,' says Stanton. 'If something wasn't going right, he would blow up. Sometimes he snapped at me, too, for no reason.'

A Beverly Hills jewellery shop owner felt he had a right to snap at the local police force during the shooting of *Straight Time*. His store was really robbed – while police were watching the intricate arrangements for filming the make-believe robbery in *Straight Time* in another jewellery shop down the street. But as Stanton recalls, the real robbers were 'pretty sloppy – much sloppier than we were. *They* were caught.'

Dustin was to be involved in a massive lawsuit over *Straight Time*, but first there were other problems to sort out. He had to convince the Press that he and Anne were still together and in love. The fights over *Straight Time* meant that they were living apart during the week and this unusual occurrence had filtered out to the media. It was not true that they had parted, but Anne had begun to assert herself and her career.

She had small parts in films herself, notably in Woody Allen's *Manhattan*. It certainly was a different life from that of a ballerina. She had loved dancing, particularly when she had toured just four years earlier with the Frankfurt Ballet, dancing with them in Birmingham, England. But a career in ballet was notoriously short and she was anxious to bank a different kind of experience for the future.

For the moment, both she and Dustin were saying that there was no conflict between their two personalities or their two careers.

Dustin, meanwhile, was off to England himself to make a film called *Agatha*. In this one, his co-star was Vanessa Redgrave. It was supposedly about the mysterious eleven-day disappearance in December 1926 of Agatha Christie (played by Redgrave), the country's most successful ever writer of crime stories and detective fiction.

Had he taken Anne's advice, he would never have made it, and doubtless would have been glad of the recommendation in the long run. As she told me: 'I was adamant that he shouldn't make *Agatha*. I was right, wasn't I?'

Just how right would become evident very soon. 'He only did the picture because he wanted out of his First Artists contract,' maintains Jarvis Astaire. He needed to make just one picture to satisfy his legal commitments and this seemed to be an easy one; and one which would give him plenty of time to think of what was coming next.

The court case with First Artists arose because they charged that he went off to Britain to make *Agatha* when he should have stayed behind in Hollywood, finishing off *Straight Time*. When he signed his contract for the first picture, he had been given the right to make the final cut provided it was done within six months of the completion of photography. He had no business, they maintained, starting a new film until the earlier one was totally wrapped up and edited.

For the present, however, he was saying very little and what he did say indicated that he thought *Agatha* was going to be as important to him as, say, *Midnight Cowboy* had ever been.

Dustin's part was as fictitious as that of Dega in *Papillon*, perhaps even more so, since Dega had been a composite figure based on several men featuring in the original true story. Dustin's role as Wally Stanton, an American journalist covering the disappearance mystery, was written by *Agatha*'s author Kathleen Tynan as a comparatively small part, secondary to that of the relationship between Agatha and her husband's mistress-secretary, played by Celia Gregory.

First Artists, however, were not satisfied with that. They instructed her to make more of Wally Stanton. They wanted their man to be a co-star and not an also-ran performer, although Douglas Brode in *The Films of Dustin Hoffman* maintains that he himself would have been happy to leave things as they were, if the film benefited from it. Certainly, that was an exceedingly unusual thing to happen. Stars usually want to be seen to be stars. In the finished product, Dustin would be seen that way, as the journalist who actually falls in love with his quarry.

'When I wrote the part of the journalist,' said Mrs Tynan, 'he was a tall blond Englishman with a supporting, small minor role. Now he's a small dark American with one of the leads.'

It wasn't an easy story to make. Doubly, it was difficult because of all the tension with First Artists. Part of the trouble was that in *Agatha*, for the first time Dustin has a producer's credit.

Everything that seemingly could go wrong with *Agatha* actually did. Kathleen Tynan worked round the clock herself to get the story right, particularly as far as Hoffman was concerned. No final script was ready when the time came to start shooting the picture. Dustin phoned Los Angeles, asking for an extension. It was not forthcoming. As he said he 'literally got on my knees and begged them not to start the film. Once you go on that floor to make a movie, it's crazy time. It's painting a picture [that analogy again] on railroad tracks, with the train getting closer. *Agatha* was every actor's nightmare. The script was literally being rewritten every day. It was a rainbow of green, yellow, pink revision pages.'

And that roughly describes the complexion of Dustin Hoffman at that time.

Not that he would ever have apologized for being difficult, even if things had gone better. 'It's not ego,' he would explain. 'But what the fuck are you gonna be [shades of *Lenny* remaining here] if you're not going to be difficult? Show up on the set and say, "Hi, I'm so and so and I'm here to do whatever you want?" I've never understood people who've held on to the job. I've never done that. I've always loved the fact when you're an actor that you can say, "Fuck you", and all they can do is fire you. You know what that feels like already, but it's so much better than doing bad work.'

Surprisingly, he was the first to recognize that the work was not always terribly good and certainly wasn't always original. 'Art is theft,' he said, 'there's no reason not to steal. If you see something good, you take it, make it your own. The trick is not getting caught.'

His problem with *Agatha* was not trying to avoid getting caught, only in making the best of a pretty bad job.

In the meantime, the others involved in *Agatha* had time to assess what it was like working with Dustin Hoffman. Among them was one of Britain's leading actors, Timothy West, who played the police inspector in charge of the Christie hunt.

'He's a proper actor, obviously,' West told me. 'He was very courteous, very nice, very easy to work with, very professional.'

But there was a 'sort of confusion' always evident.

'It was personified,' he said, 'by the production office in a Women's Institute hall in Bath, which we used as our centre.' Two sets of writers were busy working on a script that still had not been finalized. The first was writing dialogue for Dustin; the second, for everyone else.

Arthur Hopcraft was set to work on additional dialogue based on the factual events of the time, the documentary material that would bolster the romantic fiction.

'He was there pounding away at an old Olivetti typewriter with his pipe and his pint of Guinness and at the other end of the room were a group of writers doing additional dialogue for Dustin Hoffman.' The other writers were there to help flesh out the supporting role of the journalist that Kathleen Tynan had originally created and make its portrayer a star.

This work was not to be left to the original writer or the man who was there to ensure no inaccuracies or anachronisms crept in. Dustin had to have his own dialogue supplied by his own men who would somehow find a way of knitting it all together. That would not normally be considered a suitable recipe for success. It was script by committee, a group who were gradually turning a potential racehorse of a story into a camel.

Murray Schisgal also put his ten-cents' worth into the final script, says Timothy West. 'There were lots of other writers around, with secretaries, all using very smart IBM machines. It seemed to me to state the whole unjoinability of the two sides of the film.'

Jarvis Astaire was also a producer on the picture. At one time there were five of those, too. 'That caused a certain degree of confusion,' said West, 'but they all seemed to represent five different areas of funding. There was Dustin himself on behalf of First Artists, there was Jarvis Astaire, David Puttnam and Gavrik Losey and one other who came and went. Rather more than some of us thought was necessary.'

Eventually, Dustin took over entirely as executive producer, although as a producer very much accountable to what the money men in Hollywood were decreeing.

'It was better than before,' Timothy West recalls. But the problems faced by the director, Michael Apted, in bringing it all together as best he could were perhaps the toughest of all. 'He just got on with it,' Timothy West recalled. 'He was wonderful.' But there were other little local problems as well.

'Dustin, I think, was an authoritative influence who kind of brought it all together. He tolerated a lot of inconvenience. He had to do a lot of standing around, particularly in the scene where we were dragging the pond. It was a very difficult scene to organize, a tracking shot. Divers in the lake had to break the ice and the more they broke up the ice the less there was to break up in further takes; which meant that it began not to look so good. We wanted a mist, but that had to be artificial and had to be blown by fans. They wanted the sun not too far up so that it looked like early morning. There was an open car in which Dustin had to arrive and that had to stop on its marks – and the driver was not all that reliable. All sorts of things went wrong. We'd got to take 24, I think, and all Dustin really had to do was get out of the car. I know many people who would have said, "Well, call me at my hotel or my caravan when you've got this right because I can't stand around any more." But he didn't. He was absolutely spot on all the time and I admired that very much.'

One of the problems was getting the crowd artists all in place. There were about a thousand of them for the lake-dragging scene. None of the extras was paid: they were given a cup of coffee and some sandwiches and told that they were having a nice day working with Dustin Hoffman

and Vanessa Redgrave, neither of whom they could see. As the day
wore on, they grew impatient and drifted away, one by one. 'They got
a bit dispirited after lunch, I seem to remember,' said Timothy West.
'There were different ways of dealing with it. If you had one producer,
he would decide how to do it. When you had five, it was not so easy.'

Dustin was not a great communicator on the set of this picture. Very
little evidence was displayed of the famed Hoffman sense of humour.
'He didn't talk much, but I had the feeling that he quite wanted to
work alongside English actors. I felt that he was a quiet, thoughtful
person when he was working.'

It was not difficult to know of the tensions that existed during filming.
'One was always aware of them,' West added, 'because they seeped
through. You always know by the way the assistant directors behave.
If they're being pressured, it's usually from the production office. They
were being pressured and they passed that on to the work-force. There
was a lot of countermanding of orders.'

There was constantly the sound of barked instructions. 'We'll do this
scene that way'. A matter of minutes later, the order was, 'We're now
going to do it this way.' One moment an actor was told, 'We won't
need you till three o'clock', only to hear before he walked off the set,
'We need you NOW!'

'It's not uncommon,' said Timothy West. 'But I remember it very
well on *Agatha*. One was aware that orders were coming from different
directions.'

Dustin was as close to becoming schizophrenic as he had ever been in
his life. While still trying to plead with First Artists to delay the start
of *Agatha* – which they adamantly refused to do – and then actually
beginning his acting scenes in it, he was still having to think about
Straight Time.

Time, and not just the straight variety, was running out. So instead
of taking a Christmas break as everyone else involved in *Agatha* was
relieved to be able to do, Dustin flew back to Los Angeles to start
cutting the picture. When he had assembled the first twenty minutes,
he took seemingly miles of film back to Britain with him to work on it
there while simultaneously shooting *Agatha*. He had got about a third
of the way through when he heard that First Artists had taken the cut
out of his hands and were working on it themselves. He was livid – but
he had to get back to the new film.

He was not happy with that either. *Agatha* was running so far behind schedule that filming was wrapped up with a final scene Dustin wanted to add still unshot – and unshot it would remain. He has always maintained that because the scene never went before the cameras, the journalist's relationship with Agatha Christie was never properly explained. The matter would drag on for years and ultimately go before a number of courts.

Anne watched what was happening with those movies with more than merely detatched interest. 'Both these films came at the time our marriage was disintegrating and I couldn't help thinking that that was more important than the pictures,' she told me. 'But he went ahead.' Before long, it would be apparent that it was not necessarily the right choice. Neither the integrity of the pictures nor the marriage was being saved.

In the meantime, Dustin was to get involved in other legal affairs, one for real and one on screen – called *Kramer vs Kramer*.

It was seen as Dustin's return to his old form, but it coincided with a time that could best be described as Hoffman vs Hoffman.

13

The National Association of Theatre Owners had named Dustin their male star of the year. In truth, he wasn't many other people's man of any year.

He had embarked upon a period in his life which he would yearn to be over almost as soon as it had begun – and once over one he wished, above all things, he could forget. With the benefit of hindsight, it is easy to suggest that he should have seen it coming. Yet there were consolations.

Though *Straight Time* and *Agatha* had made little impact on audiences anywhere and the critics were more or less indifferent to them both, Dustin's acting ability seems to have worked its way through – even through First Artists' decision to release the first picture on a Friday without giving it a Press showing. The hope was that the momentum of the name Dustin Hoffman above the title would bring people in despite the fact that they had heard virtually nothing about the picture in question.

When critics did see it, several of them said that *Straight Time* began to pall a third of the way in. Dustin felt vindicated. That was the point when he had finally relinquished control of it. *Variety* was uncompromising in its reaction to it all: 'One leaves the theatre hoping the characters will die painfully and slowly in a hail of bullets,' wrote its critic. Even so, Leslie Halliwell in his *Film Guide* described Dustin's role as 'a resolute leading performance'.

As for *Agatha*, Pauline Kael was as prescient as ever. She wrote that the picture had a 'general air of knowingness, but seems to be missing the scenes which would explain why it was made'. How right she was. And how right Dustin had been in trying to extract that one extra scene from First Artists' budget.

But if he felt that studio bosses, audiences and critics were not all saying that Dustin Hoffman was perfect, it was as nothing compared with what was happening within himself and what was going on at home.

The conflict between the actor and the private man was more pronounced than ever. Did he want to fight the studio? Was it worth it? And what about his relationship with Anne? Hoffman vs Hoffman indeed.

For once, the stories about his marriage were right. As Anne explained it to me, she had tried desperately to separate the two sides of his personality. She tried to keep the Pressmen away from the family home. 'But I think every wife would, wouldn't she?'

Anne knew it was going to happen. 'The marriage was obviously disintegrating,' she told me. 'It was not good.'

Towards the end, she started talking to friends about her situation. 'A very old friend of mine came over and I asked him to bring some beer and for some reason or other that request became a reason to talk about my marriage to Dustin. He it was at that moment who said, "Stop complaining – do something about it." And as a result of that, the next morning I filed for divorce.'

The divorce went through amicably enough, Anne said, 'and we divided up our property fairly evenly. We really didn't have much in the way of treasures. We had only one home and hadn't really started collecting much. There were things that appealed to me more than they did to him and vice versa, so that was how we divided them.'

Anne reflected on what had gone wrong. Religion was one of the factors, not, as was usual in a mixed marriage, because of irreconcilable differences of faith, but because she wished they had chosen only one of their two different religions. She would have been happy to have become Jewish, as she has subsequently (she and her present husband Ivan Kronenfeld have a kosher New York home). 'I think it would have been better for our marriage if we'd been religious. I think everyone needs that.'

It was while all this was going on that Dustin started work on his film – about a divorce. *Kramer vs Kramer* was the last project initiated by Jarvis Astaire.

It was a picture about a tussle between a couple over the custody of their blond-haired son. The boy is a seven-year-old angelic child (Justin Henry) and Dustin, an advertising executive, gives up his job to take over temporary custody. In the end, his estranged wife wins the boy back, only to return him when she realizes that he is going to be happier with the father who had seen him through all his traumas of life at

Mingling with statesmen is part of the job – with Henry Kissinger and the producer of *Marathon Man*, Robert Evans

Sizing up to Vanessa Redgrave was the least of Hoffman's problems with *Agatha*

An off-screen moment with director Robert Benton on the set of *Kramer vs Kramer* – a director Dustin liked…

Confrontation – with Meryl Streep

Dustin, Lisa Hoffman and their son Jake at Heathrow Airport in 1983 – *(Press Association)*

Redford and Hoffman acted together in *All The President's Men*; a story Dustin wanted to buy, but Redford beat him to it

A woman's work… milking a cow with the help of Charles Durning in *Tootsie*

The greatest female impersonation of them all – *Tootsie* – a characterization based partly on Hoffman's mother

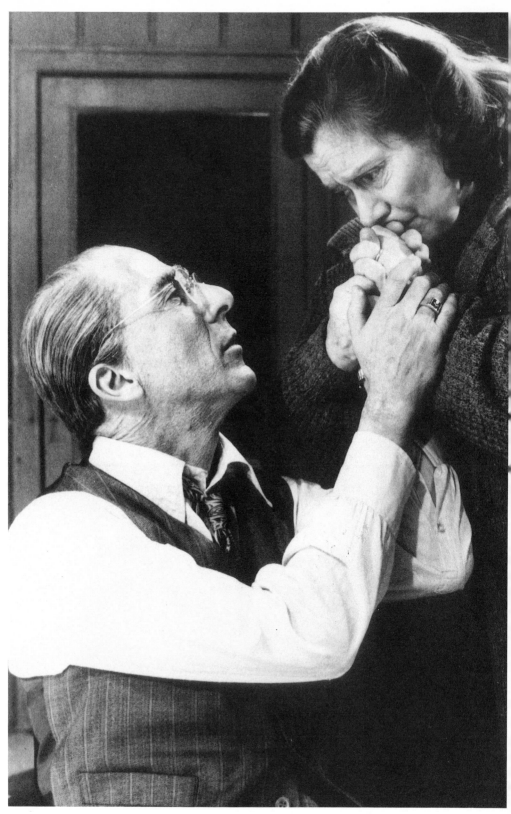

Dustin *became* Willy Loman in *Death of a Salesman* – with Kate Reid as his wife

The camel threatened to upstage Dustin and co-star Warren Beatty in *Ishtar*

Dustin as Shylock – his first foray into Shakespeare in Sir Peter Hall's 1989 London production of *The Merchant of Venice* turned into a record-breaking season (John Haynes)

The *Rain Man* won Hoffman his second Oscar and his best ever Press

school and in the playground – especially when the child is rushed off to hospital after a fall. The sight of Dustin rushing through the streets, carrying the bleeding and concussed child in his arms, beats anything from the silent days.

What the writer-director Robert Benton created was a tear-jerker of the classic kind, wrapped up in the fancy ribbons of wide screen and Technicolor. Benton won an Oscar for the picture. So did the film itself (Best Picture) and so did Dustin. Some think it was the award he would have got for *Lenny* had be behaved himself the previous time. But it was a triumph for Hoffman, nevertheless.

There was another Oscar for the picture. The woman playing his wife won one, too. She was Meryl Streep. The fission between the two on screen might have mirrored their true feelings for each other – and it worked superbly. There is no record of any great disastrous fights between them and Dustin is seen mostly without her throughout the picture, but when they get together the sparks fly and the picture is by far the better for it.

(One name originally considered for the role of the estranged Mrs Kramer was that of *Charlie's Angels* star Kate Jackson, whom Dustin had been dating after the break-up of his marriage with Anne. But the TV company would not release her.)

It was a movie, according to Jarvis Astaire, into which he had had to push Dustin.

'He said that he thought it read like a soap opera. So I had to kid the producer Stanley R. Jaffe along that Dustin wanted to do it. I knew that in the end he wouldn't take no for an answer. But it went on for a long time – like a bad cold that doesn't go away. It turned out to be an extremely benevolent cold.' But he certainly took a great deal of convincing before the bug really began to bite.

He quite clearly had no more intention – at first – of playing Kramer, than he had of going out to catch cold for real.

Dustin himself was reluctant because he had read the book by Avery Corman and did not like it. 'It seemed more contrived than I hoped it would be,' he explained. He was sent scripts, the original by Robert Benton and then a series of drafts. He did not like any of them and turned the part down, more firmly and less politely each time.

There were reasons why Dustin could be talked into it. 'I knew that Richard Dreyfuss wanted to do it,' said Astaire. 'Eventually, it was revealed that Roy Scheider was there in the background as a backstop.'

Dustin read yet another revision of the script. That one gave him

goose-bumps, he said, being no more than human as to be persuaded
to want something that someone else wanted even more badly.

Once in, he had to make the film on his own terms. He demanded
four weeks of rehearsals, a practically unheard-of luxury for a picture
of this kind. 'You can't rush quality,' he said.

There were a number of worries about taking on the picture. Justin
Henry was so 'pretty' that Dustin thought he looked as though he had
just walked out of a commercial. His immediate thought was, 'God, I
hope he isn't any good.' So he suggested that perhaps the best thing
would be to have his own daughter Jenna play the part. Instead, he
made do by thinking of Jenna and using his memories of her when he
played with the boy.

Jarvis Astaire maintains that it was not Dustin's best work, but as he
almost said, if Hoffman was going through his paces suffering from a
bad cold, it was an illness from which there was a very comforting
recovery. Hardly surprisingly, he began to think of it more kindly as
time wore on.

Once more, Dustin did not depend entirely on his own being for his
research, although it played a bigger part than in previous pictures. He
explained to Tony Schwartz in his *New York Times* piece why it was so
important to him: 'My job is to do you and the only way that's possible
is if I've got you inside me. I've got to find out what you're doing.
Nobody simply *is*, except infants.'

Which was why perhaps he spent so much time with the boy who
played his son. It was in getting to know Justin Henry that Dustin did
much of his research – although his personal crisis with Anne was
providing plenty of background information that no kind of detached
artificial study could have achieved.

Benton gives Dustin credit for making the boy other than 'just another
cute kid'. It is fair to assume that Dustin was aware of the old problem
about acting alongside children and animals. In this case, he could see
that Justin might steal a scene simply by looking at the camera . . . but
he also had the child's welfare very much in mind. Before each scene
Dustin would talk quietly, alone, with the child, to tell him what he
expected, when he was supposed to be sad, when he was expected to
be awkward.

Even Meryl Streep saw the positive side of what the man she had
once called a 'creep' could accomplish. 'If you were a little kid, Dustin
is the kind of person you wish were your father. He's very entertaining

and knows how to address a child, not as a child, but not as an adult, either – in his own language.'

Dustin spoke about Meryl Streep more frankly. He conceded that 'she's a good girl. She's decent. Smart. Stubborn. She can piss me off, boy. We had a couple of tough times in the movie'.

The toughest of all was the scene in the restaurant where Meryl tells Dustin she wants custody of the boy. Dustin explained it like this when talking to three hundred students of cinema at Los Angeles' University of Southern California:

As reported at the time, he said: 'I was sitting there, we were on location and I just couldn't do the scene. Originally she says she wants the kid up front, and I realize I can't sit here and listen to this. I would get up and leave at the beginning of the scene. So all the lights are ready and Meryl is revved up and ready to go and I don't want to do the scene.'

That was the point at which the script supervisor suggested transposing the order, asking for the child at the end of the scene. Both he and Meryl liked that. At that point, Dustin brought one of his old habits into play. He improvised. But Meryl Streep was not going to be as pliable as Laurence Olivier. They were sitting at a restaurant table, not walking up and down – and even if they had been walking up and down, a strong healthy woman like Meryl Streep could have matched him, pace for pace.

'I turn to her and say, "Just face it, you're just trying to protect all that women's lib and ERA [Equal Rights Amendment] stuff . . ." And she looked at me. She didn't know that I was now satisfied with the scene and was trying to rev myself up. I said, "You're not trying to do the work as an actor, you're trying to speak for all women," and then I walked away.'

The extras on the set just sat and stared. 'You see,' Dustin explained, 'up to that point, we had been all lovey-dovey.' Now that in itself should have set warning signals going. One should not have expected any work with Dustin Hoffman to be lovey-dovey and succeed – this was to be no exception.

Meryl herself was rattled. When Dustin suddenly broke a wine glass – again, it wasn't in the script – she was furious. 'She was very upset with that . . . She got slivers of glass all over her hair. And I just walked right out of there. Right through the extras.'

That was a violent Mr Kramer whom Dustin changed as the film moved on. He realized that the time Kramer spent with his boy tended to feminize him more. He himself thought again about how men were cheated by not being allowed to bear children themselves. He had visions of taking his case for male child-bearing to God himself, whom he imagined as a bureaucrat sitting behind a desk surrounded by the angels.

Anne says that she was never aware of the latent 'maternal' instinct in Dustin. 'He never mentioned that to me. He likes women – and that's for sure. But he never indicated to me that he wished he had any of women's attributes or gifts.'

Dustin could feel those sentiments rearing inside him in the court-room scene in which custody of the child was being settled. He improvized that throughout. At one point the judge asked him why he should be granted custody of the boy. 'Because I'm his MOTHER,' he replied – and then realized what he had said. He wanted to keep it in the picture. Bob Benton disagreed, so a possibly notable episode in film history has been lost to posterity. As far as anyone can tell, it doesn't even remain ready for inclusion in some future edition of *It'll Be All Right On The Night*.

A friend suggested that he would only have been really happy a couple of generations earlier, playing in vaudeville. He could have dressed up all he liked then and truly allowed his fancies free play.

Meryl agreed that Dustin was not the easiest person to work with. 'Dustin has a technician's thoroughness and he is very demanding, but it isn't the star temperament I'd been led to expect. It isn't vanity. He is a perfectionist about the craft and the structuring of the film and his own ego is subjugated to that.'

That was not an easy thing for him to do. Nor was it easy to subjugate the emotions he felt as he worked on this picture about a divorce when he could think of practically nothing but the break-up of his own marriage.

The effect on Dustin's two children was one of the great worries Dustin faced as he approached his divorce. He was determined that they should be affected as little as possible. One thing was certain, he would continue to be a father to Karina as well as to Jenna, and so he still is. His adoptive daughter is still his daughter.

'They became estranged for a time,' Anne told me, 'I never knew why – and then they made it up.' There were no problems with Jenna.

In *Kramer vs Kramer*, he had to sublimate all his own feelings in those of the character he played in the film.

He always saw it from the personal point of view, as it affected *him*. Above all, he wanted to know how a marriage break-up would affect children. In an off-guard moment he asked Justin which one, in real life, he would like to live with, Dustin himself or Meryl. 'Her,' he replied unequivocally.

'Oh, yeh!' protested Dustin. 'Just try living with her for five weeks and then see.' The five weeks working with Meryl to date had taken their toll. It has to be said that a great deal of it was unease for unease's sake. Dustin convinced himself that he would not get on with Meryl and had to carry the notion through even though by now it was something of a joke.

He was not alone, however, in seeing that it was little more than a brightly coloured soap opera. The British magazine *Time Out* was hardly more enthusiastic. It recorded: 'Pastel colours, a cute kid and a good script made this one of the most undeserved successes of the year; wall-to-wall sentiment.'

But more important critics found plenty of redeeming qualities in the picture. Writing in *Time* magazine, Gerald Clarke ran through a swathe of characters that Dustin had played and noted: 'But in *Kramer vs Kramer*, he has assumed perhaps the most difficult persona of all: Dustin Hoffman.'

The *New York Times*'s Tony Schwartz noted in December 1979: 'Not since Mr Hoffman made his film debut twelve years ago in *The Graduate* as Benjamin Braddock – the quintessentially callow college kid looking for love and work – has he chosen a role to which he seems so naturally suited.'

Mr Schwartz had in mind Dustin's own marital difficulties.

Dustin said he did not know whether to be complimented or offended – and he was both, in about equal proportions. He was complimented because he was, after all, trying to create an illusion. The other part offended him, 'The idea that they think I am some guy off the street who happened to fit a role . . . I'm not at a point, even now, where I have a desire to put the essential me on the screen. I'm trying on different costumes, different characters. It's like [an actor] said: "I wake up every morning and do a different impression of myself." In this movie, there are parts of me, and parts of Bob Benton, Stanley Jaffe, my brother and my father.'

What he liked about it most was that the part of Kramer had 'arc', by which he meant that it covered a wide spectrum in a curve that described perfectly the psychology behind a man who went from being a workaholic to someone who was totally devoted to his child and to the time he spent with him.

'Too often when we go through crises, we don't feel them. One thing this film does is to re-emphasize the importance of fully feeling the pain when it occurs in your life.'

The producers faced up to the fact that there would always be a crisis of sorts, working with Dustin. Stanley Jaffe was to admit: 'Someone as obsessed as Dustin creates a lot of tension and puts a tremendous burden on the people he's working with.'

Dustin himself admitted there had been fights. 'Real wing-ding' fights', as he put it. But everyone was able to tolerate them because they were all after the same thing: perfection. Well, they certainly didn't get that. But prosperity they did achieve.

Dustin was, of course, prosperous enough not to worry about where the next dollar was coming from, so he could think about what was coming after *Kramer vs Kramer* with a certain detachment. He was going to do a play if he could. One that he fancied in particular was a stage version of *Lolita*, with himself in the James Mason role, of course.

He knew what he had to do to get across to the people who paid for seats at live performances. He recalled once making love to a girl in his dressing room before going on stage. It was a mistake, he said. He needed to make love to his audiences. That night there was nothing left. Two generations earlier, a totally different actor named Al Jolson had said much the same thing. For him, every performance was nothing less than a love affair. Now Dustin had come to terms with the same fact. It was something of a discovery, an effect on his ego.

He had moved to a smart new apartment of his own in Manhattan and rented a house in Westwood, Los Angeles, near UCLA, the University of California's local branch. 'They say if you live in a college town, you never grow old,' he told *Rolling Stone* magazine. And he was pleased with the fact that he had seemed to achieve that goal. 'I like . . . that I'm ageing so well. My friends tell me I keep getting handsomer the older I get. I have no doubt that's true. I had nowhere to go but up.'

In lighter moods like that, he would describe himself as '41-year-old urban Jewish actor on the fade'. He admitted that at this age he was preparing for his mid-life crisis (there were some who were surprised and not a little concerned that he did not think it had come already). Sometimes, he woke up screaming.

He didn't scream when he and Meryl Streep went to pick up their Oscars.

He walked up to the stage without a jacket and not wearing a tie. 'Well,' he said, 'the soap opera won.'

Looking at the Award, he quipped: 'He has no genitalia and he's holding a sword.' It was time for thanks, but not the usual kind. 'I'd like to thank my parents for not practising birth control,' he said and hoped that others felt the same way about that.

It was evident, from the response he got from the audience that night, that they did.

He admitted he had been critical of the Academy. 'And with reason,' he added somewhat ungraciously. But he said: 'I'm deeply grateful for the opportunity to be able to work. I'm greatly honoured for being chosen by the producer Stanley Jaffe and the director Bob Benton.'

When it came to modesty, he had a little of that ready, too. 'I refuse to believe that I beat Jack Lemmon, that I beat Al Pacino, that I beat Peter Sellers. I refuse to believe that Robert Duvall lost.'

All that was true. Lemmon had been nominated for his spellbinding role as the nuclear power station manager in *The China Syndrome*, Pacino for the now forgotten picture *And Justice For All*. Peter Sellers was widely expected to get a posthumous Best Actor Award for his outstanding and last picture *Being There*. (Robert Duvall had been nominated for a Best Supporting Actor Oscar for his work in the anti-Vietnam war movie, *Apocalypse Now*.) Yet the Oscar was Dustin's – for the first time; at last. Those who had thought that the Hoffman star was fading were now confounded. Dustin was once again being spoken of as a super-star.

And it was only right that it should be a super-star still on the way up to pay tribute to another who had had some thirty years of movie experience behind him. Sir Alec Guinness was being given a Lifetime Achievement Award that night. It was Dustin who handed him his special Oscar.

'At rehearsal yesterday,' said Dustin in his speech, 'I met him for the first time. And I, like a fool, asked him what his favourite performances were. He looked at me, like looking at an interviewee who didn't have an appointment, and he said, "I don't have any favourites. I wish to hell I didn't make any of them." '

Dustin did not feel that about his work any more than Guinness really did either. But it did no harm to see the business of acting in a different perspective. Not that he didn't take his own Oscar very seriously. As he said himself, it was perhaps about time. 'God knows, I've done enough crap in my life to grow a few flowers.'

It was also true that he was getting back to form. And to prove it he started *buying* flowers. He would go into a florist's shop and answer the telephone, trying not altogether unsuccessfully to imitate the French accent of the proprietress. Adults were shocked, but children delighted to see him follow that performance with a session of blowing bubbles with his saliva.

But people weren't blowing bubbles at him any more. Despite his doubts and others' hesitation, the Los Angeles and New York film critics' circles both picked *Kramer vs Kramer* as the best film of 1979.

Dustin was aware of the responsibilities and problems brought by success. He thought that that one word, success, 'can really cripple you'. 'And,' he explained, 'we live in a culture based on success. But life isn't for that. Life isn't to finally get to the point where you can accept Oscars from yourself for yourself. Because the most important thing is constantly to test yourself to find out where you're full of shit in your work. And your work many times is a way of finding out how you're full of shit in your life. And when you get into the bind of simply re-creating that which is pleasing or saleable then in a sense that growth stops.'

That, of course, had always been Anne's contention. She still thought he had let the growth stop. For his part, Dustin could not totally forget his family problems. His reason for the break-up of his marriage with Anne was now public – or at least his public reason was being made public: Anne and he had irreconcilable career conflicts.

The burden of working with First Artists on his previous two pictures continued apace. While *Kramer vs Kramer* was being put out on release for the first time, Dustin announced he was suing for $33 million dollars against First Artists, their distributors Warner Bros., and Jarvis Astaire.

Included in the demand – which specified 'exemplary damages' which was intended purely and simply as a punishment, not related to actual losses he had suffered – were $2 million each for the work he did on both *Straight Time* and *Agatha*; the fee he said he would have commanded simply as an actor; he claimed that, like all the other First Artists performers, he had taken a much reduced fee in return for the artistic control that was later removed from him.

Phil Feldman, who was no longer president of First Artists, alleged that both films had gone way over their budgets. Hoffman responded:

'If you're talking about good guys and bad guys I would never cast Phil Feldman as a good guy. It was a very important experience for me. I had the shit kicked out of me and that can be very valuable in going through life. I learned not to trust anybody.'

One of the problems with First Artists was that it only made fifteen films in its eleven years of existence up to the time of the trial. The artists concerned never got together, never held board meetings and left all the details to the business executives and their lawyers. That much came out of the hearings.

The court case went on for more than a year, with Dustin alleging collusion between Jarvis Astaire and the First Artists management. The original $33 million became $65 million. He tried to sum it up. Once more, he went into the painting analogy. 'You put in a lifetime of training and once more, someone takes your paintbrush away.'

The main point of his case was that Dustin said that he had lost his artistic control. At this stage in his career – although in reality it had ever been thus – that was like saying he had lost his touch.

Depriving Dustin Hoffman of his artistic control was depriving him of his pride as well as his integrity – virtually of his life force.

(It turned out that Dustin had a much better deal with First Artists than his partners. The other artists were required to make three films for the company with a deal for 12 per cent of the gross profits and 43 per cent of the net after a certain amount had been earned. Dustin was being allowed two films at a straight 10 per cent of the gross.)

He denied that the two films were over-budget and over-schedule – First Artists were now counter-suing. They said that Hoffman 'repeatedly refused' and neglected to prepare the final cut of *Straight Time* which cost the company about a million dollars and exceeded the 61-day approved production schedule by approximately 23 days.

He also 'refused to approve or return advertising materials, stills and trailers, leading to the result that material which was less desirable and effective had to be used.'

A final budget and schedule were dependent on a final shooting script and there never was a final shooting script, said Dustin's lawyer, Bertram Fields. He not only wanted the money, but also a cancellation of First Artists' rights to distribute the picture with Warner Bros.

Dustin did not want to be dragged into too much legal jargon. 'Whether I would have made the pictures better or worse is irrelevant,' he maintained. 'It was my right to paint them. It's not ego. I can fail. I choose performances knowing full well I might not make it. But if my signature means anything, it means I haven't deceived you. Those are not my films. Only the first twenty minutes of *Straight Time* is mine. Those films are nowhere near the potential of what they could be.'

As he also said: 'I'm so proud of the work I did in *Straight Time* and so unhappy that a potentially great film wound up being a good film because it wound up in the wrong hands.' The film 'fails to lift itself beyond a kind of documentary reality. That's done in the cutting. The form is manipulative and I had a very strong point of view that I think would have transcended a depressing subject and lifted it into a metaphorical area, and that's not in the film.'

Reaching court was just a development in a long-continuing story. First Artists had tried as early as when Dustin started filming *Kramer vs Kramer* to stop him making that picture and to get back to work on their two vehicles. A judge had refused to grant them an injunction that would have stopped *Kramer* in its tracks.

At first, it seemed as though First Artists had won. Dustin had gone into a London studio to 'loop' dialogue – dub sentences that had not been recorded perfectly in the first place. But the lawsuit went on just the same.

'I looped *Agatha* really for one reason and that was simply to try to better the film,' he explained, 'and to help myself as much as I could with my own performance. But we were very careful so it did not prejudice the lawsuit and there is no arrangement for my looping *Straight Time* at all. On the one hand, I don't want to hurt a film I've been in. But at the same time, I don't want the public lied to. The films says a Sweetwall Production, which is my company. This is not a Sweetwall production and this is not my film in any shape or form. I don't want to hurt it, but I don't think it reaches the potential it could have. I hope it's successful, but I can't in good conscience promote it.'

'As for Phil Feldman', said Dustin, 'never at any point did he ever come back to me or try to dissuade me from doing that project at all. On the contrary, he thought it was a very commercial film. He had seen the rushes and he felt the love story aspect between Vanessa and me worked.'

He had no idea, when he broke off work on *Straight Time* to make *Agatha*, that the company intended no further principal photography.

They were the only two pictures he had ever worked on 'from the ground up. I saw every bit of footage of both films. I was in on every meeting. No one from First Artists was. They spotted dailies [rushes] once in a while'.

Dustin had at one stage tried to stop the films being released. His application for an injunction was rejected.

Feldman maintained that the artistic and commercial results of the pictures would speak for themselves.

What mainly annoyed Dustin was that missing scene which should have been in *Agatha*. 'That scene explains my character,' he said. Several critics had said they were puzzled by his motives.

He was telling people he cut his knees bending down to appeal to the management of First Artists not to start work on *Agatha* until everything was properly organized.

One of the by-products of this row was a continuing feud with producer David Puttnam, who went on to become, briefly, head of Columbia Pictures in Los Angeles and then returned to Britain as an independent.

What did Puttnam say about Hoffman? That 'he gave me such a bad time on *Agatha* that I became totally neurotic' – a word frequently used about Dustin himself.

There were numerous reports of rows between Hoffman and Puttnam, although with the passage of the years both seem reluctant to go into it again. Suffice it to say, neither look upon this period with any milk of human kindness in their hearts.

In January 1979, Dustin made a statement in which he repudiated *Agatha* as being his film 'in any shape or form'.

The suit dragged on for years afterwards. Eventually, a settlement was reached, the main condition being that the details of that settlement were never released. Somebody's pride needed to be protected. But nobody is going to risk contempt of court by suggesting whose.

Meanwhile, more people were expressing satisfaction with *Kramer vs Kramer*. He won a prestigious Golden Globe award, presented by Hollywood's Foreign Press Association, and in the process upset some people with a speech that was seen as criticizing the prizes but which he said was intended as consolation for Justin Henry who did not get one (the boy had also been nominated for a Supporting Actor award in the Oscar ceremonies, but failed there, too). 'I think that awards are very silly,' he told the audience at the Beverly Hilton Hotel. 'I think they pit very talented and good people against each other and they hurt the hell out of the ones that lose. And I think they relieve us that win.'

It was plainly a time for reassessment for Dustin, for among other things reassessing his attitude to women. He no longer felt that he could not be friends with women unless he had slept with them. He had several of them.

Other men worried about women taking over their jobs. Of course, Dustin didn't have that concern. As an actor, how could he? Yet in February 1980, he did not think that was a ridiculous scenario. He was just grateful that 'it never touched me'. Even so, it is strange that he thought it worth mentioning.

'My problems with women,' he went on in an interview in *Redbrook* magazine, 'are on another level – where I'm vulnerable and frightened of being around anybody who can put my life in jeopardy. Women have a tendency to make me feel very vulnerable. I think men are scared to death of women, and with good reason. But I don't know what I'd *do* without you guys.' You 'guys', in this instance, being in Damon Runyon's terminology, of course, dolls.

As for himself, 'It's true, I *am* a nice man. I'm a very nice man. It's always bewildered me why people don't like me.'

One person who plainly did like Dustin was a young woman of 25 named Lisa Gottsegen. He had known Lisa for years – since 1967, as it turned out. She was ten years old at the time and plainly not one of the women to whom his eye would stray in those early days with Anne. She was just the granddaughter of one of his mother's friends, Blanche Salter, and they met when their families got together one weekend – the way Jewish families in California or anywhere else for that matter would get together.

Dustin was unemployed and had been persuaded by Lisa's aunt to play the piano at the party. Lisa was in pyjamas, but she pushed herself on to the piano stool to sit next to him. Later, as she was sent off to bed, she told her grandmother, 'I hope he waits for me, because I am going to marry him when I grow up.'

They had met in between. When Lisa was 18, their families had another joint gathering and he offered her the chance of being his assistant. She decided to study law instead.

When they casually met again, there was a different sort of feeling between them. Of course, it was noted and of course, the Press started making predictions. Dustin had an answer for them: 'She's my attorney,' he barked, 'and if you're not careful, I'll have her sue you.' They started spending a great deal of time together. In the summer of 1980, Rabbi Lennie Berman of Los Angeles made them man and wife.

'It's not incest,' said Dustin, 'but it's probably only one step removed, because I played "doctor" with Lisa's mother when we were about six years old.' For the first time, he added, 'I can feel life when I'm not acting.' That was probably the biggest compliment he could pay anyone.

By that time, Dustin had moved on to other professional things that he hoped would help him to live when he *was* acting – and hoped that those who had reason not to like him would have had time at least to cool if not forget their reasons.

There was no doubt that Dustin had been caught up in big business, which didn't necessarily sit well with what he justifiably considered his art. Perhaps that would not compromise the principal idea he was working on now. He and Richard Dreyfuss were going to make a film about the Gershwins. Dustin playing George, Richard, Ira. But it didn't get off the ground.

What did happen, however, was a picture with a title that today conveys an instant impression of the best piece of female impersonation since Jack Lemmon and Tony Curtis put on high heels and climbed into bed with Marilyn Monroe in *Some Like It Hot*. This one was in some respects even hotter. It was called *Tootsie*.

14

She walked not exactly in beauty, but she was an attractive woman, this Dorothy Michaels who played the lead in a soap opera that all New York started talking about. A bit pernickety, it's true. Very anxious about her privacy. Not too happy about getting into long-standing romances. But a powerful, attractive woman, there was no doubt.

What no one on the soap opera realized was that Dorothy Michaels was really Michael Dorsey. And Michael Dorsey . . . well, of course, he was really Dustin Hoffman, star of *Tootsie*, the film he was determined would not be another *Charley's Aunt*, would not give the impression it was about a man in drag.

It had a simple premise: an out-of-work actor (now that really *was* a species with which he could identify) in desperation dresses as a female so that he can audition for a woman's part – and gets it.

It was an eagerly awaited film, especially by those who couldn't wait to see everyone concerned fall flat on their faces. After about three years in the melting-pot, how could those people really do anything else?

There were the usual announcements in the trade Press about *Tootsie*. Dustin Hoffman was going to make a film about actors working in New York. Before long, some writers were reporting that it was going to be about the making of a TV soap opera. Nobody had yet got the point that Dustin was going to play a woman in the picture. When that information was revealed, the tabloids in particular went crazy. What nobody knew was that it was above all a very personal statement.

It was personal on two levels: hints about the first of these were apparent to people who heard the involvement Dustin had had with *Kramer vs Kramer* and those renewed announcements about wanting to be able to bear children. This was going to be Dustin's statement that not only did he admire the way women coped with life, but that he and other men had their sensitivity and perhaps gutsiness, too.

That was the first level that you only had to study Dustin Hoffman's published quotes to understand. The second was more complicated and less obvious.

It became a factor in June 1980. His mother was taken seriously ill. She had had a heart attack. This was followed almost immediately by a stroke that left Lillian practically totally debilitated. Dustin rushed to her bedside. He chartered a helicopter to get him to the hospital in time. He arrived to find her paralysed down one side. Lillian could say nothing, but he knew he was getting through to her. He literally begged her not to give in, to fight it, to stay alive.

He knew that she was in pain, but no one could find out where. He devised in a few unplanned moments a means of discovering where. Like Carl Bernstein in *All The President's Men*, he asked her to try to smile if the parts of her body that he touched were free of pain. If they were the ones that hurt, he asked her to stick out her tongue.

Her tongue went out when he got to her feet. Doctors rushed in and realized that clots had formed there. They performed an emergency operation there and then.

'You gotta fight, Mom,' Dustin said, almost pleading with her to listen to him. 'This is a tough one.' He then looked at his father and brother and embraced them both. It was not an easy thing to do. 'Did you see that, Mom?' he asked her.

They had never been close enough to kiss each other naturally, as men can do in those circumstances, but he knew it would please her. She had always wanted to be the matriarch of a close family.

Lisa was there with him. 'We're going to have a baby,' he told Lillian.

He went back to the Columbia studios with the image of his mother's face totally impressed on his psyche. But it was not the immobile twisted face he had seen in the hospital, not the fragile, powerless woman lying on the bed surrounded by all the wires and tubes of modern, inhuman medicine, but the mother of his childhood and early adult years.

At the age of 72, she had been playing tennis and, according to her younger son, still had legs like those of Ann Miller. He remembered how, when he was very small, she used to call him 'Tootsie', which is why he was now choosing it for the title of his film.

She died eighteen months after first being taken ill. 'Not to be sacriligious,' Dustin said at the time, 'but from my point of view, God's a perverse motherfucker.'

The 'woman' he was going to play in *Tootsie* would be much kinder. She would also be a feminine person who cared enormously about the way she looked, talked and walked but who was mentally as strong as a truck driver.

It would take time before he could get that image on to film, but he was spending a great many hours, days, weeks, thinking about it and about the rows that were brewing. The only way he could completely turn off from that problem was to direct his thoughts to Lisa and the baby she was expecting.

It the eighth month of her pregnancy, Dustin was the one who pointed out that not everything looked right. He could feel that Lisa's stomach was hard and sore. When she lay down, she lost consciousness.

The cause was diagnosed immediately. The placenta – the baby's lifeline – had come away.

He went with her to the hospital, where he was told the baby would be delivered immediately by Caesarean section. He was determined to stay with his wife for the operation; the hospital doctors were equally insistent that he could not remain there. It was like a film's director countermanding an idea he had just improvised. He was furious. He said that they didn't know what they were talking about. He was going to stay. In truth, he was even more nervous than was Lisa. At least, Lisa could allow herself a few moments of laughter when Dustin struggled to put on the surgical slippers – on to his head. The surgeon persuaded him to sit in a corner for five minutes without doing or saying anything.

He later revealed that it 'blew his mind' to have to take orders from a 29-year-old woman. After all, it was *his* wife there, about to have *his* baby. What could *she* know?

When the child was delivered – he saw the surgeon dip her hand into a void somewhere and bring a baby out – 'I was hit with a baseball bat,' he was to say, going over that moment again and again.

The baby was a boy whom they called Jacob, which some thought was a further demonstration of his return to Judaism. Jacob became 'Jake', for short. Dustin muttered that he hoped he would not grow up to be a male chauvinist. A few days after his birth, the child almost died. He had an undeveloped lung which required immediate attention. The operation was successful and Dustin was able to think more about *Tootsie*. Jake was two years old when he came on to the set for the final day's shooting. By that time, a lot of fighting had gone on.

The original idea for the picture had indeed been all those feelings Dustin had had about the great advantages that women had over men. He talked over the idea with Murray Schisgal who thought it could be a small, very intimate production. Another writer, Don McGuire, was brought in to polish the basic notion.

Needless to say, the final picture hardly resembled in any way the original script submitted by McGuire, who had achieved his first fame with the magnificent Spencer Tracy film, *Bad Day At Black Rock*. Other writers took over – in fact, there were eight of them working on the project from start to finish – planning what all along was going to be a small movie that would convey the personal nature of a story that did not want to be overcrowded by detail. It seemed right that Dustin should be closely involved in the writing. He was, after all, about to start walking around with his heart on Dorothy's puff sleeves.

He needed a lot from his writers. 'I can't act a moral,' he was to say. 'The best I can do is speak personally, not say, "this is the way it is or should be," but this is true of me.'

But the Hoffman-writers relationship was more brittle than any of them had imagined. It didn't stay intact through the vicissitudes of a Dustin Hoffman picture in which the star analysed every word and seemingly insisted on working out each frame. One of the best moves on the writing front was to bring in Larry Gelbart, who was famous mainly for the brilliantly successful *M*A*S*H* TV series. Elaine May was retained, at a fee reputedly close to half a million dollars, to act as a script doctor, and she produced what was supposedly the final rewrite. Dustin said he liked that but Sydney Pollack, who had become the director, did not. He made changes.

Eventually, Dustin came up with his usual answer to problems like this: Murray Schisgal returned. Night after night and well into those nights, they wrote new scenes.

As Dustin recalled: 'Sydney would read what we'd done, reluctantly, and then we'd sit down and argue about it.' Pollack would say that he was the one who 'sat in a room with a staple gun and a pair of scissors'.

'What I wanted on *Tootsie*,' Dustin explained, 'was the same situation I had on *Kramer vs Kramer* where Stanley Jaffe and Robert Benton and I had an equal say in all decisions. We were partners and it worked wonderfully.'

He told Pollack about the Dustin Hoffman ideas on democracy and was turned down flat. 'I don't work like that,' said the director.

The real problem with Pollack was that he had not hitherto done comedy. His most outstanding success to date had been the Barbara Streisand-Robert Redford hit, *The Way We Were*. He would soon discover that working with Streisand, normally regarded as about as simple a task as munching ground glass, was by comparison a country walk on a summer's day.

Besides the fact that he could sense that he and Hoffman would come into conflict, he wasn't sure about the basic story-line. He couldn't be sure 'if it was a homage to actors, a sophisticated comedy examining sexual mores or a story about the rehabilitation of a sexist'.

Dustin, meanwhile, had to concentrate on the not unimportant role of actor.

He put himself into the high-heeled shoes of Dorothy Michaels. How did it feel to be not as sexually attractive as the girls who normally turned him on? 'It suddenly occurred to me after doing Dorothy for a while that if I'd met her at a party, I'd never have so much as condescended to talk to her, because physically she was a write-off. It's a shallow gratitude, certainly, to judge people by the way they look and I think that is what started to make me sad.' Suddenly he realized there were dozens of interesting women whom he had ignored, simply because he had not found them sexually attractive.

He knew that if he were a woman, he'd want to be an attractive one. But as he repeated: 'If I met Dorothy, me as a woman, at a party, I'd turn me down.'

It took a year to work out the kind of woman Dorothy was going to be. Certainly, he wasn't going to play a man in drag. He was not going to exaggerate a walk or use a high voice. There would be no scenes showing him balancing on those heels and keeling over. It was a serious part he was going to play, not a comedy act.

It was serious. He would be paying tribute to the women he admired so much, but also offering a paean of praise for all the hard-up, out-of-work actors trudging the streets off-Broadway the way he had done. He put his whole heart and soul into that. In one scene he declares: 'An actor waits by the phone. He has no power when he gets a job.'

The final story-line was that Michael Dorsey auditions for the same role that his girlfriend had failed to get. He realizes that he would never pass for a pretty girl, but why not a woman in the early years of middle age, who still cared about her appearance, still behaved in a totally feminine manner and who was as strong as . . . in short, his mother.

Perhaps more for that reason than any other, there were times when it was one of the hardest of his roles to perform.

'Every time I felt physically uncomfortable on *Tootsie*, like when the wig itched or the shoes pinched, I'd put on a happy face for my mother's sake. She was my inspiration.' He made that remark in an interview

with Diana Maychick in the New York *Post*, which may explain why
it sounds more cloying than usual. But the general impression was
probably correct. He maintained that Lillian had been 'very proud'
when she realized what he was doing with her 'life'. She died just as
the picture was about to go before the cameras. In a way, he knew the
film would be seen in his own mind as a memorial to his mother.

Dustin's brother Ron, by then, in 1982, an economist in Washington,
said that he was convinced that Dorothy Michaels was his mother in
spirit. 'He was keeping her alive with that part,' he said. Not that he
knew the lengths to which Dustin was prepared to go to get it right.

In fact, if one did not appreciate that Dustin Hoffman researched all
his parts that way, it could be assumed that love for his mother's
memory was precisely why he put so much into this role. He worked
on his make-up, he simulated breasts and hips and walked in the street.
No one batted an eyelid.

It goes without saying that much of the credit is due to his make-up
man Alan Weisinger, who provided facelifts for Dorothy which would
last for only four hours – by that time, the make-up would start to melt
under the hot studio lights. Sometimes, only one take was achieved in
a day. But the make-up man kept going. He gave 'Dorothy' a new set
of top teeth, to hide Dustin's masculine smile. He advised him to wear
glasses, to hide his hooked nose. George Masters, who had worked on
creating a lot of Marilyn Monroe's magic, was also responsible.

Dustin had to shave his legs, his arms and the backs of his fingers.
He had to learn how to carry a shoulder bag. He wasn't used to doing
so and the strain of it made him look like a hunchback. His dresses all
had high necks or scarves to hide his 15½ inch collar size.

A female impersonator was consulted. Not because Dustin had
thought twice about going into drag, but because he knew so many
tricks of the trade, like how to shave. It turned out that the shaving
would be more effective if it was done upwards and not downwards,
and would be all the better if done in totally damp surroundings. He
decided to do all his shaving in a sauna. But by the middle of the
afternoon the 'shadow' had reappeared and filming had to be abandoned
again.

And then there was the question of the voice. It had to sound feminine
but not a kind of falsetto, which he knew would sound . . . false. Dustin
himself chose his accent. He thought he'd make 'Dorothy' French.
When that didn't work, he plumped for a Southern drawl, which he
thought could be expanded without too much exaggeration into sound-

ing remotely like the voice of a woman, certainly more so than anything he could make of a New York snarl.

Again, he had to research it. He chose to do so with the help of the actress Polly Holliday, who had appeared in *All Over Town* and who spoke like a gal who required a mint julep before going to bed. 'It wasn't just the dialect,' he said when he was satisfied that her coaching had achieved all the results he was seeking. 'It was this other thing she has – she is a very tough lady, she is uncompromising.' So Dorothy became a combination of Lillian Hoffman and Polly Holiday. He knew he was satisfied with Dorothy when he could take her into the street.

Dustin even went to Jenna's school in all the finery of Dorothy Michaels. Jenna was furious.

'Just say I'm your Aunt Dorothy from Arkansas,' he instructed his younger daughter. Jenna did. The teacher was charming. It was extraordinarily revealing for Dustin. He discovered a new freemasonry between women. The teacher was so much *nicer* to Dorothy Michaels than she had been to Dustin Hoffman, famous actor or not.

If he could convince her, he knew he could persuade the rest of the cast of the picture, who were paid to accept him. It no longer seemed outlandish that his room-mate's father would fall in love with 'him'/her.

But there was, above all, that need to 'feel' his part. He cross-examined women visitors to the set. He asked them if they combed or brushed their hair? What foundation did they apply before their final make-up went on? Did they like his shoes? Did his bust look convincing? He would talk quite happily about the problems of his 'time of the month'.

'I'm kinda cute – in a natural way,' he told one girl and she seemed to believe him.

Dustin Hoffman as Dorothy Michaels was very convincing indeed. He arranged to meet Jon Voight at the Russian Tea Room. Both turned up. Voight failed to recognize him.

In short, he had the recipe for a great film that was bound to dance off the studio floor. Not quite.

Nothing in the story on film was anything like a match for what had happened in the studio. This was, after all, Dustin Hoffman, who required the kind of perfection normally insisted upon only by people who hold the power of life and death in their hands.

Sydney Pollack was actually the third director to be brought into the film. The first was Dick Richards who had supplied an idea for a story based on a transsexual playing in the women's tennis circuit. Tennis disappeared as fast as Richards from the director's chair. He eventually resigned himself to being just a producer of the picture. He was replaced as director by Hal Ashby. But Ashby's stay was short-lived. So much time was spent on preliminary work that he had to leave to move on to the next picture for which he was contracted.

Sydney Pollack also had two other roles in the film. He played Dustin's agent, who at first couldn't understand his client's motives and begged him to get treatment for his problem; a brilliantly acted role that was more than a cameo and seemed to permeate the whole movie. He was also co-producer of the picture. So was Dustin, through his Punch Productions company. And that was the root of what became very serious problems between them. Dustin regarded it as his project. Sydney Pollack said that as director he was captain of the ship, or conductor of the orchestra, or painter with the pallet, whichever metaphor was most appropriate for the time of day.

The rows were long and furious, although Dustin maintained they were always held in private and never in public. The newspapers, on the other hand, were full of stories, a number of which seemed to be headed 'The Troubled *Tootsie*.'

There were tales of Pollack and Hoffman actually throwing things at each other, although the director was to say that these were much exaggerated. Hoffman himself admitted there were a number of acrimonious moments between them. 'Finally [Pollack said], "Dustin, we've got to go to work. Just tell me how you want to do this scene? I don't agree with you and I'll tell the studio I don't agree, but let's do it." ' To which, Dustin said he would insist, 'No, we're not going to shoot the scene if you're not behind it. It won't be a good scene.' Eventually, there was a compromise. And it was the compromises that caused many more of the problems.

Directing Dustin was by far the hardest of Pollack's roles, mainly because he came across the Hoffman search for perfection. The real problem, of course, was Dustin's innate belief that *he* was really the director, but had to sit back and let someone else take out the paint box. Such frustrations have to find a way of working themselves out and Dustin's did via a series of shouting matches that, had there been such a category, would have won him a gold medal in the Olympics.

Pollack, interviewed on television, later accused Dustin of being a neurotic.

Dustin knew he was on the line and had an answer to the charges: 'I like to be prepared and I feel that the success or failure of a film is many times determined before you start principal photography.'

Neither was it true that he was neurotic and could only work in that frame of mind. His success in *Kramer vs Kramer* had proved the fallacy of that argument. 'I've done about fifteen films and I think I've had a rough time with about three or four directors; Sydney is one of them. Sydney and I had a rough time together and I wish that he could find it in his mind to see it as it really was and not the picture he has painted for himself, which is "I'm the normal, healthy rational director and he's the neurotic actor and I had to sit on him." ' That was really speaking his mind. As Dustin said: 'When you see the same mistakes being made year after year, you have to be an idiot not to speak up. Suddenly you're no longer a virgin. You know a couple of things.' He and Pollack never had time to become friends.

He also said that his real complaint was that he did not get time for rehearsal. As should now be more than obvious, Dustin is not one of those actors who believes he gets all the rehearsal time he needs in the rejected takes on camera. 'I was promised two weeks [of rehearsal] and was grieved that I didn't get it and that we followed the risky course of starting to shoot with a screenplay that was not completed because Sydney had decided to rewrite the script I had approved.'

Pollack was ill and the time after his return could not be spared for rehearsing. But he *was* the director and he had taken the job with the assurance that he would be allowed to make all the changes he considered necessary.

Dustin always maintained that he had insisted from the beginning that the two of them, he and Pollack, should agree on everything between them. Dustin had to give Pollack final-cut approval, but he himself had access to the cutting room after having script and cast approval.

Had he not tried directing before, this would have been the one time that he would have taken over himself, but he had learned his lesson. About this time, Murray Schisgal explained why: 'He needs acting to overcome feelings of inadequacy, but acting by definition puts you in the passive role of victim of a director. He can't do both, because he pours so much energy into acting that there's nothing left for directing.'

One director, who didn't want to be named, put it like this: 'Next to Hoffman, Streisand is a pussycat. If he weren't so talented, Hoffman would never get work. Who would put up with that kind of craziness?'

To give him credit, Dustin knew that he was causing ructions in the area around the *Tootsie* set. 'Sydney [Pollack] had said on more than one occasion that an actor's an actor and should just be an actor. The actor is usually a hired hand. Regardless of whether you're a star or not, you're still a hired hand, because when you're a star you're then working with a star director, so it evens out – you get treated the same as when you were off-Broadway.'

But he needed to be reassured during the making of this of all pictures. 'This was *my* project,' he told Mitch Tuchman, writing in the magazine *American Film*. 'Pollack's refusal to see me in any role but that of an actor was somewhat paternalistic, just the way the agent sees Michael [Michael Dorsey]. I just think that some directors are closed-minded about what an actor can contribute. You'll hear directors say sometimes, "Yes, I got a performance out of that actor; I had to push him. I had to push him further than he thought he could go." Well, there are probably a lot of uncredited occasions where actors have pushed directors into areas they haven't gone into before and I think there have been more than a few occasions where a picture is better because of the actor who is in it.'

One had to be in on all the backbiting, all the politics, to appreciate that *Tootsie* wasn't all easy and smooth for the participants. You viewed the picture and couldn't see the joins.

Sydney Pollack was asked if he would ever work with Dustin again. He had to think about that. 'After a rest, maybe,' he said.

Dustin didn't like to read that sort of thing. 'If you're trying to do good work,' he told the *Ladies Home Journal* in April 1983, 'it's stacked against you. You're spending $65,000 a day to shoot a movie, so the pressure of getting it right for the first time is enormous. With that kind of tension on a set, you're just trying to get away with your life. It is shocking to me that people don't face what the work is all about. They'll say, "That scene is just a bridge, don't worry about it." I go crazy! A bridge? How can you not make every moment important?'

Ironically and generously, Dustin has since given Sydney Pollack a lot of the credit for the success of *Tootsie*. 'Make no mistake,' he told Roderick Mann in the *Los Angeles Times* a year later, '*Tootsie* wouldn't be up there if it were not for the talent of Sydney Pollack . . . There's stuff up there against which I fought bitterly. But the audience just loves it. So I was wrong some of the time. I was also right some of the time. That's what happens when you make a picture.'

It was, in most people's judgement, quite a picture. Before long, it was apparent it had cost all of $21 million, which turned out to be

more than the total bill for the year's most vaunted epic, Sir Richard
Attenborough's *Gandhi*. 'Yeh,' joked Dustin, 'but they didn't have to
shoot in New York.' Nor did *Gandhi*'s star Ben Kingsley get $4.5
million for his role. That's what Dustin picked up for *Tootsie*.

Richard Schickel, the respected critic of *Time*, thought that its opening in December 1982 was a notable event. *Tootsie* would 'roll straight
into everyone's heart,' he wrote, 'and into everyone's mind as an unmelt-
ing movie memory.'

The film, he said, was 'more than *Charley's Aunt* updated or *Myra
Breckenridge* toned down. In telling the tale of a man forced to get in
touch with the feminine side of his nature and becoming a better man
because of the experience, it triumphantly remains a farce for our times,
not a tract for them.' He wrote of the fate of most movies that 'end up
in the ravine, bottoms up among the broken and rusting remnants of last
year's improbable dreams. A few – sensibly designed or well-balanced or
inherently powerful – seem to steer themselves into the theatres, oblivious of the uproar that attended their journey. Then, every once in a
rare while, one arrives in style, its owner-drivers still glaring angrily at
one another; but somehow the better for its terrible travails. These are
the miracles of the industry, the stuff of Hollywood legends. This year's
miracle is called *Tootsie*.'

Leslie Halliwell in his *Film Guide* summed it up: 'As with *Genevieve*
and *Whisky Galore* an unlikely comedy subject makes an instant classic.
It's all in the handling.' For once, Halliwell was only partly right.
Certainly, it was all in the handling. But the matter being handled
wasn't unlikely at all. In fact, possibly the principal handicap was that
the subject was all too likely. Men had been dressing up as women since
the days Shakespeare appeared on the stage of the Rose Theatre.

The New York Branch of Women in Film, meanwhile, announced a
new honorary member – Dustin. He said he would happily play a
woman in a film again – provided they could find an easier way of
applying the make-up.

Writing in *Village Voice* Andrew Sarris commented: 'What is particularly amazing about *Tootsie* is that every performance has fallen into
place in perfect *rapport* with the overall conception.' But it didn't all
make for perfection, not even from Dustin: 'He is teetering precariously
between an apparently pointless virtuosity and a distasteful grotesque-
ness. *Tootsie* has gotten off the ground, but not even all of Hoffman's
resourcefulness and intensity as an actor seem sufficient to make the
film fly.'

The members of the Academy of Motion Picture Arts and Sciences were, however, impressed.

Dustin was once again nominated for a Best Actor Academy Award, one of ten achieved by the picture. But the only *Tootsie* Oscar was the statuette Jessica Lange won as Best Supporting Actress. She played Dorothy Michaels' room-mate and co-actress in the TV soap opera, the girl with whom the performer whose real name was Michael Dorsey had fallen in love.

By all accounts, Dustin and Lisa were just as much in love. But the Dustin Hoffman career was still a priority. So what next? The answer came from once more thinking about his relationship with his parents. This time, the emphasis was on his father.

15

It was one of those times in his life when everything seemed to be going right. Without even Sydney Pollack to go 'neurotic' over, there was an element of perfection in the Dustin lifestyle.

'I realize,' he said, 'how sad the world is.' But he added: 'I am happier now than I have ever been.' He wasn't going to rely on it. His laurels were not for resting upon. 'I think if God gets wind that Hoffman's been happy for three straight days, he'll level me.'

With no new film to make, no new play to move straight into, he was looking for new audiences. *Rolling Stone* magazine's Gary Smith went with him into a dentist's surgery. 'Did you know that cunnilingus is the best thing to prevent tooth decay?' he asked his dentist. The man was quick off the mark, knowing that oral sex was not a remedy he could easily recommend to his other patients. 'Then why are *your* teeth going bad?' he asked. Dustin couldn't spend too long working that one out and neither did he have to. 'Heredity plays a part, too,' he said, but added that we were living in a society that worships the orgasm. He could have pleaded guilty in that department, also.

Dustin was not going to give up in his search for new fields to till. When he heard that people wanted to go to acting school, like a girl in a dress shop or the man in charge of renovating his apartment, he made the arrangements and paid the bill. He once saw a cripple struggling to walk in the gutter of a street near Broadway. Dustin went to help him. When he heard that he, too, wanted to go to acting school, he tried to help there, as well, although the man was found to be unsuitable.

It was as if playing in *Tootsie* had not just brought back to him memories of his mother, but had reawakened inside him the peculiar feelings he had of *déjà-vu*, of what it had been like to want to get an acting job but to have got no further than manning the cloakroom of a Broadway theatre when the most exciting thing to happen to him 'professionally' had been to handle the coat of Eleanor Roosevelt.

He said that he missed 'Dorothy'. She had plainly become very much part of him – so much so that he kept the dresses he wore in the film in a trunk in his office. Several people asked for them – including Lisa and her grandmother. There were requests to donate them for charity, but Dustin kept them in the trunk and the trunk stayed in his office, in the way that old vaudevillians – the link was quite obvious – kept their props for posterity. Lisa said that was OK with her, providing he did not try wearing them again.

That certainly was not his idea, although as he said he would not mind playing a woman in a picture again, if the right one came along. Certainly, the last one had been a huge success, topping all charts for the best part of five months. It also won him the British 'Oscar', the BAFTA award, which he shared with Michael Caine for Best Actor. (Caine's was for his masterly performance of the inebriated lecturer in *Educating Rita*.)

But Dustin was the last person to want to dwell exclusively on the past. He was able once more to indulge himself in plans for the future, most of which he probably knew would not come off. He contemplated a stage comeback with a new version of *Inherit The Wind*, about the famous 'monkey trial' of the 1920s – a 'Bible Belt' community disputing the right of a school to teach Darwin's theory of evolution – which had been a brilliant film starring Spencer Tracy and Fredric March. But that didn't happen. There was talk of his playing the part of Arkady in the film version of *Gorky Park*, but it was made without him. Then, he was going to star as a baseball player-manager in a comedy called *Long Gone*, but that never happened. Columbia Pictures bought a book by a Toronto film director, Martyn Burke, called *Laughing War* which they hoped Dustin would make. He wouldn't. Blake Edwards, the successful producer/director of the Pink Panther series – who was almost as well known as Julie Andrews' husband – was trying to persuade Dustin to make *The Man Who Loved Women*, a comedy which had been a moderately successful French movie. The title made it seem amazingly appropriate for Dustin, but Edwards wouldn't forgo his cutting rights.

The woman he loved most these days was, of course, Lisa. When she told him she was having another baby, he told everybody that he loved her more than ever, which was probably totally true. He was with Lisa at the birth in March 1983 and said afterwards he had helped 'coach' her during the delivery. The new baby, Dustin's fourth child – if one includes Karina, who might have been estranged from him, but whom he still considered as his own – was a seven-pound, 12-ounce daughter to whom they gave another Old Testament name, Rebecca.

Only a few people had known that Lisa was even pregnant. After the difficulties attending Jake's birth, they wanted to keep out of the public eye with this one. It was not so much superstition as a refusal to tempt fate. (He seemed to think much the same way about ski-ing. 'You need a lot of snow – and a lot of Blue Cross,' he quipped, although he was wealthy enough to run his own Blue Cross operation).

The new child, of course, gave Dustin reason to take his mind off his career, but only momentarily. Stirring at the back of that mind now was a project that had been part of his very being for as long as he had been interested in the theatre: *Death of A Salesman*.

He still thought of his father as a Willy Loman figure. Not that Hoffman senior had been a total failure. Towards his last working years, he had succeeded in business beyond his earliest ambitions. But he had been fired before being allowed to retire gracefully. What was more, his relationship with his family had remained complicated. He never had reason to quote the speech of the son in the play: 'Pop, I'm nothing, Pop. I'm a dime a dozen and so are you.'

Dustin still remembered the first time he read *Salesman*. It was the very first play he had ever read; Ronald had given him an anthology in 1954 and *Salesman* was included. As he devoured its pages, he could sense that the whole family history was being exposed to public exhibition. 'I felt like my family's privacy had been invaded. I couldn't talk about it for weeks.'

Certainly, he had never been able to talk about his relationship with his father. Until now, that is, and the connection was so obviously in his mind that he couldn't hold it back entirely. But it was to speak in guarded terms, such as: 'We all love our fathers, but we had some hard times.' Or, 'My father was a successful travelling salesman, but I don't think he was successful in his own eyes. In our house, we lived in a state of great friction.'

As Jarvis Astaire had told me, there was no ease between them. That much in common with Willy Loman he and Harry still had. The death of Lillian had made the elder Hoffman even more isolated than before. A man who could say that he had neglected his family relationships trying to scrape together a living had to pay a price.

Dustin related Willy Loman to Harry Hoffman all the way through. He remembered that, to his father, neither he nor his brother Ron had done well – not in Depression terms, in which triumph meant going out with a suitcase and coming back with a full order book and a cheque from your employer. Actually, Dustin could understand that. 'The Depression,' he once said, meaning every syllable of his spoken thoughts, 'you never know when it's going to hit.' That would always be the Dustin Hoffman philosophy. Don't be too happy. Tomorrow, it might rain.

Arthur Miller was the first to encourage him to do the play. He knew of his feelings for it, had heard the record directed by Ulu Grosbard that had starred Lee J. Cobb and featured Dustin in the small role of Bernard, the friend of Willy Loman's son Biff.

Arthur Miller had conceived his Willy Loman being a little man, just like Hoffman. Or perhaps not quite like him. His original script had referred to him as 'a shrimp', and dialogue changes were made for Cobb, who was physically very much more powerful (and most agree equally so in performance).

Dustin decided not to try to put on weight, but to lose it. He was portraying a man in the last days of his life. He was mentally as well as bodily a wreck. 'Willy can't sleep, can't eat, he's wired.'

He could relate to the significance of Willy Loman failing to complete a sales trip for the first time in his life. 'That's like an actor not finishing a play,' he explained to writer Mel Gussow.

The idea came to fruition, however, in the country home Dustin and Lisa now owned at Roxbury, Connecticut near their neighbour, Arthur Miller. They sat and talked one day, idling the time away, discussing their various new work projects.

'You don't want to do *Salesman* do you?' Miller asked almost casually. It was like a small boy being asked if he wanted an ice cream or a little girl invited to go to the ballet. Yet, even so, Dustin wondered whether it was too soon. Was he ready for it yet? He and producer Robert Whitehead had talked about doing the play before *Tootsie* became a viable project, but neither of them had been ready for a commitment then.

Behind most of Dustin's doubts was the single thought of Lee J. Cobb – 'and,' as he put it, 'his sixteen-inch guns as Willy. God! How I think about what I saw on the stage! That has been the most intimidating factor for me as an actor. Cobb's scenes are there, playing in my mind.' They were stronger than memories of his own attempt to get a group to perform the play during his years struggling in summer-stock.

Cobb was a memory so brilliant, it was almost sacrilege even to attempt to equal it. 'He was like a rock by Rodin.' Another time, Dustin described seeing him in the part as like watching a boxing champion in the ring. 'No performance has ever affected me more.'

He had seen a National Theatre version in London, starring the British actor Warren Mitchell – best known in Britain for his amazingly successful part of Alf Garnett in the outrageous *Till Death Us Do Part* TV series, the forerunner of the American *All In The Family*. He had thought Mitchell splendid. Miller said that the most recent version he had seen was in Peking with a Chinese actor. He hoped Dustin would take the part. He would even add the old lines about Willy Loman being 'a shrimp'. Dustin didn't say whether he thought that was a compliment. Being asked to take the part, however, certainly was.

Without too much persuasion, Dustin accepted.

The writer saw it, though, mainly in artistic terms. 'You look at him at work and you say, "What a plucky little guy," ' noted the playwright. 'Which is exactly the way you should feel about Willy, too.'

What Dustin felt was that he was acting out the life of his father. But he also realized that he was almost worshipping at the shrine of Arthur Miller as well as that of Lee J. Cobb. He went hunting in the archives for Miller's original notes. He talked to the author about his experiences with Cobb – who was about to be fired because up to ten days before the opening he 'just sat there like a lump' only to sit up 'at the kitchen table and he *was* Willy Loman'. He heard how Elia Kazan had directed the original production.

Then, it went into production. The Broadhurst Theater had been selected for a Broadway run of about four months. There would be out-of-town try-outs in Chicago and Washington, D.C.

On reflection, once it got into production, *Tootsie* might have seemed a lot easier, although there were no rows reported with the play's director, the American-born Michael Rudman, who had also directed the Warren Mitchell version in London.

Rudman was Dustin's own choice. Since Hoffman was, with Arthur Miller and Roger L. Stevens (no longer shying away from a Hoffman production), a co-producer of the venture, his thoughts were avidly listened to and rejected at peril.

'I wanted to get on a wavelength with Arthur,' Dustin insisted. 'It's shorthand to put two people on stage and ask the author, "Is that the animal you mean?" You're working out – and you're getting free rehearsal time.' He knew he was beginning to crack the part when he found himself saying Willy Loman's lines in Miller's 'rhythms'.

Casting of the other roles was vital, and Dustin actively concerned himself with it. He wanted Gene Hackman to play Charley, the achieving neighbour that Willy secretly envied and admired, but he was not available. David Huddlestone was chosen – after Dustin kicked around the idea of not having an actor play the part at all, but a former basketball coach, Red Holzman.

He had a few other bizarre notions – like asking Robert de Niro to play his son Biff. De Niro wasn't over-impressed. 'You want me to be your son on stage?' Mel Gussow recalled him saying, and not filling in the details of what he did not say. When the two met – de Niro accepted Dustin's invitation to at least come and talk – it was obvious that the two men were simply comparing notes about each other. In the end, the part went to John Malkovich, although the production had to be delayed for four months until he had finished another project.

'Everyone told me not to do it,' Malkovich later recalled, 'because [Dustin] was such a horrible man, so dreadful to work with. I found that charming. It intrigued me. I never had the least trouble with him.' In the role of Willy's wife Linda, Kate Reid was chosen.

People wondered whether Dustin wasn't too young for the role, even though he did have his hair cut so that he was virtually bald on top. Loman was to appear with what was virtually a crewcut, grey going on white. So Dustin shaved off most of his own hair for the wig he would wear as Willy to fit better. But he *was* 46 and Lee J. Cobb in his celebrated Broadway version had been a mere 38. It was Miller who finally put his mind to rest on that matter. 'You won't have the physical strength for the role at 56,' he told him.

Even at 38, Cobb had found it too hard and after four months of over-working as Willy Loman and over-eating and over-smoking as Lee J. Cobb he had had to be replaced. He couldn't take it any more. With that thought in mind, Dustin embarked on the project as though he were remaking *Marathon Man*. He went jogging, but seriously and strenuously. During the day, he ate nothing more than a salad. 'The first thing I say when I look in the mirror in the morning,' he said, 'is, "Did I eat too much last night? Is it showing on my face? Have I been working out enough every day? Am I retarding the ageing process as much as possible?" '

Seemingly, every off-duty moment was spent chewing – not gum, as he had with Susan George, but inordinate amounts of garlic as if to exorcise a vampire or some angry spirit. He said it was simply he was convinced that by doing so he would avoid catching a cold.

Nevertheless, he knew that by the time he got to the theatre to play

Loman he had to feel as well as look 'fragile'. He also took an afternoon nap. It was like a boxer who always required a post-lunch sleep.

If nothing else, he would have felt fragile about the court case with First Artists. In the midst of his *Salesman* preparations, the settlement had finally been reached after all sorts of allegations going to and fro and Dustin complaining about the 'lies' his opponents told.

Dustin knew he had the advantage of having Harry Hoffman on whom to base his character.

But just as Lillian eventually became only *part* of the amalgam that formed Dorothy Michaels, so Harry was only a section of Willy Loman. He was the base, but into the salesman Dustin incorporated a lot of the Arthur Miller whom he knew, too – and a great deal of his own invention.

As a demonstration of how much he had got into the part, he refused to have his name on a brass plate outside his dressing room. Instead, the plate read: 'Dave Singleman'. Willy Loman refers in the play to Singleman as the one who died the death of a salesman.

Arthur Miller had no doubts at all that Dustin was right for the part when the play opened at the Broadhurst Theater on 29 March 1984. But he had never kidded himself it would be easy. 'Dustin Hoffman is full of his own contradictions,' he said without going into too much detail, as though listing the contradictions would only bring more. He remembered when Ulu Grosbard had commended him all those years before when he was assisting (he was virtually no more than the stage manager at first) in his production of *A View From The Bridge*. Miller said that he remembered that he looked 'as if he had barely gotten out of high school.'

There were no rows between author and actor. Dustin respected Miller from the top of his head to the soles of his shoes. He was more mature now than he had been in *Marathon Man* and he would not subject the writer to the kind of problems that he had presented to Laurence Olivier, one of the few people for whom he had had anything like the same amount of regard.

But it all got together. Thanks to Miller who, Dustin told *New Yorker* magazine, produced *Death of a Salesman* in a way not dissimilar to how Mozart whistled his symphonies before getting them down on paper, and thanks to Rudman and Dustin, too, it all finally got on the road.

The play had a mixed reception during the Chicago try-out. To the city's *Sun-Times* critic it was perhaps more convincing than it needed to be. 'Underneath the old crow, we have to have hints of the young bantam rooster,' wrote its critic. 'Before this show goes to Broadway I would suggest [throwing] out Stanislavski and go back to the streets.'

In the *Chicago Tribune*, Richard Christiansen said Dustin 'genuinely seems to have been an old-line salesman working the New England territory for the last thirty years.'

The audience wasn't so sure. They 'didn't seem knocked out', reported *USA Today*.

Dustin was plainly affected by it all. A reporter was heard to shout to him: 'I'll call you next week.' Dustin couldn't guarantee to be there. 'I may be in Forest Lawn,' he replied, referring to the best-known cemetery in Los Angeles. But the play sold out in Chicago, without the startling notices, and was an apparent triumph by the time it got to Washington, ready for the Broadway opening. But even though most of the problems had been ironed out, at every intermission there would be notes from Dustin passed to the other players on how he wanted things done differently next time. It was, someone noted, like watching the rushes of one of his films.

In Washington, things were very much better than on the first stage of the run. In America's capital city, there were no critics ready to go out on anyone's limb to say anything other than how successful it all was. The *Washington Post* described it as 'riveting'. Hoffman's performance was 'harrowing and affecting'.

Mell Gussow noted in *The New York Times* that 'this is a different, more centred Hoffman'. He added: 'From the moment that Hoffman came on stage carrying his heavy sample cases, there was no question [but] that he was an old Willy Loman worn down by life. By the time that he and Malkovich had their final showdown, the play had achieved cathartic heights.'

Dustin himself said that playing the part was his 'deepest wish coming true'. And he added: 'You hear God singing and it scares you.'

He comforted himself by knowing that he was playing a part to which the public who bought tickets could relate. When he wasn't on stage at the Broadhurst Theater, he had a chair in the wings. From there he could look at the audience. Always there was someone sleeping. He wasn't offended by that. He was pleased to see it. That sleeping man thought that Willy was himself. There was no reason not to say 'Goodnight' and nod off.

The way the play was received, both by public and by critics, convinced all the people involved at the top – Miller and Dustin, in particular – that it ought to be seen by more people. A longer stage run didn't make a great deal of sense; nobody could afford to tie up Dustin Hoffman in a play for years until all the potential customers were exhausted, and by that time Dustin himself would have been exhausted, too. Neither could he be expected to take the play on the road, to all the people who might be able to afford the price of a theatre ticket but most certainly could not stretch to fares to New York.

Naturally, there was talk of a movie. But there had been one in 1951 starring Fredric March and although this totally removed the Jewish element of an essentially Jewish story, it was a brilliant success. Stanley Kramer, the director, had excelled himself.

Lee J. Cobb had also done a version, which Arthur Miller dismissed as 'an abbreviated television thing', which 'chopped off all the climaxes almost like a lawn mower.' There was now going to be a television version, but a very different kind of production on a very different kind of television. For one thing, it would cost $3.5 million.

What was now proposed was a TV special, virtually filming the play, except that the actors who had got used to projecting voices had to modulate and adapt them for the intimacy of a televised play.

CBS agreed to put up the money, and they were wise to do so – particularly with both Dustin and Arthur Miller acting as executive producers.

Nothing was cut. One line was added. The set was in an *idea* of a Brooklyn house, not a real one.

Dustin made his own stipulations; that he should be left 'alone', to 'create'. He didn't want to get involved in meetings with management. Unless he could help it, he didn't want to be introduced to any of the executives.

The film would eventually be released to play in movie theatres, too. Before then, however, Dustin could reflect that even if it came at the bottom of the ratings, 20 million people would still have seen it.

Of course, it couldn't be merely a reprise of the theatre version. It was redesigned by Tony Walton and a new director was brought in to convert the wide spaces of the stage to the much smaller confines of the small screen. Volker Schlondorff succeeded well enough with the three-hour production.

Certainly, well enough for Arthur Miller and Dustin Hoffman. 'I've never been happier about something of mine in my life,' said the play-wright. 'Me neither,' said Dustin.

They were not alone.

Writing in *Vanity Fair* magazine, Stephen Schiff commented: 'It's not just another televised play; it's a new work, more refined than the Broadway show and more touching. One feels Hoffman's stubborn drive behind it; it has his jitters, his whine, his awkward fervency. He has done with this straw-hat-trail war-horse what he has wanted to do with every vehicle he's ever worked in; he has made it his own.'

It was the definitive *Salesman*. 'Not *a* Willy Loman, but *the* Willy Loman.'

The performance hadn't merely been toned down, wrote Schiff, it had been reconceived. 'This new Willy groans his lines, pumping them out from a well of fatigue.'

What he really pumped them from was much more simple – his heart. As Dustin said, '*Death of A Salesman* is the reason I've been an actor.'

16

Dustin was now experiencing a syndrome familiar to small boys who have just received a good report from school: the problem of trying to follow it next time.

As usual, there were the fears that he couldn't possibly do it, followed by the self-confidence that indicated that, well, of course, he could. The trouble was proving it.

He put it well enough in January 1986, while the applause for the TV *Salesman* was still ringing in his ears. What he worried about was 'prolonged happiness'. Just how long could it go on? Experience had told him to be suspicious of it. 'As soon as things are really good, I always have a feeling the rug is about to be pulled out from under me. On a beautiful day in California, there's always a thin layer of smog. With me, there's always a thin layer of fear.'

Life was not just precious, it was temporary. Not long before, he had toyed with playing Faust. If the devil had come to him then with the offer of the greatest part in the greatest play ever written – but doubtless not written yet, because by now every existing role was virtually his for the asking – in exchange for the rest of his life, he would have signed the contract instantly. Now, early in 1986, he would have taken a bit longer to get out his pen.

There were, he would say, demons inside of him. Would he, for instance, ever rid himself of the one that haunted him every time he kissed his children as he left the house in the morning? On each occasion, he pondered inwardly the one thought: would he ever see them again? Perhaps the biggest demon of all in his life, his relationship with his father, had been tamed considerably. The older Hoffman had married again, this time one of Lillian's nurses, and the relationship seemed not just to work but to have transferred itself to Dustin. Father and son were getting on better than they had for years.

People looked at fabulously wealthy people like Dustin, saw his relationship with Lisa, heard how thrilled he was when she became pregnant again and gave birth to a third child and second son, Max, late in 1985, and imagined everything was perfect. When they read that he was asking up to $6 million for a film role, they just could not imagine such success, or contemplate such earnings.

It was essential for him to talk in figures like that, even though he certainly didn't need the cash. Each nought on a cheque represented status. To take fewer noughts would be to recognize a drop in that status. No, he would say, he wasn't interested in money for money's sake, although he had houses and cars on both sides of the Atlantic. There was his home at Broad Beach, close to the Pacific Coast Highway in Malibu, a 92 acre estate at Roxbury, Connecticut, and another at East 65th Street in the smartest part of Manhattan and he had just paid £1 million for a house in Kensington, London. (He had rented a luxury New York penthouse close to the Dakota Building where John Lennon was shot, and then complained that the heating and hot water were inadequate for the $7,000 a month he was paying.)

He had four cars in England alone, including a £40,000 Rolls-Royce and a Mercedes stretch limousine. He said he chose which to use according to his mood.

But money was not just for the keeping. For instance, he had given away most of the $4 million he had made from *Tootsie* to a camp in California for child cancer sufferers, a place where those children could enjoy themselves without being laughed at for their disabilities. The idea had come to him when he heard about Lisa's cousin, who had suffered from leukaemia for most of her life.

As usual, there was a whole stack of projects awaiting his attention. And as usual there was a whole stack of rumours about other stacks of projects that he was definitely going to do, like making a filmed biography (biopic, in the vernacular) of President Harry S. Truman. A lot of people blamed Truman for the ills of the world, since he was the man who gave the OK to the dropping of the atom bombs. But Dustin had much more of a villain in mind: he still wanted to play Hitler, he told a largely Jewish audience of singles at New York's Young Man's Hebrew Association. 'It's like a *shtetl* here,' he said introducing the crowd to whom he was lecturing to, first, his doctor and then, his brother the economist.

Sometimes, things went further than mere rumours. In the spring of 1986, Cannon Films – run by Israeli cousins Menachem Golan and Yoram Globus, who were being spoken of as the new Hollywood moguls

– published advertisements bearing Dustin's photograph and declaring that he was going to star in their next movie, *La Brava*, about a retired Secret Service agent involved in blackmail.

The idea had originally been taken up by Universal, only to be cancelled by them. They became interested again when Dustin expressed enthusiasm, but they once more cooled off at the thought of the price he was demanding: $6.5 million and 22 per cent of the gross box-office take. Other studios showed a certain enthusiasm too, until they also heard Dustin's financial demands. The Cannon group, anxious to rid themselves of their reputation for producing cheap, sleazy pictures – like a dreadful version of Zola's *Nana* – took it up with wild abandon. 'For the first time,' said Golan, 'Cannon is over-excited.'

It had reason to be. And to regret that over-excitement.

Dustin maintained that he had a clause in his contract with the producers guaranteeing him the right to approve all advertising. But when thumbing through his copy of *Variety* and then the *Hollywood Reporter* he saw full-page colour advertisements that he knew he had most definitely *not* approved. If Golan and Globus could do that, maintained his lawyers, what was in store further down the road? So Dustin cancelled his contract. Yoram Globus insisted that 'there is no problem whatsoever', and that the picture would be made with the 'deal still in place.' He added that 'there might be discussions about a few points.' The discussions, such as they were, concluded that *La Brava* was not going to be made, at least with Dustin Hoffman in the lead.

A few months earlier, Dustin had been seen in the South of France, tagging on to spectators watching the Tour de France, the cycle race which had previously given him just about the same sort of enthusiasm as when offered a bowl of cold rice pudding. But there was an idea afoot that had been at the back of his mind on and off for five years; a film based on the book *The Yellow Jersey*, about a 38-year-old racing cyclist at the end of his career. Dustin was talking about getting a cycling coach to help him, should he play the lead. With him were two other men, each anxious to show how seriously they were taking the project. Colin Welland, the English actor-writer who had written the Oscar-winning *Chariots of Fire* was busy working on a script and Michael Cimmino, who had directed the biggest flop of all time, *Heaven's Gate*, was making the preliminary inspections before starting work as director of this picture, too. But it was never to materialize.

Those who doubted whether playing a cyclist made sense for Dustin, probably thought that the part of a lawyer was more up his street. That was why he optioned movie rights on the successful novel by Stephen Greenleaf, *The Ditto Bit*. That wasn't all. He did the same with the novel by former prisoner Edward Bunker, *Animal Factory*. Neither of those came to anything. The interest flattered the authors, but took their work off the market for the length of time his options lasted. Dustin meanwhile went on to other things.

It was announced he was going to update – and Americanize – the Alec Guinness hit of nearly forty years earlier, *Kind Hearts and Coronets* in which he would play the whole series of parts himself. But that also has come to nought.

Nevertheless, the name Dustin Hoffman still made headlines, even when he had only the vaguest associations with the story in question. In early 1986, a film producer was arrested on charges of molesting runaway boys. Dustin visited him in jail – and it was his name in the papers. A month later, a woman schoolteacher was found dead in a hot tub on Dustin's Roxbury estate. Dustin was not in residence and the woman was a friend of the estate caretaker, but it was Hoffman upon whom the reports concentrated.

He would undoubtedly have preferred to have been featured in the media solely for his work, particularly for that which did materialize, like a four-part TV series made for the prestigious Channel 13, called *Strokes of Genius*, in which Dustin told the stories of leading abstract painters, like Jackson Pollock, Willem de Kooning and Franz Kline and the sculptor David Smith. It was the first time he had played himself, and he found difficulty reading from the auto-cue, an aid which he didn't usually use. 'How *does* Marlon Brando manage?' he asked somewhat unkindly.

People were soon to ask how Dustin Hoffman managed, for he was embarking on a new film, to be called *Ishtar*, which some saw as a remake of the Bing Crosby-Bob Hope opus *The Road To Morocco*. The problem with this picture turned out to be not so much that it was a bad film or a hard journey along that road, but that this stretch was paved with dollar bills – mostly going out, not coming in. Before long, it achieved the dubious reputation of being, *Heaven's Gate* apart, practically the most expensive movie ever made – at a cost of close to $40 million. It was a figure practically impossible to recoup. Add to that the fact few critics were greatly enthusiastic and that consequently it came and went from cinema circuits with as much fluidity as the sand in the desert in the film, and it is hardly surprising that very few people remain with much enthusiasm for it.

The best that can be said for the picture is that Dustin seemed to be having fun. So did his co-star, Warren Beatty. In fact, they looked so good together that there was talk, the almost inevitable talk, of a regular partnership. For good or ill – and on balance and even without much equilibrium, it must be mainly for good – it hasn't happened.

The strange thing is that, despite Dustin's reputation for seeking perfection, he and Beatty had created nothing less than a turkey.

To be sure, there seemed to be a lot going for it. There were a number of laughs and quite a bit of music, some of it sung by Dustin, some of it allegedly written by Dustin, too, and a script by Elaine May, who had contributed so much to *Tootsie*, as well as scoring notable successes of her own with such work as *A New Leaf* and *The Heartbreak Kid*.

In *Ishtar*, Beatty and Hoffman played a couple of songwriters, Rogers and Clarke by name, who should not in any way be confused with Rodgers and Hammerstein or Rodgers and Hart.

Maybe it's a little unkind to the duo who did so much for Dustin's first film, but the pair who are advised to try their cabaret act out of town – and go to Ishtar, a mythical land near Morocco, to do so – seem more based on Simon and Garfunkel than anyone else. It's a film that invokes the name Gaddafi at one stage, and any picture that condemns the Libyan dictator can't be all wrong. Except that Rogers and Clark are never sure whether Gaddafi is a man or a place.

What went wrong with *Ishtar*? Perhaps it was simply that Dustin had been pushing his luck and had allowed that incredible instinct of his to slip. Maybe, more, that he had reached a stage that no one wishing to be thought of as simply an actor, rather than as a star, should approach without extreme caution. Suddenly, it was as if he were taking a holiday from the triumphs everyone else seemed to take for granted. It was Harry Warner, the senior Warner Brother, who had first directed people in search of a message to go to Western Union. Dustin had always had a message of his own and for the first time in years had forgotten to listen to it. This was all beneath him.

Dustin is an actor who, for all his research and the pain that it causes, works by instinct and then brings his Method into play. This time Method became madness. The instinct let him down. Somehow, he just thought it would work and it didn't. 'After I read the script, Warren and I talked on the phone and thrashed everything out,' he was to say. 'We found a commonality of taste and we've just gone on from there. Mind you, we don't hang out. I'm married with kids. He's not. I go to bed early, he doesn't.'

Was it really so exciting that Dustin should play a man who has as many women swarming around him as Beatty had flies? It was usually the other way round, Warren was the stud, Dustin the *nebbech*. But Elaine May thought the role change would have people howling. The titters came from the few people who understood the in-joke.

It may also have been funny to realize that a not inconsiderable part of the budget went on looking for a blind camel. The prop men on *Ishtar* saw a camel, but in the fond belief that one should never go for the first thing on offer, decided to look for another one. Before long, they decided that first was best. They approached its owner again. 'Sorry,' said the man, 'we've just eaten it.' Dustin had other problems of his own with camels. As he explained: 'When a camel cushes [gets up or sits down] it moves forward suddenly and then back. If you're not wearing a camel-adapted athletic supporter, your gonads go forward and then tuck under. I found this extremely painful, but Warren did not. He has famous gonads and people have been throwing darts at them for years.'

They each admired the other's ability – tenacity and ferocity were words bandied about quite considerably.

By the time the film was all wrapped up, Dustin quipped that he felt as though he were at the Last Supper. He should have known better than to start the meal in the first place, especially to get involved in a story that turns Beatty and him into fodder for a gang of spies, an idea that really went out at about the time that Hope and Crosby were packing their bags for the last time. Both of the men falling in love with the same beautiful girl – Isabelle Adjani, a French actress currently having an affair with Beatty – was calculated only to make audiences yearn for Dorothy Lamour, *almost* dressed in a sarong and materializing from a mirage.

As far as Dustin's career was concerned, it would be charitable to think of *Ishtar* itself as being a mirage. But, unfortunately, it wasn't. Columbia lost a good slice of the $40 million it invested in the film, and Dustin, Warren Beatty and Elaine May and the others drawing mega-salaries – Dustin down to the mere $3.5 million that Warren Beatty also picked up; Elaine May getting almost $1 million for writing and directing the opus – laughed all the way to the bank.

First indications that things were going wrong came when Columbia bosses saw a credit for Pepsi-Cola at the end of the picture. The firm is owned by *Coca*-Cola. Dustin explained that having Coke in the film would look as if they were 'kissing ass'.

No one was doing that about the film. The usual flattery enjoyed by big stars was decidedly absent.

Dustin told *People* magazine: 'Warren doesn't want me to talk about money, but, man, there's just been too much death-wishing about this picture. My unconscious can't take it. I mean, don't they realize that you can't make a movie with two big stars for under $35 million today? And that's without Morocco.'

It didn't even begin to get its money back in the United States. In Britain, it opened in London and lasted there only a matter of days before being sent round the provinces, where it came and went like . . . a mirage.

Newsweek magazine had the temerity to ask: 'Does the $40 million really show in *Ishtar*? You'd have to say No.'

Richard Schickel in *Time* was a lot kinder. He almost waxed lyrical about it. '[Elaine] May, whose painstaking ways and modest grosses do not usually commend her to the studios, gets to work in something near her best vein. Hoffman has a role nicely suited to the comic whine of his neuroses. Beatty, 50, has one in which his distracted air, and his lack of traditional star presence, can be made to look like modesty . . . The rest of us can enjoy a movie that is reasonably genial and diverting. At a cost of $10 million or $15 million, it might have made the studio happy. But even the misery of its unrecoupable costs is cushioned: the management that initiated the project has been replaced and the new team can cheerfully disown it.'

Nobody called the picture, 'Hoffman's Gate', but if they had, most would have tried to avoid going through it again.

For the first time in years, Dustin was not over-happy with something he had done. He tried his family for consolation and usually he got it, like narrating a performance (along with Ossie Davis) of *Peter and the Wolf* at New York's Central Park which the Hoffman clan thoroughly enjoyed. Or simply just meeting his children from school. He called for Becky – as Rebecca was inevitably to be known – at her school one day. 'Look,' she said, waving a picture, 'I made this for you – and your friend, Mommy.'

Lisa *was* Dustin's friend and he needed her. Now, though, he was going to take a new look at that career of his.

17

If *Ishtar* was going to be seen as a temporary aberration, something had to be done and done quickly. It was. Dustin made *Rain Man*. Suddenly, as though caught in a rainstorm, the chattering finished. The death-wishing was over. For the first time in his life, Dustin Hoffman was being spoken of as the world's greatest actor.

It had been years since anyone in Hollywood had earned that sort of plaudit, yet now that was precisely what was being said about him in *Rain Man*, the picture which in March 1989 earned Dustin Hoffman his second Oscar, a statuette for which nobody made excuses. No one suggested that it was for past services. Not a word was mentioned about its really being for *Ishtar*. Heaven forbid. Had he had qualms about that picture – and loyally, he would never admit that he had – he deserved the pride that the story of the autistic patient with the trapped brilliant mind earned him. It was nothing less than a triumph.

Should there be any justification in the cliché that huge people fail only hugely, then there must be equal credit paid when the reverse is the case.

Rain Man turned out to be the picture that said the five-foot-six-inch tall Dustin Hoffman was really a giant who happened to look small. He also turned what might have started out as a lesser part into a *tour de force*.

In a way, this was history revisited. He was with another actor throughout the picture, but not on the equal terms he had been with Warren Beatty. It was almost a reprise of Ratso in *Midnight Cowboy* or of Dega in *Papillon*. Once more, Dustin Hoffman was the *nebbech*, a role all knew he could play better than anyone else. Once more, he was playing second fiddle to another actor – and once more he had left the other one far behind by the time the final credits started to roll. It was as though Dustin was at his very best when he had someone else acting as a pace-maker. He was encouraged by the sight of seeing another

performer in front and he was pushed on by the notion of being able
to breathe down that man's neck and then see him puffing behind.

It would not be true to say that that was always his intention.
Uniquely, he had never been worried too much about billing; never
quibbled about anyone else getting the best lines. Just so long as he can
do what he likes with the ones he *has* been given, which is usually like
giving an arsonist a can of petrol.

Rain Man is the story of two brothers, one avaricious but normal,
the other locked away in his mind every bit as much as he is locked
away in an institution with others like himself – autistic men and women
need their own surroundings, insist on a consistency of routine which
demands a certain chair to sit on at a certain time; the same television
programme on the same evening; five, not four, not six pieces of cut-
up fish for supper on Wednesdays.

Originally, it was thought that Dustin would be good as the brother
who is mentally normal – normal, that is, if one can forgive his greed,
his determination to wrest the fortune left by their recently deceased
father from the clutches of his abnormal sibling – only to find that he
becomes attached to and protective of the weaker one.

Dustin said that, on the contrary, he wanted to do what he was good
at doing best: playing the character, the *nebbech*. But he didn't come
into the action until fifteen minutes had gone by. Since that had not
bothered him with *Midnight Cowboy*, why should it worry him now?
Besides, the other brother was being played by Tom Cruise – whom he
described, over-generously, as 'the top star of the day'. Wasn't it right
that he had a couple of reels for himself?

Dustin had not known much about Cruise. But his daughter Jenna
had. She told him about the handsome man she liked so much and with
whom she so badly wanted her father to work. There was really little
more persuasion needed.

Actually, matters were somewhat less simplistic: Dustin and Cruise
were with the same agents, who decided that there was ample reason
for a good marriage within the family.

It really all began with a meeting that the writer Barry Morrow had
had with an autistic man named Kim. Kim was locked in his own mind,
while able to do mental arithmetic with the speed of a fork of lightning
striking a tree.

He wrote his story *Rain Man* and offered it to a production company,
who presented it to United Artists. Early in 1987, the first draft was

given to Dustin, via the president of the Creative Artists agency, Michael Ovitz.

Ovitz was the one who thought of Dustin for the part of Charlie, the brother who will do anything for an easy buck, including kidnapping his elder brother. It was, after all, the big part; the star role.

Dustin was captivated – but wanted to play Raymond, the man whose little brother when a child could make nothing more of his name than 'Rain Man'.

Once determined to play Raymond, an actor had to be found to play Charlie. And that was why Cruise, aged only 26, was chosen. For once, the prospect of two middle-aged men on screen simultaneously was not considered good box office. With the experience of *Ishtar* behind him, who was Dustin to argue? Ovitz also represented Cruise, who had become an idol of young girls of Jenna's age, but girls who spent most of their money on pop records, yet had spared some of it to see films of his like *Top Gun* and *Cocktail*.

Dustin said he was pleased to work with Cruise. Like himself, Tom liked to rehearse and he 'made me realize how time was passing by.'

It was a picture that would either finally establish Hoffman as that greatest actor in the world or place him firmly on the escalator marked 'Down'. This was a time for actors to start seeing their lives flash before them. All Dustin could see were the memories of the mental hospital where he had worked during the time he was praying for June and summer-stock to come round again. He would go out for lunch and find himself mimicking those patients of thirty years before. To his fellow-lunchers, either Dustin Hoffman had himself gone mad or was becoming remarkably insensitive to the problems of others. On the contrary, Dustin Hoffman was beginning his research.

Dustin met Kim, spent weeks with him and watched other autistic patients in a home that specialized in looking after people with the disability. He studied fifty of them, although 'studied' is a cold, clinical term that does not do justice to the kind, unpatronizing way in which he made them feel they were his friends. Getting that far was quite an achievement in itself.

His enthusiasm for the project had been fired actually before he saw Morrow's first draft. There had been a film on television about sufferers and he was amazed at the story of a girl who had never been taught to play the piano, but who had sat down at a keyboard for the first time and produced the most beautiful music.

He sat and talked with the families of autistic people, like the mother of 28-year-old Joe Sullivan, who always ate cheese puffs with toothpicks. Raymond in the film was to eat cheese puffs with toothpicks. Joe Sullivan kept writing notes; totally unimportant details were painfully recorded on pieces of paper. Raymond did that, too. Dustin imperson- ated Joe in front of the mother. She wasn't hurt by it. To her, it was a contribution towards getting people to understand what Joe was all about.

He noticed how autistic people talked, how they concentrated on issues that became magnified into matters of the utmost importance, how nothing would sway them from the item under consideration. He watched their facial movements, how they kept their heads down as though afraid to face a world that they didn't understand and which didn't really understand them. He noted the stilted, monosyllabic pat- terns of speech.

He studied the reasons behind autism. He asked doctors what it was, how it was caused. No one really knew – although the prevalent theory was that they lacked a part of the brain that makes people care for the welfare of others. But despite what the doctors said, it was fairly obvious that there was *no* reason; certainly no really satisfactory explanation.

He said that he wanted to ask, 'Where are they?' It was, he said, like a man coming home to his wife, his mind elsewhere. She talks. He stands there, but doesn't hear a word. 'Where were you? You can repeat what they said, word for word, but you really weren't there.'

That was why he and Cruise never face each other. Dustin told him at the very beginning that there would be no eye contact between them. There were the problems that had to be faced on most Hoffman films. Morrow's concept of the picture was different from Dustin's. He didn't like the idea of Tom Cruise playing Charlie because he thought it was improbable that a man so much younger than Raymond could realisti- cally be his brother.

In the end, Ron Bass was brought in to write the final script, although Morrow's contribution was always recognized. But the film, as it turned out, was all due to Dustin.

Morrow had made the man like, as Bass put it, 'a lovable sweet, a Cabbage Patch doll. Dustin wanted to make Raymond autistic, totally withdrawn, unable to show or receive human affection. Now he's iras- cible, quirky, someone you have to reach out to. Suddenly you have two guys who will never get together. It's tougher, more dramatic.'

Marty Brest was the first director employed on the film. He left because of Dustin's intensity. 'He's like a microsurgeon,' he said, meaning that he didn't like the way his star was trying to paint the picture. *He* thought that Raymond should be allowed to improve mentally as the picture moved on, to work towards a happy ending. Dustin was adamant that the doctors to whom he had spoken had advised that, unfortunate as it may seem to the audiences, Raymond would not advance out of his shell. 'I think the worst thing that can happen is that the movie succeeds on a fraudulent level,' Dustin maintained, and Brest was out. Dustin's way was better, he believed, than making the film succeed simply by using the good box-office approach that Brest had wanted. That was why his research was as important for *Rain Man* as for almost anything he had ever done before. Perhaps much more so. It was not a fun picture. This time, he wouldn't get the girl riding on a camel out of a sand dune.

He still would never admit to actually enjoying film-making. As he once said, 'It's great for the director because he's always cooking, but for an actor there's so much time to sit around.' But that was unfair on himself. Even when he sat, he seemed to be studying. Sometimes, the research was nothing less than painful. He needed to walk over the locations, to see if they were right. One of them was an inter-state highway, closed for shooting one of the scenes in the middle of the night. A serious road accident was being simulated and glass had been liberally distributed over the surface. Dustin, as usual, had to take time out to tell a joke. Because it was a Hoffman joke, it had to be with actions. In the course of those actions, he tumbled over, broke his fall with his hand – and landed in a mass of glass. Weeks later, the hand was still bandaged (when not filming) while the glass worked its way out.

Naturally, the real drama in the picture came from the very brilliance of Raymond. Dustin knew that all autistics weren't also *savants*, but he also wanted to get over the message that the world did have clever people who are trapped in this way, who never surface, are never appreciated.

But he was worried about one thing – a lack of humour. So Dustin improvised. In one scene in a telephone box, quite unexpectedly, Dustin broke wind. 'I like to fart when I'm among my men friends,' he said. This one was 'a good one, a cracker'. Tom asked him – again unscripted – 'Did you fart?' It was retained in the picture.

Dustin was not any easier on this film than he had been in any of his others. Even when he was not improvizing farts, he wanted scenes done his way. Barry Levinson, who had taken over as director, allowed him most of them.

In the end, this tougher, more dramatic film became the top box-office draw of the winter of 1988–9. It cost $250,000 less than the $24 million which had been budgeted, even taking into account Dustin's own fee of $5 million.

Dustin tried not to paint the lily too much. The film, he said, was simply about two guys in a car.

The reviews were ecstatic. But the one he treasured most was a letter from a mother who said that she took her autistic son to see the picture. As she was leaving the theatre, the boy turned to her and said, 'I love you, Mummy'. She wrote to say 'thank you' to Dustin.

She was not alone. There was the English autistic teenager who was much like Raymond, but who drew the most accurate and brilliantly beautiful architectural drawings.

Dustin went along to see 15-year-old Stephen Wiltshire and was overcome by the artistic talent – to say nothing of accuracy – of the youngster who had been mute until he was seven years old and who introduced himself at their meeting, organized by the *Mail on Sunday* newspaper's magazine *You*, by saying, 'My name's Stephen Wiltshire. I am aged 15 and was born in 1974.'

'I bet you don't know when *I* was born?' said Dustin.

'Fifties? Forties?' asked Stephen. 'Worse than that,' said Dustin. 'The Thirties.' And he told him that he himself couldn't draw anything. Stephen said that he knew that Dustin had won an Oscar for *Rain Man*.

It made the actor all the more grateful, not just for the success of his career, but for his family – the ever-growing Hoffman family. There was now a fourth child for Lisa and him, their second girl together and his fourth daughter, Alexandra. He was planning to send their two elder children to a small private school in London during the autumn of 1989.

For once, it was possible to believe that the movie didn't always come first in his life.

18

Rain Man confirmed it: Dustin Hoffman, close to 52 years old, was at the peak of a remarkable career. The man who had almost always had good reviews, but who had done a few regrettable things in his time had surmounted them all. There wasn't an actor in greater demand, a star with a bigger following. When more than one newspaper on each side of the Atlantic began talking about his being the world's greatest actor, it was time to take stock and join in the cheering.

There was always a risk, of course, that people would cheer him because that was the thing to do. In a crowded room he could recite verbatim the world-famous broadcast recording the crash of the Hindenburg airship or imitate Winston Churchill. He'd get a standing ovation at a private party for those. He enjoyed most of all the cheers for his film. He'd sneak in the back of theatres that were playing the picture and just wait for the audience's reactions.

Not that there weren't the expected snipes. On an American TV programme, Dustin talked about the need to understand a part, to live it and, inevitably, to research it. Bette Davis was on the same show. She looked at him with one of those glances that turned Jack Warner and his brothers into stone. 'Why,' she asked, 'don't you just act?' Laurence Olivier was supposed to have asked the same question, adding his usual 'Dear boy' for good measure.

He had to learn to take the snipes. He liked to recall the story of the sculptor Jacques Lipchitz, slaughtered by critics who said that it looked as if he just threw clay on to the ground. He thought that was an interesting idea and did just that – developing beautiful abstract patterns in the process. As Dustin said: 'You use it against them. That's the only way you can survive.' Others would have liked him not to survive at all.

But that certainly wasn't the way most people thought about him. After Rain Man and the 1989 Oscar ceremony?

He was not just on top, but was being fêted at the top. In England, he met the Duchess of York, 'Fergie' to the Press and public. He spent hours practising his bow as though it were part of another film role. He was told to call her Ma'am. He said he hoped he would say anything but 'Hi, Fergie'. But they chatted and she told him she was impressed by his performance – and that of Cruise. 'You look like brothers,' she told him. 'I'm convinced of it.'

Most other people were convinced by Dustin Hoffman. Now, though, a new public would see him in a totally new role. For the first time in his life, Dustin Hoffman was going into Shakespeare. Sir Peter Hall, formerly head of Britain's National Theatre, had formed his own company and was about to launch a new production. It was *The Merchant of Venice* and Dustin Hoffman was playing Shylock.

That, too, was the result of the usual teething troubles, although compared with some of the things that Dustin had experienced, it was like lying in a punt gliding down the River Isis on a summer's afternoon in Oxford.

Oxford wasn't going to be on the Hoffman agenda. But Bath was. The play was to have its opening at the Roman spa town. Yet it had all started a year earlier. And in Los Angeles.

Dustin had heard about Hall's new company and rang to ask if there would be a part for him. It was unexplored territory that he now wanted to venture into.

'He actually said that he wanted to play Hamlet,' Sir Peter recalled for me.

'Years ago, I think he conceived the idea of playing Hamlet and who shall blame him? It is the greatest test, the greatest part for an actor. For one reason or another he never did it.'

But in the summer of 1988, he asked Hall: 'Do you think I can play Hamlet?'

The British producer-director was adamant. 'I said, no, he couldn't. He asked me why and I told him, "Because you're too old", which I think he is. Also, I think it's madness to take on Hamlet as your first Shakespeare assignment.'

He also told him to avoid the 'biggies' at that stage. No Lear or Richard III until he had done something small but 'showy'.

So Hall suggested Shylock. Dustin knew the play, said Hall, 'although I don't know how well'. In fact, Dustin himself was quoted as saying: 'Because of my ignorance of Shakespeare, I didn't know until I read it that the play's a time bomb, very controversial.'

What he discovered, of course, was that it was probably the most controversial of all Shakespeare's plays, in some ways the most controversial play in the English language. All over America, schools have banned it from their curriculum. In some parts of the United States, public performances are barred. In Britain, too, every time a production of the play is staged, there is a public outcry.

There are two schools of thought about it. One – and that is the reason for its numerous bans – is that it is anti-Semitic. The other – and this is the interpretation of Sir Peter Hall – is that it is a play about anti-Semites; an indictment against their prejudices and a fair reflection of Shakespeare's (and Shylock's) times. That was how Hall was going to stage it. He would ridicule the Christians and their lack of Christian charity the way he believed Shakespeare had done.

Dustin was convinced. 'He is, after all,' Sir Peter told me, 'Jewish to the roots of his being, even if he didn't come from a religious family. It was very much a Jewish family. Ask me to define Jewishness and I'd find it difficult, but I know it when I see it, and I respect it.'

In fact, Hall said that it would be impossible today to cast anyone but a Jew as Shylock, just as only a black could play Othello.

There was another reason why he thought Dustin would be tempted. It was a small part, just five scenes, Dustin was used to smaller roles than usually went to stars, wasn't he? 'But,' Hall told me, 'it's also a play-stealing part; a very great part. Portia runs the play, puts in all the energy, but Shylock attracts all the attention.

'I also thought that his mixture of comedy and pathos which shows through in all his acting was uniquely suited for this part.'

So a deal was struck, for £2,000 a week, which to Dustin Hoffman is barely enough to put coins in the coffee machine. But for once, money – or the prestige it represented – didn't matter. Neither did billing. His name wouldn't be featured in lights. On the posters proclaiming it to be a Peter Hall Company production it would appear before that of Geraldine James, who played Portia, but after that of John Cater who played the tiny part of Old Gobbo. All the billing was in alphabetical order.

That would be how it would happen in Bath, prior to the London opening at the Phoenix Theatre. Except that it didn't go to Bath before opening in London. Weeks before it was due to play there, Dustin heard that his father had had a stroke and was in a coma. Dustin considered his duty was to be with Harry and not his audience. It looked as if his father might die and if he did, he wanted it to be an honourable death with his family around him – a death of a salesman.

Harry got a little better; in fact, Dustin, when he accepted his Oscar for *Rain Man*, referred to the old man watching the show on a rented television in the hospital. His condition in May 1989 was not bad enough to warrant postponing the opening in the West End later that month. The play would go to Bath after the London run.

It was a reasonably sympathetic production, sympathetic enough for it to be seriously considered for a tour in Israel.

Shylock spoke like a Jew, but not like an exaggerated Jew. He sounded neither as though he manned a pushcart on Delancey Street nor a barrow in Petticoat Lane. His voice was slightly American, but only in the sense that it wasn't an English accent he had. He practised being Shylock, walking through Kensington Gardens, saying the lines to himself.

Dustin under-played the part. He tried gentle persuasion – sitting on a bench, legs apart under his 'Jewish gaberdine', as he tried to reason, 'Prick us, do we not bleed? Tickle us, do we not laugh?' Hall had Antonio literally spit into his face. Shylock barely turned a hair in the beard he had grown for the occasion (he also wore a black yamulka skullcap and sidecurls; the latter were probably an anachronism and certainly not the usual style of a Jew from Venice). In the courtroom, he sharpens his knife on the sole of his shoe, ready to exact his pound of flesh, a piece of business Peter Hall inserted and which had not been used for about a century.

In at least one preview performance, Dustin fluffed a couple of lines. But he seemed comfortable enough with the iambic pentameter, the meaning of which he said he didn't even know before starting work on Shylock. Peter Hall sent him a tape, indicating pauses where the breathing should come.

'But he had no trouble with it,' said Hall. 'He's very musical. He has a very good voice. He got the rhythms just right.'

Sir Peter was happy with Dustin, who put in his own ideas, as he always did. 'I can't see why an actor shouldn't put his own interpretation into a part,' the director told me. 'After all, he's acting it. He's using himself as the raw material. The director's job is to edit that and try to make it right for the play; balance the play and try to help the actor to give it things that perhaps he didn't know he had. I had no disagreement with him at all.'

So what did he put into it? 'Absolute obsessional energy,' Hall replied.

Others had been known to say as much before. 'Concentration, hard work – an ability to try twenty things while most actors are trying to think of one. He's terribly quick, terribly brilliant, not easily satisfied. Most of all in rehearsal, he takes the most enormous risks – which I've always found great actors do. They dare to be very bad in order to try to find something.'

He tried 'umpteen different ways' of playing the big speeches.

The execution of the play changed night after night; 'the balance of each scene against other scenes was assessed. The interpretation did not change.'

It could all turn, Hall told me, into a classic Shylock. 'If Dustin Hoffman was just an actor, I've no doubt it'd become a masterpiece. Because he's Dustin Hoffman, it might not.'

The critics were almost convinced. Michael Billington, writing in the *Guardian*, noted: 'Mr Hoffman's humorous approach pays handsome dividends – not least in his little smile of triumph to the Duke early in the trial scene – it also means a loss of the tragic dimension. What goes missing is what Hazlitt, writing of Kean, called "the hard, impenetrable, dark groundwork of the character of Shylock." ' And Irving Wardle in *The Times* took up the same theme: 'Hoffman's is much the most genial Shylock that I have seen. He may vow implacable enmity to Antonio in a first act aside, but you would never guess it from his welcoming smiles and open embraces . . . he makes himself agreeable even to his fleeing servant Lancelot . . . What does not come off are the directly emotional climaxes which strain his voice to the limit and substitute rhetoric . . . for his particular and priceless capacity for expressing the secrets of a man's mind through low-key unguarded utterance.'

The *Daily Telegraph*'s Charles Osborne noted the 'discreet charm of Hoffman's Shylock'. The much-respected Milton Shulman reviewed it in the London *Evening Standard* in a piece headed: 'Shylock, where is thy sting?' He wrote: 'Hoffman's performance is sound and well spoken, but it is never fierce enough to make Shylock an interesting monster nor despised enough to make him an oppressed victim.' Yet in *The Sunday Times* John Peter called it a 'masterly performance'. 'His Shylock is tough, shifty and unpleasantly resilient; an unattractive operator.'

The public certainly was impressed. When it was announced that his Bath debut was being postponed until after the London tour, there were near riots in the streets as people queued for more tickets. In London, Dustin felt ill one night and an understudy was told to go on. Ticket buyers were not amused. There were more shouts and even fights as three-quarters of the projected audience demanded their money back.

It turned out to be the most successful play of the season – absolutely unique for Shakespeare. Advance bookings had been the biggest in history for a non-musical. All of which was an indication of the power of being Dustin Hoffman.

News of the Shylock triumph crossed the Atlantic, where a New York production starring Dustin was being seriously considered.

Time magazine's William A. Henry III wrote: 'Hoffman carefully modulates his five scenes, using familiar but effective gestures, the shy grin, the hunch of the shoulders, the sudden stare, the deliberate monotonous thud to denote anger. His performance, anything but a star turn, is intelligent, confident and touching.'

Dustin himself was unnerved by it all. For two days before opening, he was running backwards and forwards to the lavatory, suffering from acute diarrhoea. The worst part of his nerves, however, affected Lisa. He said that he was so wrapped up within himself that he couldn't make love to her. After the first night, he couldn't wait to get to bed with her.

A celebrity-packed première followed more than a week of previews. Paul McCartney came backstage to offer his congratulations. So did Sir John Mills and Dame Peggy Ashcroft.

Leigh Lawson, who played Antonio, sent Dustin a present which he nailed to his wall – a plastic female breast, which he claimed weighed about 16 ounces. Underneath was the legend: 'You wanted it, you got it.'

What Dustin Hoffman really got was a different kind of award, the satisfaction that as an actor he could do practically everything. It is not given to many to claim that – and be justified.

There was still a great deal of admiration in him for the work of others, usually those gone before, like Charlie Chaplin, who in the film *City Lights* abandoned three months of shooting. 'Imagine if I did that today? And when you spend time trying to get everything right before you start shooting a film, you hear this stuff about being a perfectionist – as if being a perfectionist is so bad.'

Dustin said that if he were going to have an operation and heard that the surgeon was a very, very nice guy but not a perfectionist, he'd wake himself from the anaesthetic and try to get out of there quick.

He has never minimized what he did, and as he contemplated a new film, *Family Business* with Sean Connery, latest in a long line of male co-stars, there was enormous concentration on the work in hand – as always. He was looking for surprises, which was the very life-blood of Dustin Hoffman. 'I want people to go into a cinema and not know what I'm going to do,' he said.

The trouble with him was that old school report syndrome. People knew he would surprise them. They expected to be surprised.

He knew he was obsessive. He envied people who could just go to sleep at night without bothering about their problems. He thought it would be wonderful just to *enjoy* a sunset. He couldn't. 'I'd want to shoot it.' As he also said: 'I'm so tired after a vacation that I need a vacation.'

But he did sometimes see what he did in fairly basic terms. There was a lot of admiration for success, as an actor or as anything else. 'I mean, if a guy is talking to a girl at a party and she asks him what he does for a living and he says he's a scientist and he's just invented the vaccine for polio, then you *know* he's going to get laid.' But he also said: 'A child eating an ice cream is all wrapped up in it and you look on as an adult and think that this is the way you would like your life to be. I do.'

Meryl Streep had once described him as 'the most wonderful combination of generous and selfish. He wants to be the greatest actor who ever lived.' That won't come about. But his status today means that he might get on to a short list.

He no longer planned his own obituary, probably realizing it would now certainly get more than the paragraph in *Time*'s Milestone section he had once expected. But he thought about his means of dying. He was sure that the actor David Burns handled his own death perfectly. He was a comedian, so when he fell head first on stage, he got a laugh. 'The perfect exit,' said Dustin.

But he did still worry about the future, was petrified about a state of affairs which he acknowledged was 'too good to be true'.

Lisa had brought him firmly back to his Judaism, not the kind epitomized by the anti-Semites who had seen Shylock so differently. But they observed the holidays now. There was no Christmas tree, but on Chanukah, candles were lit on the family menorah.

'Lisa is great for Dustin,' said Robert Benton, one of the directors with whom Hoffman did not have a bust-up. 'She's got his number. Few people have. And he knows it.'

He believed he had total happiness. He did not have total love. Anne, the first Mrs Hoffman, told me that she thought of him with no affection

whatever, had not seen a Hoffman film since *Tootsie*, which she considered over-rated. 'I was quite surprised. I didn't think it was that
good.' She still thought that he would have been a better actor had he
stayed on the New York stage.

What about all the plaudits of late? 'Unfortunately, today in the
theatre, acclaim and expertise are not always the same. I don't single
him out. It's true of a lot of people. When you become as famous as
that, people say you're very good even when you're not.'

That is a personal, very subjective view. For most people, what he
produces *is* exceptional. Even he doesn't expect miracles of himself. If
he could, he might really be a Rain Man.

Index